USING SPEECH RECOGNITION SOFTWARE:

DRAGON NATURALLYSPEAKING AND

WINDOWS SPEECH RECOGNITION

Second Edition

Calais J. Ingel

Using Speech Recognition Software: Dragon NaturallySpeaking and Windows Speech Recognition, Second Edition

Copyright©2011 by Calais J. Ingel
Published by Ingel Publishing, distributed in the United States by Lightning Source and Ingram

Cover design by Beth Regardz

ISBN: 978-0-615-38512-9

Requests for press review copies, instructor guides and other information should be directed via electronic mail to ingelpublishing@gmail.com.

Printed in the United States of America.

TABLE OF CONTENTS

NOTES ABOUT USING THIS BOOK

The Speech Recognition Method: Use Your Voice

✓ In this book, you will use your voice for dictating text (words you want typed) and commands (actions). Using your computer primarily by voice is called the Speech Recognition Method, and the principles are taught in this book. (Using your hands is the manual method.)

Bold Type, Italics, Quotation Marks: What They Mean

✓ **Commands** are always highlighted in **bold type**. They should be spoken aloud. (For example, **Scratch That**.)

✓ Text that must be manually typed is in *italics*. This is not a common occurrence.

✓ Items which require a mouse click are in quotation marks (for example, Click "Next").

The Exercises: Read Through Before Beginning

✓ An **exercise** usually follows an explanation of a new fact or skill. Always read all the way through a section (instructions and the exercise) before beginning to dictate.

Basic Computer Skills are All You Need

✓ This book presumes basic PC skills; for example, how to open, close, and save a document, and how a mouse and keyboard function.

Are You In A Class? Or, a Class of One?

✓ Some students using this book will be in speech recognition classes where they are expected to save and turn in the Exercises. Some people using this book will be working on their own (a class of one). Exercises are written to be useful to both groups; however, if instructions say to print work, or to write a paragraph reflecting on your experience, make the choice appropriate to your situation.

✓ The appendix contains useful reference material, such as a list of voice commands. More help is available online, at nuance.com, microsoft.com, and the author's blog, usingspeechrecognition.com.

New in the Second Edition

New in this edition are expanded instructions, more images and explanations of confusing items, and more, including the following:

Dragon NaturallySpeaking:

- ✓ Updated information for Dragon 11 and 11.5, including new commands.
- ✓ Expanded coverage of the user profile training options available in Dragon 11 (and 11.5), including the option to read the text without prompting.
- ✓ The addition of helpful subheadings in longer exercises to explain parts of an exercise.
- ✓ Visual improvements: more screen shots, images, and improved text appearance.
- ✓ New exercises, including those for the Dragon Sidebar.

Windows Speech Recognition in Windows 7

- ✓ Expanded explanations of difficult concepts in Windows Speech Recognition.
- ✓ New exercises, including a timed writing using Windows Speech Recognition.

More Guidance

- ✓ New "Trouble?" sections to guide you through difficult concepts or confusing areas.
- ✓ More frequently asked questions, grouped in "Question Time!" sections.
- ✓ More "True Stories" of actual speech recognition users and issues they have faced.

How to Get More Help:

The Author's Website

The author of this book has a blog to focus on speech recognition issues, which is found at this address: usingspeechrecognition.com. On this site, find updates, tips, answers to (even more) frequently asked questions, and other useful material. Drop by and say hello!

Assistive Technology Specialists

If you have a severe physical limitation, or a degenerative condition, look for an assistive technology specialist in your area who can help you set up your computer for hands-free work, and recommend adaptive devices to meet your unique needs. Trackballs, head-pointing devices, and other modifications can make input easier. Also, consider Dragon NaturallySpeaking Professional, which allows the creation of macros, or scripts, to automate tasks.

Acknowledgements

A book like this one only comes together after years of trial and error and the help of many people. The author would like to thank the many hundreds of students who have learned to use speech recognition software in the AT Lab at Cabrillo College. Specifically, thanks to Michael Edwards, who taught me everything I needed to get started, and to certain students who made a difference in my teaching: Sally McCloud, Bob Bogard, and so many, many others. I am very grateful to the amazing staff in the Computer Technology Center who never fail to help: Jamilah Vittor, Ann Schwartz, Barbara Durland and Rhea Leonard. Thanks to the DSPS office staff—Nikki Oneto and Alta Northcutt make so much possible for so many. My appreciation goes to Dr. Jim Weckler for his unbridled enthusiasm for technology, and to Dr. Margery Regalado for her support of assistive technology. My talented colleague Steve Larson gave valuable advice, as is his custom—thanks for being in my corner. To all of the technology writers who have addressed speech recognition, but especially to the amazing David Pogue, I tip my microphone.

Beth Regardz, a fantastic artist and colleague, dropped everything to make the lovely cover to this book and give advice about style—twice! Rabbi Paula Marcus reminds me what is important, and to look beyond the screen. The wonderful Van Adams enrich my life—thanks.

My family showed amazing patience and encouragement with me when I was ready to throw my laptop out the window. They cooked, they soothed—they are the best! Here's to Micah and Mahalia, the best kids any mom could want. Mark, you are the song in my heart, and my beshert. This book is dedicated to you.

Introduction

A Game-Changer

Speech recognition is a major game changer. For most of human history, people could only record their ideas and thoughts at the speed that their hand could write or type. The average person working with a pencil or pen (or a feathered plume) writes between 10 and 20 words per minute. When typewriters came along, they offered a huge increase in speed—doubling the speed of handwriting. When word processing was developed, people who had typing skills could continue to use those skills in a more flexible format than typing directly onto paper. It required learning computer skills, but the advantages in editing, formatting, and revision were huge—not to mention the advantage of automatic spellchecking.

> Think about how long it took you to learn to type well—speech recognition takes only a few hours to learn to do well.

New Skills, New Opportunities

Speech recognition is a similar leap ahead. The computer skills you already have are useful, including knowledge of keyboard commands. But there is an entirely new skill set to learn, and it takes some time. Think about how long it took you to learn to use a computer, and how long it took you to learn to type (if you do type). Now consider this: with a much smaller investment, you can type twice as fast by voice as you can manually.

Speech recognition has other benefits as well. For one thing, speech recognition software never misspells a word. Add to this the freedom of being unchained from your keyboard: you can pace back and forth while you compose the Great American Novel, or with a wireless headset you can dictate to your computer from various locations in your home or office. With a digital voice recorder, you can dictate anywhere—in the car, on the beach, between meetings, etc.

Speed and More Speed

Speech recognition levels the playing field for students, office workers, medical and legal professionals, and writers. Students use the software to write papers quickly—something every busy student knows is important! People whose work involves using a computer appreciate being able to compose reports, write e-mails, and just generally speed up daily writing tasks. Writers, for whom the act of composing written work is their primary task, benefit greatly from the ability to dictate from 100 to 150 words per minute instead of typing at 30 to 60 words per minute. Medical and legal professionals benefit from all the advantages above, plus the ability to save on transcription costs by dictating their own work.

Use Speech Recognition Methods: Hands-Free or Combination

In this book, the two variations of speech recognition use are taught: first, the "hands-free" method, which uses speech only. Understanding the hands-free method for completing any task is important for good speech recognition skills. If you have any kind of hand, arm, shoulder, or neck problems, the hands-free method can make a big difference in how much pain you experience when using a computer. And, for a person with a severe physical limitation, the hands-free method makes it possible to use a computer independently.

Working hands-free can reduce injuries and pain from keyboarding and mouse use.

The second method is called the "combination method", or combo method, because of the combination of speech recognition techniques and traditional manual techniques. While the hands-free method is faster once it has been mastered, the combo method is useful in certain situations. Most speech recognition users use both methods, depending upon their needs at any given moment.

Myths and Realities

There are many myths about speech recognition: that it is hard to use, that it requires a stilted way of speaking, and that the technology is inferior. Like most myths, there are truths within: the early versions of most speech recognition programs really *were* hard to use, they did require a stilted way of speaking and, by today's standards, the technology was inferior. Some low-quality speech recognition programs are still on the market, which unfortunately reinforces these stereotypes.

However, two high-quality speech recognition programs for PCs using the Windows operating system are widely available: Dragon NaturallySpeaking (Premium or higher edition) and Windows Speech Recognition. Nuance, the maker of Dragon NaturallySpeaking, also produces the premier speech recognition program for the Apple computer, Dragon Dictate for Mac. While Dragon Dictate for Mac is outside the scope of this book, it relies upon the same basic speech recognition principles used in these chapters.

From The Author

I have taught speech recognition software to college students for over a decade—since the early days of the software—when it took many hours just to train a user profile (a process that takes 15 minutes today).

Hundreds of college students (of all ages and abilities) have taught me many important lessons: to make every effort to explain a concept clearly and concisely, to remember that the learning curve is steepest at first, and, to encourage everyone to continue through the first difficult hours to the other side when using speech recognition software.

When you dictate twice as fast as you can type, dictating can feel like flying!

It really does get easier with practice, and when it does, typing by voice can feel like flying. So, prepare to be patient with yourself and the computer, and get ready for a truly modern, exciting way of working with the computer—by voice!

Note: This book was dictated using Dragon NaturallySpeaking and Windows Speech Recognition. If I can dictate this book, you can dictate your projects as well!

Why are there questions and answers interspersed through the chapters?

As this book's author is also a college instructor who has taught hundreds of students to use speech recognition software, she knows the questions that come up repeatedly for new users. To make life easier, these **frequently asked questions** are included in the relevant sections, or in groups under the heading "Question Time!".

CHAPTER 1

Beginning Speech Recognition: Training A User Profile

About Speech Recognition Software and This Book

Speech Recognition software makes it possible to type and control the computer by voice. Most users can dictate at speeds near 100 words per minute, and many can work significantly faster—with few errors! It requires a good, noise-cancelling microphone and (at first) a bit of patience. Talking (dictating) to a computer is very different than typing and using a mouse and it takes a while to learn how to do it efficiently and well. (Think back to how long it took you to learn to use a keyboard to type well—probably many hours!)

> Would you like to dictate 100 words per minute or faster, with 97% accuracy?

This book walks you through the new methods you will use, step-by-step, increasing the complexity only after you have practiced the basic skills.

As you read the chapters, study the examples and practice the skills in the exercises. Frequently asked questions are answered throughout the chapters, and a list of commands introduced in each chapter is found on the chapter's last page.

Dragon NaturallySpeaking

Dragon NaturallySpeaking has been the premier speech recognition product on Windows-based computers for over a decade. Newer is **Windows Speech Recognition,** built into Windows 7 (and Windows Vista). This book addresses both Dragon NaturallySpeaking and Windows Speech Recognition.

In This Chapter

- ✓ About Speech Recognition Software
- ✓ Train a User Profile in Dragon
- ✓ Discover the DragonBar
- ✓ Learn to Control the Microphone
- ✓ Special Topic: Dictating text vs. Dictating Commands
- ✓ Use DragonPad
- ✓ Dictate text, punctuation and basic commands
- ✓ Timed Writing I
- ✓ Dragon Help Files
- ✓ Dragon Tutorial
- ✓ Frequently Asked Questions
- ✓ 8 Exercises
- ✓ Command

How does speech recognition work? What does speech recognition software do?

These are the two most frequently asked questions from computer users when they first hear of speech recognition software (also sometimes called "voice recognition software.") Here is the answer: When you dictate to the computer, it matches the sounds you make with words in its vocabulary. Then, **the software tries to match what you said with something that makes sense in context**; for example, if dictating a sentence, you say "period" at the end of it the software will type a period (.) instead of typing out the word "period." However, if you dictate a sentence with the word "period" in it, such as "The Jurassic period was long ago" Dragon types the word, not the punctuation. Finally, if you say a command like "Click Save" the software clicks on the Save icon.

Each person who uses Dragon must train their own user profile.

Accurate speech recognition is not hard to achieve if you follow the methods in this book. User training, which is the process of reading text aloud to match your voice to the words on the screen, is the first step toward good speech recognition. In Chapter 2, the second essential technique for good speech recognition is added: correcting misrecognitions. Excellent speech accuracy (97% or greater) is possible through use of these two techniques: dictating proficiently and correcting errors.

Benefits of Using Speech Recognition Software

People who use speech recognition software do so for various reasons. Some people need to be able to work faster. Students appreciate being able to speak their thoughts quickly when writing a paper, instead of slowly writing or typing their work. Authors who struggle to get their thoughts down "on paper" find a speaking solution improves their writing.

Some industries, including healthcare and law, are increasingly using speech recognition to improve efficiency and reduce transcription costs. Finally, many computer users have developed hand, arm or other injuries from keyboard and mouse use. Speech recognition provides a pain-free alternative. Speech recognition offers a completely new way to use and enjoy the computer, more quickly and without overworking your hands!

Does this mean I can throw away my keyboard and mouse?

Probably not. While speech recognition software can be very accurate, a keyboard—and especially a mouse—is quicker in certain situations. Speech recognition is excellent for dictating into documents and e-mails and replaces the mouse in many situations, but some programs and web pages don't work well with speech recognition. Programs that require a lot of clicking and dragging with the mouse (like image-editing software) are especially challenging to use with speech recognition. For computer users who are physically able to do so, a combination approach that primarily uses speech recognition software, but includes the keyboard and mouse when needed, is optimal.

Which is the best speech recognition program?

The best speech recognition program is the one that works best for you—one that you feel comfortable using because it has a high degree of accuracy and the options that you need. This book covers Dragon NaturallySpeaking and Windows Speech Recognition, two leading speech recognition programs.

Dragon NaturallySpeaking is available in several versions, each with their own options. Dragon NaturallySpeaking is also known for its high level of accuracy. However, Dragon NaturallySpeaking needs to be installed on each machine you want to use it on, and a license must be purchased and activated to use the software. For this reason, many Dragon NaturallySpeaking users install their software on a laptop, so that their speech recognition can travel with them wherever they go.

Windows Speech Recognition has fewer options, and with only one version, there's less opportunity to customize your experience. However, Windows Speech Recognition is preinstalled on Windows 7 and Windows Vista, making it the low-cost choice that is automatically available on newer Windows machines. For example, if you go to visit relatives for a week and you use their computer, you could have speech recognition available to you there.

This book addresses **Dragon NaturallySpeaking** in Chapters 1–5, **Windows Speech Recognition in Chapters 6 and 7**, and **advanced features** for both in Chapter 8. Suggested is to work through this book and then decide which speech recognition software is the best match for you.

TRUE STORIES

An obviously bright student came to see me about using speech recognition software. He said, "I don't know if I can learn this. You see, I have such severe dyslexia that I basically can't read, and I fail classes because my spelling is so bad that teachers won't read my papers." After learning to use Dragon NaturallySpeaking, including how to play back text, the student was able to dictate his papers instead of typing them—and he began passing his college classes.

Dragon NaturallySpeaking: Prepare to Train

When you start Dragon NaturallySpeaking, the first of a series of windows to begin the user profile training process appears. (If it does not, see the "Trouble?" section on the next page.) Training a user file requires setting up a microphone, performing audio checks, and speaking text aloud to the computer. The process takes about 10 minutes, and you need to complete it in one session, so plan ahead.

There are several options for completing the training process. Each option is presented with step-by-step directions and explained on the following pages in Exercise 1.1.

First Step: Train a User Profile

To use Dragon NaturallySpeaking, first set up a unique file for your speech, called your **user profile**.

At first, the recognition might not be as good as you would like, but it improves as you work with it.

After only a few sessions of use, not only will you be better at dictating to the computer, but your speech recognition will have improved as well.

Before you train Dragon NaturallySpeaking, determine which **version** number you are using. These instructions are for versions 11 and 11.5. (If you are training an earlier version of Dragon, the standard training process is similar, but the windows will look different. Dragon 10 is covered in the previous edition of this book.)

Wait—I need to install Dragon NaturallySpeaking! Now what do I do?

If you need to install Dragon NaturallySpeaking, follow the directions in Chapter 8, or the instructions that came with the Dragon DVD, if available.

What About A Microphone?

You need a good quality, noise-cancelling microphone—preferably one designed for speech recognition. A headset microphone is most common, but microphones can also be handheld or sit on the desktop. Voice array microphones are useful for people who have difficulty wearing a headset. (With Dragon version 11.5, iPhones can be used as microphones as well.) Plug in or set up your microphone before beginning. **Note:** if you are using a digital voice recorder, and you do not plan on using a microphone to dictate directly into the computer, see the recorder manufacturer's instructions and Dragon Help to set up your user profile.

Exercise 1.1 Train a User Profile in Dragon NaturallySpeaking

DIRECTIONS: For best results, read through page 15 before beginning. Follow all steps carefully. Note: This is a very long exercise—the longest in the book—so be patient and read each step carefully.

Start the Dragon NaturallySpeaking Program

Double-click on the Dragon icon (looks like a green flame) on the desktop, or choose Dragon NaturallySpeaking from the Start menu to open the program.

Create a User Profile

After Dragon NaturallySpeaking opens, the first of a series of windows opens which takes you through the user profile setup process.

Click "Next" to continue. (Tip: Pressing the Enter key will also activate the "Next" button. After you train your user profile, you can speak the names of buttons to activate them—but not yet!)

Trouble?

If the training windows do not appear automatically, go to the **DragonBar**, click on the **Profile** menu, then choose **New User Profile**.

When the New **User Profile** window appears, click the **New** button on the right-hand side, and continue with the instructions on the next page.

Exercise 1.1, Continued

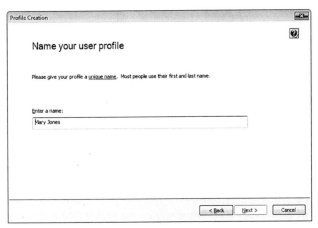

Choose Your User Profile Settings: Name

Give your user profile a name, such as your first and last name. Type the profile name into the text box, then click "Next" (or press the Enter key).

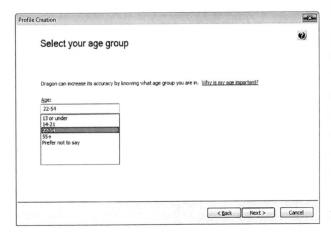

Age Group

On the next screen, called "Select Your Age Group", choose an age group from the list box (or choose "Prefer not to say"). Click "Next". (*Why?* Because Dragon customizes the recognition based on the age of the user: for example, adolescents have a different sound to their voices than do older adults.)

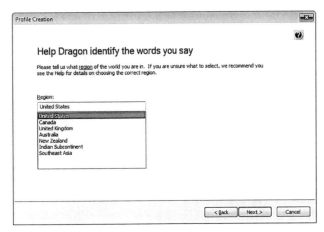

Where In the World Are You? Set Regional Vocabulary

The next screen, titled "Help Dragon identify the words you say" asks you to choose the region of the world that you are in. This is because there are different vocabularies in different parts of the world. For example, in US English, one says "period" at the end of a sentence, while in UK English one says "full stop". Click "Next" after making a location selection.

Exercise 1.1, Continued

Do You Have An Accent?

If you have an accent, choose the accent from the list in the next window (called "Help Dragon understand how you pronounce words"). For example, an English speaker from Cambodia might choose SEAsian (for South East Asian). If you aren't sure, or your accent doesn't seem strong, choose "Standard". Click "Next".

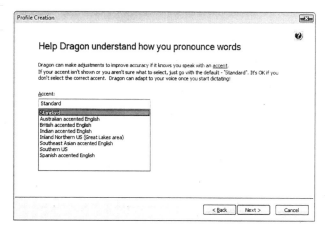

Microphone Input Method

Look at your input device (microphone) and choose the options in the window which best describe it. (If you have a microphone connected already, the best choice is often pre-selected for you.) Dragon calls this window "How do you talk to your computer?" but perhaps a better title would be "With *what* do you talk to your computer?"

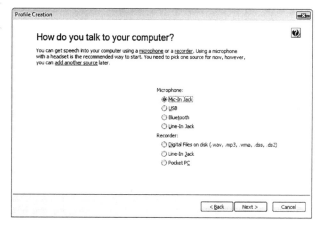

Review Your Choices

Check that the options you selected, which are summarized in this window, are what you want them to be. When you are ready, click "Create". (If not, click the "Back" button and make changes.)

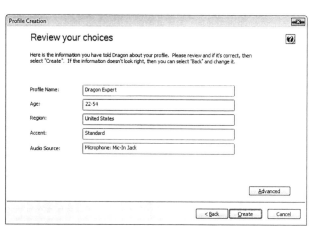

11

Exercise 1.1, Continued

Your Profile is Being Created

Please wait while Dragon creates your new user profile. This can take several minutes, but when it is complete, you will be able to begin training.

Position Your Microphone Headset

Put the headset on and adjust the band so that it is comfortably snug—not too loose or tight. This is important, as your microphone can easily slide out of place if the headset isn't properly fitted.

Get the Microphone in Place

Once the headset is comfortably snug on your head, put one hand on the band to hold it in place while you pull the microphone arm (the thing that holds the microphone itself) down toward your chin. Keep the microphone just over a thumb's distance from your mouth (put your thumb against your lips to check) and just slightly off-center to your mouth, to avoid the microphone picking up your breathing.

Use your thumb to position your microphone—one thumb's distance between your mouth and microphone is perfect.

If the arm is flexible, be careful not to bend or contort it out of shape. Not only will you look silly if the microphone arm is bent, your recognition won't be very good!

Note: Instructions for positioning presume a microphone headset, like the one pictured on this page. If you are using a different type of microphone (array, stand microphone, wireless microphone, etc.) set it up following the manufacturer's instructions. Click "Next" to continue.

Exercise 1.1, Continued

Tip: When you take a short break from dictating, don't take off your headset. Swivel it up out of your way, or just leave it where it is and turn off the microphone pick up in the software. Commands to control the microphone are covered later in this chapter.

Dragon Volume Check

The next screen begins the first of two "checks". The first check is to see if the software is picking up enough volume from the headset.

To test this, click on the "Start Volume Check" button in the window, then read the text in the box aloud, in a "quiet conversational" voice—as if speaking to someone nearby. It beeps when it is finished—probably before you have read the entire passage.

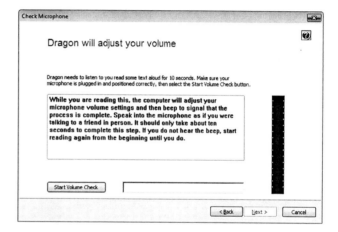

Click "Next" to continue.

Trouble?

If you don't hear a beep, perhaps the sound to your system is turned off. No problem: just watch the text. The text passage will turn gray when it is finished adjusting the volume.

I got an error message that the volume was too low. Help!

If an error message states the volume is too low, try disconnecting and reconnecting your headset from the computer—even if it seems fine. Move the microphone a little bit closer to your mouth—a finger's distance. If you still get the error message, restart the computer or try another microphone. **Do not** speak louder to compensate—fix the equipment issues instead. (For recommendations on microphones, try a reputable website, such as cnet.com, usingspeechrecognition.com, etc.) Note: the headset that comes with Dragon software is not automatically the best choice for you. Shop around, buy one you like, then save the freebie that came with Dragon as a backup in case something happens to your primary microphone.

Exercise 1.1, Continued

Dragon Quality Check

The second "check" screen checks the quality of sound from the sound system.

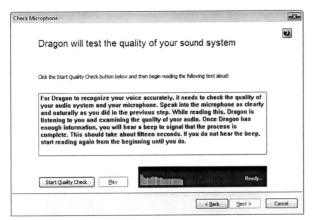

Click the "Start Quality Check" button to begin, and read the text in the box aloud. Use a steady, relaxed voice (not loud, not whispering.)

It beeps when it is finished, and the audio check is "passed" or "failed". If it passed, click "Next" to continue.

Trouble?

If the check has "failed", click the "Back" button and try it again—often this works. However, if you are still having sound problems, check the following:

✓ Headset is connected properly—microphone plugged in the mic in jack. With a USB headset, make sure the connection is good and that the computer recognizes it. It may look fine, but unplugging it and plugging it back in might just do the trick.

✓ Is it a noise-cancelling headset, designed for speech recognition software? This is not the same as headsets used for gaming, mobile phones or VOIP (voice over IP). For recommendations on high-quality headsets, visit nuance.com/naturallyspeaking and look for a "recommended hardware" link.

✓ With Bluetooth or wireless headsets, check the battery in the headset.

✓ Are you reading the text fluently, to give the software a good voice level? If you find yourself starting and stopping reading, practice it a few times before running the checks.

✓ Restarting the computer will frequently resolve a problem.

Exercise 1.1, Continued

Choose a Training Option:

Option 1: Show the sentences to read in an interactive window. This is how most users will train the software, and it takes less than 10 minutes. Instructions for this option begin on the next page.

Option 2: Show the whole training script at once: a good option for increasing accessibility, as you can make the text larger, or read as slowly as you need to. (Dragon calls the second option "Show text without prompting".) Instructions for this option begin on page 20.

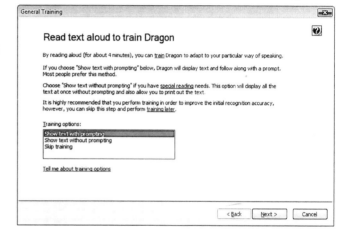

Option 3: Skip reading the training text. Instructions for this option begin on page 25.

Which option is right for me?

The first option, called "Show text with prompting" (also known as the "standard training option") is right for most people. It works best if you don't have any difficulty reading or speaking, and you can spend 10 minutes or less (Dragon says "about 4 minutes", but 5-10 minutes is a reasonable estimate) to train a user profile to understand the way you speak. Choose this option unless you have a reason not to.

I have dyslexia. Which option should I choose?

Choose the second option, called "Show text without prompting", following the steps beginning on page 20.

I am in a hurry. Can I skip the training?

Yes, but you should plan to do some additional training later, to compensate for skipping the training now.

I need large print, or more accessibility. What should I do?

Follow the steps for Option 2, "Show text with prompting" beginning on page 20. These instructions also apply to people with speech difficulties or other limitations, who will do better with a more accessible option.

Exercise 1.1 Option 1

Option 1: Show Text with Prompting

DIRECTIONS: Follow the instructions carefully.

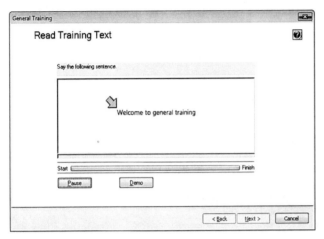

Welcome to General Training!

Check that "Show Text with Prompting" is selected, then click "Next".

Click the "Demo" button for a demonstration of how to speak the text.

Click the "Go" button, wait a second or two until a yellow arrow appears, then say the phrase on the screen, **Welcome to general training**.

If it recognizes your speech, the next window will appear.

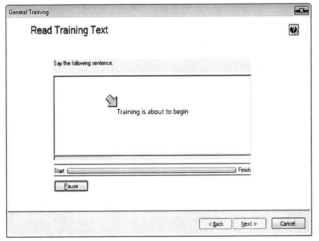

Training Is About to Begin

Dictate the second phrase, **Training is about to begin**, then wait. It may take several seconds for the window on the next page, which lets you choose a script to train, to appear.

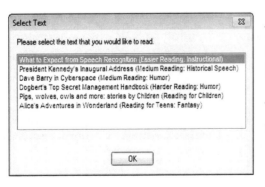

The **Select Text** window appears. Choose "What to Expect from Speech Recognition" and click "OK".

The text will appear in the training window one sentence or so at a time.

Exercise 1.1 Option 1, Continued

Click the "Go" button (it turns into a "Pause" button, as shown), wait quietly for a second or two, and the yellow arrow will show where to begin speaking.

Read each sentence out loud, in a calm, natural voice. You do not need to speak the punctuation.

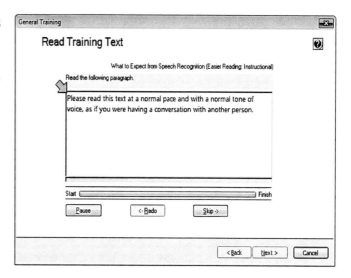

Trouble?

If the yellow arrow gets stuck on a phrase, try it again. If it still doesn't recognize your speech, click the "Skip" button and skip the problem section.

When you have finished, a message of congratulations appears. Click "OK" and Dragon will adapt your dictation into your user profile.

This takes a few minutes, which is a good time to drink some water to keep your vocal chords in good shape!

Tip: If you have a hard time reading the text passages smoothly, make it easier on yourself! When a text window appears, click the "Pause" button. Then, read the paragraph until you feel comfortable with it. When you are ready, Click the "Go" button and dictate the text. Continue until done.

Trouble?

If this doesn't work for you, choose the second training method, beginning with the instructions on page 20.

What is in the Training Passage?

The training passage gives useful information about how to use speech recognition software. If you skip the training, or use the alternate method, you can get the same information by reading the script below.

Dragon's "What To Expect From Speech Recognition" Script

Below is the text from the recommended training script.

Dragon will now collect an audio sample so it can adapt to the characteristics of your voice and begin learning how you pronounce words. Please read this text at a normal pace with a normal tone of voice, as if you were having a conversation with another person.

You are not required to say punctuation while reading this training text, but it's a good idea since you will need to say punctuation when you dictate documents and e-mails. Dictating with Dragon is different than talking to another person. People can easily filter out noise, which lets us understand each other even in a noisy restaurant.

Computers need help separating speech sounds from other sounds. As you read, make sure you are in a place without too much noise. You should also check the position of your microphone. Your microphone should always be about an inch away from the corner of your mouth. When people talk, they often hesitate, mumble, slur their words, or leave words out altogether. But we are still able to understand each other.

For example, we use our experience and common sense to decide whether someone said "I scream" or "ice cream". Dragon doesn't understand what words mean, so it can't use common sense the way people do. Instead, Dragon recognizes words that appear next to other words. It learns this from the way you speak to it. You need to help it understand how you speak and the context of the words you use.

Dragon calculates how frequently words and phrases are used and can offer you suggestions when it makes mistakes. You just need to know how to operate it properly. It's best to dictate in complete sentences, speaking clearly and evenly, in a natural manner. The idea is to speak to Dragon normally, at a consistent speed and volume. Try not to hesitate, exaggerate your pronunciation or talk loudly or slowly. Try to think about your whole sentence before you start to speak it. This will give Dragon the context it needs.

The software lets you dictate punctuation and symbols, such as: Question Mark, Open Quote, Plus Sign, and Hyphen, even things like smiley face.

Dragon also comes with hundreds of commands, including: **New Paragraph, Backspace 5, Mouse Move Up, Drag Mouse Down, Correct That, Undo That, Copy That, Cap That, Delete Line, Go to End of Line, Press Enter, Press Escape, Press F2, Press Tab.** Pause briefly before saying a command and Dragon will instantly recognize that the command is something you want it to do, rather than something you are dictating. When you first start dictating with Dragon, it's important to be patient. As with anything, practice is important.

Try to avoid saying extra words you really don't want in your document, like "you know". Dragon has no way of knowing which words you say are important, so it simply transcribes everything you say. Think about what you want to say before you speak. This will help you to dictate in complete phrases.

To understand what it means to speak both clearly and naturally, listen to the way newscasters read the news. For the best results using speech recognition, copy this style when you dictate. If you dictate something by accident, you can delete it by saying **Scratch That.** You can delete full sentences, a phrase, just one word, or a symbol.

You can apply formatting using a word processor. Just select the word by voice, then you can capitalize, change font size and style, and apply bold, italics, or underlining. Dragon enables you to perform many everyday tasks by just using your voice. (©Nuance.com)

As you can see, there is good information in the training script—how to speak to a computer, and some of the most common types of commands. If you skip this, however, don't worry—it will all be covered later in this book as well.

This wasn't the exact training text I saw! What's up?

The training script allows users to "skip" difficult phrases. If you skip phrases, you will get additional phrases at the end of the script, which aren't given here.

Exercise 1.1 Option 2

Option 2: Show Text Without Prompting

DIRECTIONS: Read this section through before beginning, so that you know what to expect. Follow the steps carefully.

1. At the "Read text aloud to train Dragon" window, choose "Show text without prompting", then click "Next."
2. At the "Read Training Text" window, click "Next".
3. At the "Read Training Text: Text Display" window, choose whether you want to read text from the screen, or if you want to print it and read it from the paper printout.
   - ✓ **To read from the screen**, select that option and click "Next".
   - ✓ **To read from printed text**, click the "Print" button, then modify (enlarge, etc.) the text and print it on your printer. **Follow the instructions beginning on page 23 under the heading "To Read from a Printed Page".**

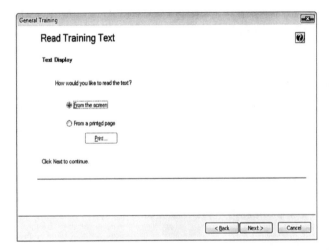

Trouble Deciding?

If you choose to read the passage **on-screen**, you can use assistive technology, such as screen reading or screen magnification software. If you choose the "Print" button instead, the text will open in a **document window**. From there, you can enlarge the text, or add spacing between lines, or whatever works best to make it easier for you to read. If you aren't sure, try reading it on screen, and see how it goes. If it doesn't work out, you can always print it, practice reading it aloud a few times, and then try it again.

Exercise 1.1 Option 2, Continued

Option 2A—Read Onscreen:

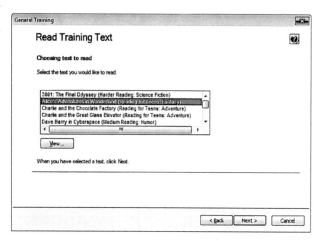

1. At the "Read Training Text: Choosing text to read" window (pictured at right), choose a selection of text to read. (Note: if you think you might get the giggles or crack up at a funny selection, do not choose the humor selections.)

2. Click the "Next" button.

3. At the next window, click the "Begin Training" button to open the text training window.

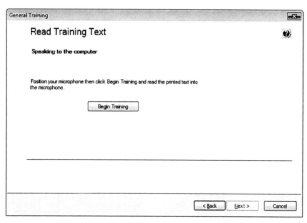

4. Click the "Next" button.

5. Pre-read the page of text that appears in the window. When you are ready, click the "Begin Training" button.

6. Begin speaking the text aloud in a calm, clear voice. (For tips on how to read text aloud, see Dragon's "What to Expect From Speech Recognition" script on page 18.)

7. When you need to pause, click the "Pause Training" button. Click this same button again when you are ready to continue.

Exercise 1.1 Option 2A, Continued

8. When you have read at least 4 minutes of text, the **OK** button will become available (it will be gray and inactive until you have read enough text aloud) and you can stop. However, if you want to perform additional training, continue reading aloud, clicking the "Next Page" button as needed.

9. After you click "OK", a new window appears with a button for you to click to "Start Adapting" your speech into a user profile.

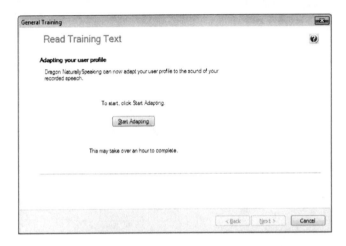

10. Click the "Start Adapting" button. While the window claims that this may take over an hour to complete, a 4 minute recording may take only 20 minutes or so—it depends on several factors.

 You could use this time to read the "After You Complete Training" section of this book on page 26, or to get a drink of water—or both.

11. When the adapting has finished, click "Next" if necessary.

12. The training window closes, and the three windows to set accuracy options appear. These options are described on page 26, in the section titled "After You Complete Training".

Tired of setting up your user profile? Don't worry, you are almost done! Soon you will be able to talk to your computer and see results!

Exercise 1.1 Option 2B

Option 2B—Read from a Printed Page (*continued from page* 20)

Reading text from the printed page allows for much more text formatting customization than on-screen reading does. For example, you could make the passage double-spaced, to make it easier to see each line individually. Or the font could be enlarged, made all capital letters, or changed to an easier-to-read font face. For people who read better with color, the font color (or highlighting color) could be adapted. People with learning disabilities, low vision, or those who just prefer to read text from paper rather than the screen, will want to consider this option.

Follow the steps below to train the script from the printed page(s):

1. Continue with these instructions after completing steps 1-3 on page 20.

2. Click the "Print" button to open the text in a word processing program (WordPad, for example—which program will open depends upon which word processors are installed in your computer.) If you do not like the program the document has opened into, select the text, copy it, and paste it into the word processor that you prefer.

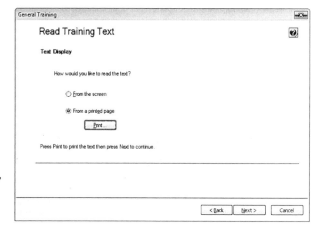

3. Within the document window, **make any changes** to font style, size, or line spacing that make reading easier for you.

4. **Print** as many pages as you wish to read—try to do at least 500 words (two pages at the default font size), or more. **Don't** print the whole passage, unless this is what you really want, as they can be more than 10 pages long!

5. **Close the document** after printing the selection you want to read aloud.

6. Return to Dragon NaturallySpeaking. (This should happen automatically when you close the word processor. If it does not, perhaps you minimized the Dragon window to the Taskbar and you can restore it now.)

7. Click "Next" to go to the training window where you will read the printed text out loud in a calm, clear voice.

Exercise 1.1 Option 2B

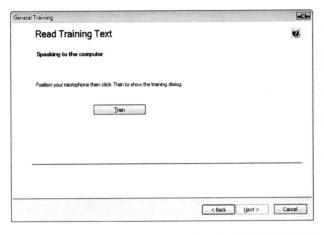

8. When you arrive at the "Read Training Text: Speaking to the computer" window with the "Train" button, click the button, wait a few seconds, then **read aloud the text you have printed**.

9. Notice that the window tells you that the computer is listening. Continue reading text aloud. Read for at least **4 minutes**—longer is acceptable, but less than that won't work. (Don't worry if you pause between sentences, or if you need little breaks. The timer only advances when you are actually speaking.) **Note:** try not to make other sounds into the microphone while you are recording your speech. If your microphone turns on and off, turn it off if you need to cough, talk to someone else, or have a drink of water, for example.

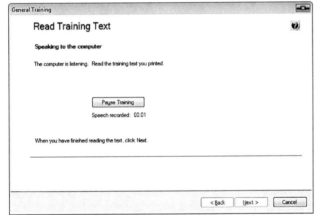

10. When you have finished training, click "Next".

11. Dragon will adapt and save your user profile. This may take several minutes, which is a

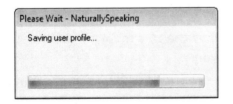

good time to drink some water and read ahead in this text.

12. When your user profile has been adapted and saved, the three windows to set accuracy options appear. These options are described on page 26 in the section titled "After You Complete Training". Go to that section and complete your user profile setup process.

Exercise 1.1 Option 3

Option 3: Skip Training

DIRECTIONS: Follow the steps below if you choose to skip training.

If you skip training, the computer will make more mistakes when you dictate to it. **This will require more correcting of misrecognitions**. However, this can be a good option for people who do not wish to do training, or who are unable to complete the training process.

If you choose this option, plan on doing additional training at a later date (found in the Accuracy Center, see Chapter 5) to increase your recognition.

1. At the window pictured below (called "Read text aloud to train Dragon"), choose the "Skip Training" option and click "Next".
2. Wait for a few minutes while Dragon creates a user profile for you.
3. Go to the next page and continue choosing options to complete your user profile setup.

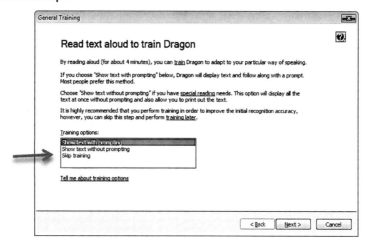

True Stories

Phil was a student in my speech recognition class. He did the standard training option the first time he used Dragon, but it didn't work well for him because he would stutter under the pressure of training. After several tries, he decided to skip training. He had many more corrections to make for the first 5 or 6 hours of speech recognition use, but eventually his user profile was accurate and working well. He felt less stress, so he spoke fluidly and clearly, and at over 100 words per minute!

Exercise 1.1, Continued

After You Complete Training (Or Skip Training)

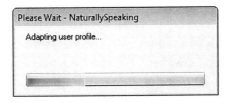

A window with a progress bar will appear, letting you know that Dragon is adapting your user profile (getting it ready for your use). You may see the "Saving user profile" window as well.

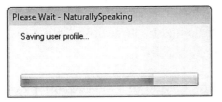

If you are saving the profile on a flash drive, this can take several minutes—otherwise, it shouldn't be more than a minute or two. (This is a good time to take a drink of water to keep your voice in good shape!)

Three Accuracy Options: Set Them Later

After completing the training, Dragon offers you several options. These include adapting your documents and e-mail to improve your recognition, running accuracy tuning on a scheduled basis, and running data collecting. All of these items can be set later.

To get started dictating sooner, decline the options (for now). To learn more about these options, and change any settings later, see the Accuracy Center in Chapter 5.)

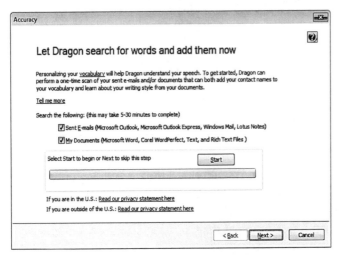

1. The "Add Words" Window

In the "Let Dragon search for words and add them now" box (pictured at left) uncheck the checkboxes by "Sent E-mails" and "My documents" and click "Next."(See "Why should I skip adapting for now?" on the next page for more information.)

2. Improve Dragon's Accuracy

In the "Let Dragon automatically improve your accuracy" box (pictured at right) uncheck the checkbox by "Automatically improve accuracy" and click "Next."

Note: The accuracy which will be improved is Dragon's, not yours. YOUR accuracy in dictating is improved by learning the correct ways to talk to your computer and correct misrecognitions.

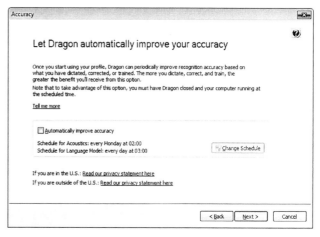

3. Data Collection

In the "Help us improve Dragon" box, choose the radio button for "Don't run Data Collection" and click "Next". (See Dragon Help for more information on Data Collecting.)

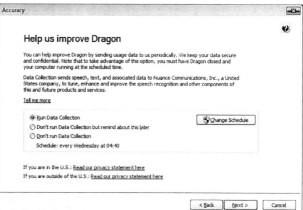

Your Profile Is Ready to Use!

The final window of the setup process says "Congratulations, your profile is ready for use!" You could open the Dragon tutorial, or click the link to see what is new in version 11, but since you have this book to walk you through all that, just click "Finish". (The Dragon Tutorial is covered later in this chapter.)

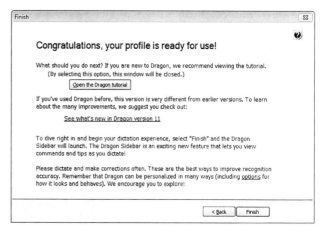

CONGRATULATIONS! You have now completed Exercise 1.1 and trained your first user profile!

What happens now?

The training will close, but Dragon will load your user profile so that you can begin dictating.

The **Tip of the Day** window appears; read it and **close it**. (It will appear every time you start Dragon, unless you uncheck the box next to "Show Tips at Startup".)

The **DragonBar** opens across the top of the screen, with the microphone turned off. The DragonBar is explained on page 31.

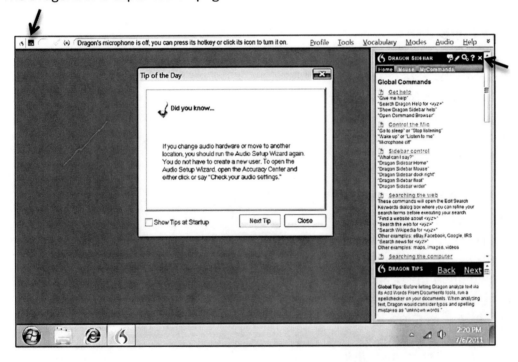

The **Dragon Sidebar** opens on the right side of the screen. This window displays commands to help users learn them. **Close it for now by clicking on the X** in the upper right-hand corner of the Sidebar. The Sidebar is covered in Chapter 2.

Can I stop now and come back later?

Yes. In fact, the next exercise takes you through the process of shutting down your user profile, exiting the program, and then restarting Dragon to continue working.

Exercise 1.2 Save User Profile, Exit Program, and Restart

DIRECTIONS: Follow the steps to save your new user profile, exit the program, and restart the computer. (*Why?* Not only does this exercise teach you how to do these skills, it helps you make sure that your training worked, and that there aren't any unforeseen problems.)

1. On the DragonBar, click the "Profile" menu and choose "Save User Profile".

2. Wait a minute or two for the software to process the request.

3. Then, from the same Profile menu, choose "Exit Dragon". Dragon will save (if needed) and close.

4. Restart your computer, then open Dragon NaturallySpeaking. While you wait, read the frequently asked questions below.

5. When Dragon has started, you should see the DragonBar across the top of the screen, the Tip of the Day window, the Dragon Sidebar, and the Open User Profile window.

Profile

New User Profile...
↣ Add audio source to current User Profile...

Open User Profile...
Open Recent User Profile ▸
Close User Profile

→ Save User Profile
Manage User Profiles...
Prepare User Profile for Use...

Backup User Profile
Restore User Profile

→ Exit Dragon

6. Click on your user profile name in the Open User Profile window, then click "Open".

7. Wait several seconds while your user profile loads. Once your profile is loaded, it is ready to use. The microphone is off. (You will learn to turn it on, off, and put it in a standby mode called *sleep* in the next exercise.)

8. You are now ready to continue with this chapter.

Trouble?

If you see an error message as you restart your computer, or restart Dragon Naturally Speaking, you will need to fix the problem. Here are the most common problems and their solutions:

? **Error message:** "User training has not been successfully completed for this user" or similar (see example).

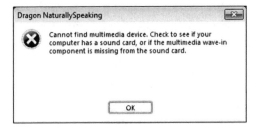

  ✓ You either need to re-train your user profile, or you may have only missed a few steps which you can complete now. Click "OK" to load the user profile and see what appears that needs your attention. Complete the training steps as needed.

? **Error message:** "No audio device detected" or similar message (see example).

  ✓ Plug in your headset again— or troubleshoot wireless headsets and handheld microphones. Dragon will not load a user profile if no microphone is detected.

? **Other error messages**

  ✓ Visit nuance.com/naturallyspeaking and look up the specific error in their support pages. Some errors can be challenging, but persevere. If you don't find answers at nuance.com, you can also post your question at usingspeechrecognition.com.

On the next page, read an overview of the DragonBar. The DragonBar menus, and options for displaying the DragonBar (called modes), are covered in Chapter 2.

Discover the DragonBar

The DragonBar is the main interface between the computer user (you!) and Dragon NaturallySpeaking. You will use the DragonBar in the rest of the exercises in this chapter, so it is useful to learn briefly about it before beginning. Read the steps below to learn about the DragonBar, the main Dragon interface.

1. Beginning with the upper-left corner of the window, notice the green Dragon icon (looks like a flame) to the left of the words "DragonBar", indicating that this window is the DragonBar. On the right are the standard three buttons for minimize, maximize and close.

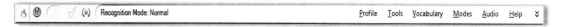

2. Next to the Dragon icon is the microphone icon on the left, an oval-shaped volume display bar, a green or gray checkmark called the "Full Text Control" indicator (tells you if Dragon works fully with that window, or in a more limited way), a "recognition mode" button (more on this later) and the **message area**, which displays messages about the status of the microphone and more. In the example above, the message tells that the Recognition Mode is Normal. (More on this later as well.)

3. There are six menus: **Profile, Tools, Vocabulary, Modes, Audio** and **Help**. To the right of the Help menu is the **Extras** toolbar icon, which is the shape of two down-pointing arrows (also called chevrons). The Extras toolbar holds the correction button, the playback toolbar, and the transcribe button—useful with digital recorders.

> Dragon's six menus hold the program's features. Learn about these in detail on page 83.

4. The **DragonBar** can be displayed in five different ways. Learn about these, and explore how to select the one best for you, on page 83. Below is an example of the DragonBar in "floating" mode.

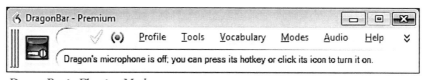

DragonBar in Floating Mode

Special Topic:
Dictating Text vs. Dictating Commands

Dictating Text: Clear and Steady

Dictating **text** involves several important techniques: use a clear, conversational voice, which is relaxed and steady. Remember to speak at your regular speaking pace or slightly more slowly. Your microphone is very near your mouth, so you do not need to speak loudly at all. Finally, never speak text one…word…at… a…time with long pauses in between words. Your recognition will be much better when you speak normally.

> Speak calmly and in a relaxed, conversational tone when dictating.

Dictating Commands: Speak "Commandingly"

In the next section you will begin dictating **commands**. To dictate commands effectively, use the technique of <u>pausing slightly</u> before speaking the command. (How slightly? A one-second pause would be plenty!) Then, speak the command as if it were one word ("**gotosleep**") and <u>pause again</u> before resuming regular text dictation. In this way, the software will know that you meant to dictate a command and not text to be typed. Speaking a command a little more loudly than text can also help. All commands in this book are in **bold type**. (Items which must be typed, by contrast, are in *italics*, and items which must be clicked on manually are in quotation marks.)

> Speak commands as though they were one word, and "commandingly".

Alternate Commands

For many commands, there are alternate commands that perform the same function. For example, in the next section, there are two sets of commands to make the microphone go into standby mode and wake from standby mode. The primary commands are given first, but if you have any trouble with them, use the alternate commands. A list of commands appears in the back of this book.

> Pause slightly before and after a command for best recognition.

Learn to Control the Microphone

Good control of your microphone is necessary to become good at speech recognition, so it is worth the time it takes to get these commands (or their alternate commands) to work for you. Controlling your microphone by voice involves three essential commands:

- **Go To Sleep**
- **Wake Up**
- **Microphone Off**

Use the keyboard, the mouse, or alternate voice commands to control the microphone. Below is a table of the three positions of the microphone, what the icon looks like in these positions, and the various ways to achieve these states. While it is immensely helpful to learn to control the microphone in at least two ways (i.e., voice and keyboard), ultimately the best method is the one that works best for you.

Control The Microphone

Microphone Status	Icon	Spoken Command	Alternate Command	Keyboard Shortcut*	Mouse Action
On		**Wake Up**	**Listen To Me**	Number Pad + key Number Pad / key	Click mic icon to turn on
Asleep (Standby)		**Go To Sleep**	**Stop Listening**	Number Pad / key	
Off		**Microphone Off**	---	Number Pad + key	Click mic to turn off

The Keyboard shortcut is a "hot key" that toggles between two settings: Number Pad + key toggles between on/off; Number Pad / key toggles between asleep/on.

Why are there multiple ways to start and stop the microphone?

Flexibility! Notice how there are three ways to turn the microphone off? This is common in using a computer with speech recognition: there may be one way to do something with the mouse, one way to do it with the keyboard, and a way (or several ways) to accomplish the same task by voice. If one way doesn't work for you, try another.

Exercise 1.3 Microphone Commands

DIRECTIONS: Follow the steps below. Speak the text in **bold** aloud. Do not say anything else, or you may have unexpected results. Refer to the chart on the previous page as needed.

Turn On Microphone

1. To turn on your microphone, click with the mouse on the microphone icon on the Dragon Bar or press the plus (+) key on the number keypad. When the microphone is on, the microphone icon turns green and the icon "stands up".

Put the Microphone into Sleep Mode

2. Say, **Go To Sleep**. Wait a few seconds while the computer processes the command. The microphone should now be asleep.
3. If it does not respond, try it again, speaking clearly and "commandingly".

"Wake Up" the Microphone

4. After it is asleep, wait a few seconds, then say **Wake Up**. The microphone should wake up, and be in the "on" position. (You might also see a message box prompt you with a message like "Please say that again". This is normal.)

Practice Microphone Commands

5. Practice sleeping and waking your microphone by first saying **Go To Sleep**, then **Wake Up**.
6. Do this several times, speaking clearly, pausing for about 5 seconds between commands.

Turn Microphone Off

7. Say **Wake Up** one last time, pause, then say **Microphone Off**. The microphone will turn off.

Review: How did the microphone commands work for you? If you are a polite person who generally doesn't speak commandingly, you might have a hard time telling the computer what to do—you may have to force a "bossy" tone until you get used to giving commands! (Imagine commanding a puppy to "sit"; this is the type of vocal firmness to use.)

Help! It isn't working!

If you have trouble getting the commands to work, you may be saying it too quietly or too slowly. Remember to speak commands as if they were one word, without pauses. If the above commands don't work, try the alternate commands, **Stop Listening** and **Listen To Me**.

Where is the Microphone On command?

You cannot turn ON your microphone by voice. Why? Because the microphone is *not on to hear you!*

What's so great about the Go To Sleep command?

The **Go To Sleep** command is one of the most useful Dragon commands. The purpose of this command is to mute the microphone while leaving it on. This is very useful if you need to answer the phone, have a side conversation, or just take a quick break or a drink of water.

Why is the volume level green, yellow, red or gray?

The volume meter on the Dragon Bar is green for good volume levels, yellow for acceptable (but possibly low) levels or red (input is too loud) as it works.

If you see red in the volume meter, your voice or your headset level is too high. Either speak more softly, or move the microphone back away from your mouth a half inch or so. A gray bar means that the microphone is asleep.

The Results Display

When you have the microphone turned on, a small green flame icon animates to show that Dragon is listening and is processing your speech. When you pause, the text appears.

If Dragon does not understand what you said, the results display shows "Please Say That Again" to prompt you to repeat your last dictation.

`Please say that again`

The results display can be moved out of the way by dragging it with the mouse; once you have it positioned where you prefer it, you can anchor it to that spot by double-clicking or right-clicking on the flame icon or text box and choosing "Anchor" in the menu that appears.

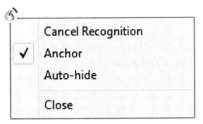

Finally, if you prefer to not see the results display, you can choose "Auto-hide" from the results display menu, and results display will "auto-hide" according to the settings. (See Chapter 8 for more on settings and options.)

Time to Talk to Your Computer: Dictate Text and Commands into DragonPad

Dragon has its own simple word processing program, called DragonPad, which is optimized for creating dictated documents. (The same skills you learn here can be used later in other word processors like Microsoft Word or OpenOffice Writer.) In the following exercise, open and close DragonPad, and dictate some basic text and commands to move the cursor.

Commands you will use in Exercise 1.4, in addition to the microphone commands from the previous exercise, are the following:

- **Start DragonPad** or **Open DragonPad**: opens the DragonPad program.
- **New Line**: Moves the cursor down a line (like pressing the Enter key).
- **New Paragraph:** Moves the cursor down two lines, and begins a new paragraph.
- **Click Close** or **Close Window**: Closes the open program window. The effect is the same as clicking the close box with the mouse.

Tip: Read the entire exercise before beginning; it will make your dictation better.

Go to the next page and begin Exercise 1.4.

Exercise 1.4 First Dictation

DIRECTIONS: Complete the exercise, following the steps carefully (see example below). The text in **bold** should perform a function, not be typed as text. If Dragon types something different than what you dictate, **leave it** for now. You will learn how to delete gibberish and make corrections soon.

Start DragonPad

1. With your microphone on, say **Start DragonPad** or **Open DragonPad**. *Wait 10 seconds for DragonPad to open.* If the DragonPad window does not appear after 10 seconds, repeat the command.

Dictate sentences, punctuation, and commands

2. Locate the blinking cursor (also called an "insertion point") in the DragonPad window. Now, dictate (say) this simple sentence: **Today is the first day of the rest of my life.** (Say **period** at the end.)

3. Look at the sentence. If it went perfectly, great! If not, don't worry—it will improve soon.

4. Say **New Line**. This will move the cursor down to the next line.

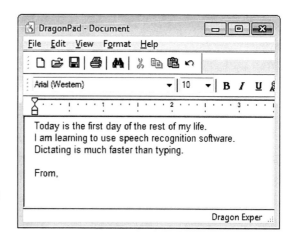

5. Dictate this sentence: **I am learning to use speech recognition software.** (Say period.)

6. Say **New Line**.

7. Dictate this sentence: **Dictating is much faster than typing**. (Say period.)

8. Say **New Line**.

9. Say **From,** (say **comma**)

Put the Microphone into Sleep Mode

10. Say **Go To Sleep.** You should see the microphone icon move to the sleeping position. If not, wait 5 seconds and then repeat the command.

Exercise 1.4, Continued

Save and Print the Exercise

1. Save this document by clicking the "File" menu, then choosing "Save As...". Name it "Exercise 1.4" and save in an accessible location (the Documents folder, a removable USB drive, etc.).

2. To print, click the "File" menu, then the "Print" option. In the print window, check the settings, make any changes as needed, then click "OK" to print.

3. Legibly sign your name below the closing ("From,") on the paper printout. The exercise is now complete.

Close DragonPad

1. Put your headset back on, if needed. Adjust your microphone to one thumb's distance from your mouth and slightly off to one side.

2. Wake up your microphone with the command **Wake Up**.

3. Dictate the command **Click Close** (or **Close Window**) to close DragonPad.

4. DragonPad closes. (If a message appears asking if you want to save changes, you probably haven't saved the document and should do so now.)

Review: How did it go? Was it mostly correct, but with a few errors? If so, this is normal and expected! (No errors? Lucky you!) In the next chapter you'll learn to correct errors, but just leave them for now. In the future, **only commands** will be in **bold** in exercises: text to be typed on the screen will appear in a slightly larger font, like this: Hello!

Note: In Chapter 2 you will learn the **essential Dragon warm-up exercise,** which is similar to Exercise 1.4, and helps you gauge how your recognition is working.

Help! I can't get DragonPad to open with the voice commands!

If both **Start DragonPad** and **Open DragonPad** aren't working for you yet, go to the **Tools** menu on the DragonBar and then click the "DragonPad" item. (Don't worry if this command doesn't work the first time you use it. However, if it doesn't work for you by the time you have finished the exercises in this chapter, train the command following the steps on page 60.)

How can I remove some unwanted text quickly?

If something you dictate is misrecognized (i.e. you say "cat" and Dragon types "rat") then you need to make a correction. Corrections are covered in Chapter 2. If, however, you just want to erase some gibberish, use the command **Scratch That**.

Scratch That!

Scratch That is an essential command that you will use often. It tells the program to remove the last "utterance" or "unit" of speech. This might be a word, but more often it is a phrase or a sentence. Use this command after noticing unwanted text (maybe you coughed), or you have changed your mind about what you have dictated. Just say **Scratch That** and it will be erased!

For Example:

- You dictate a sentence about the day of the week. You say, "Today is Monday."
- However, you look at the calendar and it is, actually, Tuesday.
- You say, **Scratch That**.
- Your text will disappear. Dictate the correct sentence, "Today is Tuesday." and it will appear.
- Now you have the sentence you meant to dictate.

What if I don't like saying Scratch That. Is there an alternate command?

An alternate command for **Scratch That** is **Strike That**. They both delete the last bit of text.

I used Scratch That, but it didn't work. Why?

The command **Scratch That** is designed for small amounts of text only—a word, a phrase, or a sentence. For longer units of text, say **Delete That**. Warning: when you use **Delete That**, the text may be permanently deleted (depends on the program and its settings—but it is best to consider "deleting" to be irreversible).

Oops! I scratched some text, but I want it back! How do I undo that?

To get back text after you have "scratched" it, say **Undo That**. (This works best if done immediately.) Finally, an "oops" button!

Undo That

Undo That works in other situations as well—which is especially helpful if you aren't sure what went wrong or how to fix it. So, when you notice something has gone haywire, try saying **Undo That** right away. (Also, the keyboard command for **Undo That** is Ctrl+Z.) The reverse of **Undo That**, if you change your mind, is **Redo That**.

About Punctuation

Do I have to dictate "period" and "comma"?

No, but Dragon works best if you <u>do</u> dictate punctuation. Dragon can automatically add commas and periods, but **it can be hard to get it to work correctly**. To try the automatic punctuation feature, say **Auto-punctuation on**. When auto-punctuation is on, the software puts in a comma when you make a short pause, and a period when the pause is longer. To turn off auto-punctuation, say **Auto-punctuation off**. It is recommended to leave auto-punctuation off until you have more experience dictating.

What about other punctuation, or symbols and special characters?

 Punctuation involves a lot more than commas and periods! While we use punctuation every day, speaking punctuation aloud is not something we usually do. Also, some punctuation is less common and requires practice. The following exercise (Exercise 1.5) shows how to dictate punctuation and common symbols.

How Will I Know What to Say?

In the following exercise, you will see punctuation, symbols, and special characters in a column, with the word to be spoken next to the item. Many will already be familiar to you.

What if some of these symbols and punctuation don't work well for me?

If you have trouble getting some of the punctuation or symbols to work, make a note of this. In Chapter 2 use the Spelling box to correct words, punctuation or symbols that don't dictate properly. Try any challenging symbols again when working in the Spelling box.

 Most students of speech recognition have difficulty with one or two items at first. Most common is the colon [:] symbol. The tilde [~] can be tricky as well! Speaking symbols like the ¾ (three-quarter sign) can take practice. However, if you have never dictated a "smiley face" :-) or a "winky face" ;-) you just might have some fun with this exercise. ☺

Exercise 1.5 Punctuation and Special Characters

DIRECTIONS: Open DragonPad again with the command **Start** (or, **Open**) **DragonPad**. Dictate the left column of punctuation and symbols, then the right column. (Don't make columns; just dictate one item on each line—this makes it easier to proofread.)

Say **New Line** after each symbol; this will create a list. If any of these aren't typed properly, say **Scratch That** and try again. If it still doesn't work, leave it for now.

Item	Dictate as...	Item	Dictate as...
.	Period (or Dot or Point)	§	Section sign
,	Comma	&	Ampersand *or* And Sign
:	Colon	#	Number Sign *or* Pound Sign
;	Semicolon	_	Underscore
?	Question mark	¶	Paragraph sign
!	Exclamation Point or Exclamation Mark	$	Dollar Sign
--	Dash (may look like one long dash, or two short dashes)	¢	Cent sign
...	Ellipsis	€	Euro sign *or* Euro *or* Euros
-	Hyphen	:-)	Smiley Face
'	Apostrophe	:-(	Frowny Face
's	Apostrophe S	;-)	Winky Face
/	Slash or Forward Slash	%	Percent sign
\	Backslash	¼	One-quarter sign
"	Open Quote *or* Begin Quotes	½	One-half sign
"	Close Quote *or* End Quotes	¾	Three-quarters sign
(	Open Paren	^{1}	Superscript 1
)	Close Paren	^{2}	Superscript 2 *or* squared
[	Open Bracket	^{3}	Superscript 3 *or* cubed
]	Close Bracket	+	Plus sign
~	Tilde (say "Til-duh")	-	Minus sign
@	At sign	÷	Division sign
©	Copyright sign	=	Equals sign
™	Trademark sign	×	Multiplication sign

Sleep Microphone and Check Your Dictation

Sleep or your microphone with the command **Go To Sleep**. Compare your work with the list above. Go to the next page.

Exercise 1.5, Continued

Save, Print and Close

Save your work as "Exercise 1.5". Print if needed. Close DragonPad by turning on or waking your microphone and saying **Click Close** or **Close Window**.

Review: How did it go for you? If one or two symbols stubbornly refused to be dictated, this is not unusual. If you had trouble with more than five of the items in Exercise 1.5, you may want to teach Dragon to understand your dictation of those especially difficult items. The Spelling box (covered in Chapter 2) is useful for this task. **Note:** Don't train these items now—it may not be necessary, as Dragon improves as you work with it. Wait until you have learned to use the Spelling box in Chapter 2 to make these changes, if they are still needed.

About Timed Writing Exercises and Exercise 1.6

 A timed writing exercise gives instant feedback on your dictation speed and recognition. Expect to see many recognition errors in this first timed writing; your speed and recognition will improve as you work through the next few chapters. You will need a reliable timer handy.

✓ The timed writing passage (on the next page) is 150 words long. **Do not try to finish it in one minute**; in fact, it was written so that you likely do not complete it. (Just stop speaking when the timer goes off.)

✓ However, if you do complete it, say **New Line** and then start dictating again from the beginning.

✓ If you have trouble reading the text aloud (you skip words, get lost in the text, etc.) try the old grade school trick of focusing on each word, one at a time.

✓ You may have many errors. Think of this first timed writing as a kind of pre-test—before you have honed your user profile by dictating text and making corrections. At the end of Chapter 3 is another timed writing—compare your work then to this first timed writing.

✓ Feel free to try this exercise more than once. Often, it takes a try or two in order to get used to speaking normally while a timer is running!

✓ Punctuation spoken in this timed writing is **period** and **dash**. Your dash may look like this (--) or like this (—). For this exercise, both are fine.

Exercise 1.6 Timed Writing I

DIRECTIONS: Read the steps below before beginning.

1. Set a timer for one minute, but do not start timing yet.
2. Turn on your microphone and say **Open DragonPad**.
3. Say **Go To Sleep** to put your microphone to sleep.
4. **Pre-read** the timed writing passage, to make your speech more fluid and less error-prone. Notice where the dashes and periods are.
5. When you're ready to begin, turn on your microphone and start the timer.
6. Dictate at your normal rate of speech, or just a little more slowly and deliberately. Remember to dictate punctuation.
7. When the timer goes off, turn off your microphone immediately. This prevents unintended dictation.
8. Look over your work, and count how many words you dictated (use the guide at the right-hand side of the page to help you).
9. Subtract the number of errors (wrong words) from the total number of words. This is your adjusted WPM (words per minute).

Timed Writing 1 *Dictate the text below*	Words Per Line	Total Words
New users of speech recognition software are often surprised	9	9
that it can be difficult to work with the computer in a new	13	22
way. There are several reasons for this. For someone who has	11	33
been typing for years, it takes a while to get used to how	13	46
quickly you can dictate e-mail and create documents.	8	54
Learning the right commands for any situation — and	8	62
remembering them when you need them — is challenging at	9	71
first. If you frequently reach for the mouse or revert to typing	12	83
on the keyboard, stop and dictate the command to learn what	11	94
you can say. Finally, it's easy to become irritated or frustrated	11	105
with the computer when it misunderstands. After all, we tend	10	115
to become irritated or frustrated with people when they	9	124
misunderstand us. Don't take it personally. Just keep in mind	10	134
that you're talking to software, not a person, and that it will	12	146
get better with practice.	4	150

Total words – errors = adjusted words per minute

Exercise 1.6, Continued

Review: How did it go? If you had a lot of errors, it can be disappointing. Consider this a practice test. After you learn to make corrections in Chapter 2, your recognition will improve significantly. Follow the directions below to save, print and close your work.

Save and Print Your Work

Save your work as "Exercise 1.6". Print if needed (this can also make it easier to see errors).

Close DragonPad

Close DragonPad by turning on your microphone and dictating the command **Close Window** (or, **Click Close**).

QUESTION TIME! HERE ARE FREQUENTLY ASKED QUESTIONS:

What if some words were formatted differently—such as "email" instead of "e-mail", "it is" instead of "it's", or a long dash instead of two short ones?

No problem! Don't count these as errors. If your computer formatted some items slightly differently, but your recognition was good (it was the correct word or punctuation), then count it as correct. If you do want to change the formatting of any words or punctuation in the future, use the techniques for correction and training presented in Chapter 2.

How many words per minute are considered good?

New users of speech recognition software wonder how many words per minute they should be trying to achieve with a timed writing. There is no speed goal for this timed writing. However, consider how fast you can type and measure your speed against that; if you are dictating faster than you can type, then speech recognition software is probably a useful tool for you! (Did you wonder about the helpful Dragon command mentioned in the timed writing passage above? The command to get a list of useful commands in any particular situation is: **What Can I Say**.)

Does the software know every word I might speak?

Yes—and no. While speech recognition software can recognize most English language words, numbers, symbols, punctuation, names, and many common acronyms, it can't know everything. If you need to dictate words not in the standard vocabulary, you can add them. Some examples of words you might add are names with unusual spellings, words imported from other languages, and specialized terminology. Also, speech recognition tries not to let you embarrass yourself in print: certain vulgarities (swear words) are replaced with other words (i.e., "fark").

So, I really shouldn't eat potato chips while dictating? Or chew gum?

Have you ever tried to knit while typing? Can you imagine what would happen? Go ahead, try to picture it! Eating and chewing gum while dictating is the speech equivalent—and it's **not** a good idea! You will have poor recognition, and your voice won't be consistent. You should, however, drink water while dictating (just not while actually speaking, for obvious reasons!)

Is there anything else I shouldn't do while dictating? Can I have the radio on?

Dictating is a very localized activity—mainly centered around your mouth. Having a radio on (or a TV, or a person talking across the room) usually isn't a problem. However, loud noises like doors slamming or vacuum cleaners can cause problems with speech recognition. Try to work in a reasonably quiet area, without too many distractions.

Author's Note: That said, I once dictated demonstrations of Dragon while in at a very noisy conference exhibit. Sometimes even I couldn't hear what I was saying over the roar of the crowd—but Dragon picked it up just fine!

What if my recognition accuracy doesn't get better soon?

The Accuracy Center organizes the many useful tools Dragon NaturallySpeaking provides for increasing accuracy. For example, you can import a list of specialized vocabulary used in your business or academic field. For more about The Accuracy Center, see Chapter 5.

What's Next?

Up next: the last two exercises in Chapter 1. In these exercises, DragonPad is not used (close DragonPad if it is open). You do, however, need your Dragon user profile open and your microphone on.

What are the last two exercises about?

Practice speaking names of items on the screen to activate them (instead of clicking with the mouse), while learning more about Dragon NaturallySpeaking, in the last two exercises of this chapter: Exercise 1.7 Help Files, and Exercise 1.8 Dragon Tutorial.

About Exercise 1.7

The Help area, with topics and subtopics, is designed to replace a paper manual. Help topics are useful for getting more information about Dragon Naturally Speaking, as well as lists of commands, troubleshooting help, and more.

The "Search Dragon Help" Command: Quick and Easy

This excellent command will search the Dragon Help for any topic you request—even if you don't have the Dragon Help area open! For example, if you are working in Microsoft Word, but you need Dragon Help, say **Search Dragon Help for [*topic*],** where you substitute the word or phrase of your topic instead of the word "topic". Try this out in the exercise below to see how it works.

Note: While the Help area can be completely accessed by voice, the commands necessary to do so are covered in later chapters. Therefore, you'll need to use your mouse for parts of this exercise. (If this is not feasible for you, skip this exercise for now. You can always return to it after you have learned the commands to move the cursor by voice introduced in Chapter 2.)

Exercise 1.7 Help Files

DIRECTIONS: Follow the instructions to open the Help area, view topics and subtopics of the Help files, and close the Help file.

Commands used in this exercise are **Give Me Help**, **Close Help** and **Search Dragon Help for [*topic*]**.

Open Dragon's Help Area

1. Check that your microphone is on, then say **Give Me Help**. The Help area will open. (See the example on the next page.)
2. Look for the words **"Getting Started"** next to the book symbol in the list on the left side of the window. Click on the **plus sign** to the left of "Getting Started" with the mouse to open the list.
3. Click on the **minus sign** next to the item to close the list again.

Look Through the Subtopics and Links

4. Look for a **subtopic** of interest to you, such as "Using the DragonBar" to learn more about the DragonBar.

Exercise 1.7, Continued

5. In the main area of the window, there are **links** to learn about what is new in your current version, to visit nuance.com, to go to the Accuracy Center, and more. If you scroll down this window, you will see other options.

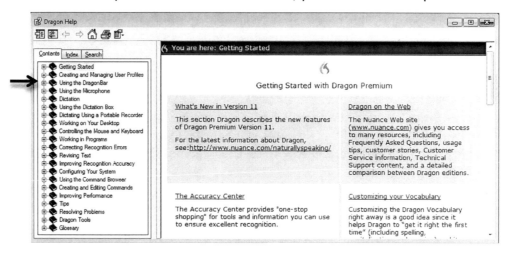

Close the Help file

6. When you have exploring, close the Help file by dictating the command **Close Help** or **Click Close**.

Search by Voice

7. From the desktop, with the Help area closed, say this Dragon Help search command: **Search Dragon Help for *Microphone***. The Help area should open again, with information about the microphone displayed.

8. Try one more Help search by voice. With the Help open, or closed (your choice), say: **Search Dragon Help for *DragonBar***. The Help area should now display information about the DragonBar. Look it over, then say **Close Help**.

Reflect and Write

9. Write a short paragraph summarizing what you read in the Help area. Describe at least one new fact or command that you discovered. Title this paragraph "Exercise 1.7".

Review: How did this go? An alternate way to open the Help file is to click on the "Help" menu in the DragonBar. From the "Help" menu, click on the "Help Topics" item.

About Exercise 1.8 "Getting Started" in the Dragon Tutorial

Dragon NaturallySpeaking has an extensive tutorial. This useful area contains overviews of Dragon topics, step-by-step instructions and in some areas, short instructional videos. In this next exercise you will explore the Getting Started area, which covers many of the topics you've learned about in this chapter.

Exercise 1.8 "Getting Started" In The Dragon Tutorial

DIRECTIONS: Learn to use the tutorial, and review much of what you have learned in this chapter, by working with the first two topics in the **Getting Started** section of the Dragon Tutorial. Try to complete this exercise by voice. Use your mouse only if voice commands don't work.

Open the Tutorial

1. Say **Click Help** to open the Help menu in the DragonBar.
2. Say **Tutorial** to open the Dragon Tutorial.

Get to Know the Tutorial Window

3. When the Tutorial opens, look over the window.
4. Notice the areas in green along the upper portion of the window: Home, Getting Started, Dictating Text, Correcting/Editing and Using Applications.

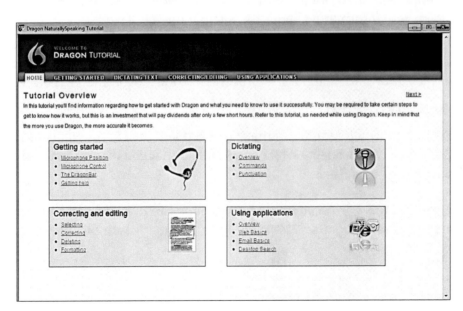

Navigate the Tutorial by Voice

5. Say **Click Getting Started** to open the Getting Started area.
6. Notice the first topic is **Microphone Position: Overview**.
7. Say **Click Back** to click the "back" link and return to the **Home** tab.
8. Say **Click Microphone Position** and that area opens again.

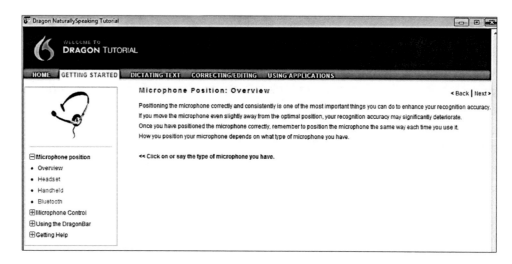

9. Say **Click Headset** to open the Headset area. Read the text there.
10. Say **Click Handheld** to open the tab called Handheld. Read the text there. Finally, say **Click Bluetooth** to see that area.
11. Say **Click Microphone Control**. The Microphone Control area opens, and after a minute a video usually plays which demonstrates how to turn on, off, and sleep the microphone.

Close the Tutorial

12. Say **Click Home** to return to the opening Tutorial screen.
13. Close the Tutorial with the command **Click Close** or **Close Window**.

Reflect and Write

14. Write a short paragraph summarizing what you read in the Tutorial area. Give at least one new fact or command that you discovered. Title this paragraph "Exercise 1.8".

Review: Notice how navigating the Tutorial by voice was different from navigating the Help area by hand. Also, speaking links is different from dictating text. You will use this technique for dictating links when working with programs—especially web browsers (covered in Chapter 5).

Is my user profile getting better even when I don't save a document?

Yes, provided you save the updated speech information (the commands you dictate, for example) into your user profile. Every time you use the software, you are training it to understand you better. Below, learn how to **save your user profile by voice** every time you finish a session working with speech recognition software.

Save User Profile and Exit Dragon By Voice

Save your user profile with easy voice commands before exiting (closing) the program when you are finished with your Dragon NaturallySpeaking session. Here's how:

1. Dictate this command: **Save User Profile.**
2. Wait while Dragon processes the command; check the DragonBar for progress.
3. Close the program by saying **Click Profile** to open the Profile menu in the DragonBar; pause a moment, then say **Exit Dragon** in a clear, normal voice. Wait to see if Dragon understands. If not, pause for a few seconds, then try again.
4. You do not need to turn off your microphone—the software will do this for you when you close Dragon.

Are there any other methods for saving my user profile?

Yes. This can be accomplished by clicking on the Profile menu and choosing the **Save User Profile** option.

Can Dragon save my user profile automatically?

Yes. You can automate this task by setting it up in the **Options** area. To do this, go to the **Tools** menu in the **DragonBar** and choose **Options**. The **Options** window will open: click the **Miscellaneous** tab. Next, check the box next to "Automatically save the profile changes" click "Apply", then "OK". The Options window will close, and Dragon will now save your updates to your user profile every time you close Dragon NaturallySpeaking.

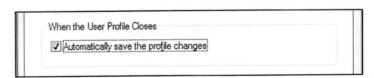

QUESTION TIME!

I won't ever have to train a user profile again, will I?

You don't need to train a user profile again, provided your new profile is working well, but you may choose to at some point in the future. If you get a new computer, or use more than one computer with Dragon, you will likely train a new user profile. Don't fear training another user profile—it is much easier the second, third, and fortieth time!

If I get a new microphone, do I need to train a new user profile?

If you get a new microphone, you do not need to train a new profile in order to use it. Instead, load your user profile, then go to the DragonBar's Audio menu and choose "Check Microphone". The audio settings windows which you completed when you trained your user profile will appear. Perform the training, then the new microphone will work. This does not work if you are going to use a digital recorder—in this case, train a user profile just for this device (it is okay to have more than one user profile, just give them different names, like "Jane Smith-Recorder").

Where is the User Profile Saved?

Dragon NaturallySpeaking user profiles are stored in the hard drive of the computer you train, unless you specify a different location. For example, user profiles can be stored on removable flash drives, or other storage drives. If you need to store your user profile somewhere other than the default location (your computer's C drive), see the instructions in Chapter 8. To move a user profile to another computer, see the directions in Chapter 8 for exporting a user profile.

Completion of Chapter 1 includes: the initial set up and user profile training, learning commands to control the microphone, using DragonPad, practicing punctuation, examining the Help files and the Tutorial, and finally, saving your user profile.

Command Review

Note: A cumulative list of commands presented in this text is in the Appendix at the end of this book.

Commands in Chapter 1 are:

Go To Sleep	Redo That
Wake Up	Close Window
Microphone Off	Auto-punctuation On
Listen To Me	Auto-punctuation Off
Stop Listening	What Can I Say?
Start DragonPad	Give Me Help
Open DragonPad	Click Help
New Line	Close Help
New Paragraph	Search Dragon Help for [*topic*]
Click Close	Click [*name of item*]
Scratch That	Save User Profile
Strike That	Click Profile
Delete That	Exit Dragon
Undo That	

CHAPTER 2
Dictating Text and Making Corrections

After training your Dragon NaturallySpeaking user profile and trying dictation with DragonPad in Chapter 1, you're probably eager to learn how to dictate text effectively, use the right command in any situation, and correct misrecognitions. These items are the primary focus of Chapter 2.

To help you in these goals are the following: **core instructions** to follow when using speech recognition software, a **warm-up exercise** to prepare you to dictate successfully, **commands** to navigate by voice around your text, and an orientation to the **DragonBar menus** and **Sidebar**.

By the end of this chapter, you should begin to feel comfortable dictating text and commands to the computer and making corrections.

Dictating Text

Dictating is Simple!

Dictating text is simple: you speak the words and punctuation into a word processing program, such as DragonPad or Microsoft Word, and it is typed on the screen. The difficulty comes when you need to do one of these things:

1. Apply formatting to text or numbers
2. Dictate a word or phrase new to Dragon (e.g. names or acronyms)
3. Dictate your own work (compose)
4. Make corrections

In This Chapter

- ✓ Best Practices When Dictating Text
- ✓ Core Instructions
- ✓ Warm-Up Exercise
- ✓ Continuous Speech Recognition and Misrecognition
- ✓ Making Corrections: Three Levels
- ✓ Commands to Control the Cursor
- ✓ DragonBar modes, menus
- ✓ Dragon Sidebar
- ✓ Control Dragon windows by voice
- ✓ 12 Exercises
- ✓ Frequently Asked Questions
- ✓ Command Review

All of these situations are covered in the next few chapters. However, most dictation situations are not difficult—if the best practices for speech recognition are followed.

Best Practices for Excellent Speech Recognition

Working with speech recognition is different from typing—and not just because you are speaking rather than pushing keys on a keyboard. Using keyboarding and mouse methods will lead to frustration; learn and use these best practices instead.

1. BEGINNER'S TIP: USE PRINTED TEXT

When learning to dictate text, it is best to **begin by reading printed text**. Reading text aloud is something you are probably familiar with doing. It is **harder to compose your thoughts in your head while dictating**, so until you are fluent with the software, read printed text aloud to practice dictating.

Reading printed text, such as the exercises in this book, will help you learn to dictate effectively.

Later, when you are experienced with dictating and seeing the words on the screen, try composing your own writing (see page 165). This avoids the frustration that comes with trying to learn speech recognition while composing writing in your head and trying to dictate fluently.

2. DICTATE FIRST, FORMAT SECOND

When working with word processing in the past, you might have typed a title to a document and then spent a moment to make it centered, bold, and perhaps even a different font. When you dictate with speech recognition software, it works better to dictate all the text for the document first, correct it, save it, and then make formatting changes afterwards.

Not only does this make it easier to dictate a document without having to stop to format it, but it avoids several potential problems. First, Dragon can get "stuck" in a formatting style and it requires extra effort to undo it. If you dictate first, and format

Dictate unformatted text first, make corrections if needed, then go back and add formatting.

second, this rarely happens. Second, occasionally a formatting command will lead to unintended results (for example, you say **Bold That** and instead the paragraph disappears) which take time to correct and might disrupt your train of thought as you write an academic paper or work report.

54

3. MAKE CORRECTIONS, BUT NEVER INTERRUPT A SENTENCE

When you type, you usually correct a typo as soon as you notice it—often, right after it occurs. With speech recognition software, when you see an error in a sentence, ignore it until you finish your sentence. Always wait until after you dictate the punctuation at the end of the sentence before you make a correction, because often the software will change it before your eyes, frequently making it closer to what you had intended. Also, speech recognition software uses a language model based upon units of speech—such as sentences—and interrupting a sentence can create more misrecognitions. However, it is not necessary to make corrections after every sentence—that can get tedious.

> Never interrupt your dictation of a sentence to make a correction.

Instead, **make corrections after every paragraph or so**. Many users find that after they have worked with speech recognition for several sessions, their recognition is good enough that making corrections every few paragraphs or every page is about right.

4. FOLLOW CORE INSTRUCTIONS

When typing manually on a keyboard, there are basic instructions to follow. Speech recognition also works best if you follow certain guidelines, and these are called *core instructions*. The core instructions for speech recognition will increase recognition accuracy and help prevent injury.

Core Instructions

1. Do a warm up exercise (2–5 minutes of generic practice)
2. Take frequent sips of water (to keep your voice as healthy as possible)
3. Take regular breaks (e.g. 5–10 minute break each hour)
4. Read the step before you do it *or* plan ahead what you mean to say and do

On the next page, learn about the warm up exercise, then practice this new skill in **Exercise 2.1, The Warm Up Exercise.**

About The Warm Up Exercise

The warm-up exercise takes five minutes or less, but performs a valuable service.

First, it tells you how well your speech recognition is currently working. If you dictate the warm up exercise and all is well, you can be confident that your user file is ready to go. However, **if you notice many errors** in your recognition you can take steps to improve your accuracy right away, before any bigger problems occur.

Second, the warm up exercise **keeps you from beginning your dictation session in an important document** that might be harder to fix if something goes wrong.

Exercise 2.1 The Warm Up Exercise

DIRECTIONS: Read the entire exercise before beginning. Turn on or wake up your microphone and say **Start DragonPad**. Leave mistakes for now. Items in **bold** are commands, and should produce an action, not be typed as text. Items in brackets [ ] give instructions and should not be spoken. (See example.)

[Start Dictating]

Hello computer, are you ready to work today?

New Line

I am using speech recognition software.

New Line

Dictating is much faster than typing. **New Line**

Today is the first day of the rest of my life.

New Paragraph, **Microphone Off**

[Stop Dictating]

Review: Notice how some words are fine but others may be misrecognized. By doing this exercise regularly, you will come to know how your recognition is doing from just these few sentences! Some words may appear as contractions (*I'm* or *Today's*): notice these, but don't change them. Soon you will learn how to correct errors, but just for now save your exercise—without correcting errors, as you will do this in the next exercise—by clicking on the "File" menu and choosing "Save As". Name the document "Exercise 2.1" (don't type the quotation marks) and use it with Exercise 2.2 (on page 63).

Trouble?

If you had difficulty with the warm up exercise, read these tips and then try the exercise again:

1. Dictate the four sentences of the warm up exercise in a normal, relaxed way.
2. Try not to watch each word as you dictate, as it will interrupt the flow of your speech.
3. Instead, look at the screen after you have completed a sentence and dictated the sentence's ending punctuation.

 # QUESTION TIME!

How many mistakes are typical in the warm up exercise? How many are too many?

The first time a new user dictates the warm-up exercise, anywhere from one to 10 errors are typical. After making corrections using the techniques in this chapter, the number of misrecognitions is usually reduced by 50% or more. Therefore, don't be discouraged if you have several misrecognitions in your first warm-up exercise. However, if you still have three or more misrecognitions in the warm-up exercise after several sessions of working with the program, use the Accuracy Center (see Chapter 5) to improve your recognition accuracy.

My recognition was fine yesterday—why would it be worse today?

There are many possibilities. Your microphone connection might be loose, your computer's antivirus software might have chosen that moment to run a resource-intensive computer scan, you might be chewing gum (gasp!), or you might be coming down with a cold. Dictating a warm-up exercise gives a quick heads-up to a potential problem.

If I have a cold, is that a problem?

If you have a cold, nasal stuffiness due to allergies, or a sore throat, your recognition will be worse than usual. In fact, sometimes the first indication of a cold among speech recognition users is an unexplained decrease in accuracy! If you are feeling unwell it is probably best to save speech recognition for another day.

QUESTION TIME! (CONTINUED)

Is "misrecognition" just a fancy word for error or mistake?

Misrecognitions are a very specific kind of error that speech recognition software makes. So, yes, **misrecognitions** are in fact **mistakes**—but <u>not just any random error</u>. Misrecognitions are like incorrect guesses—if you give the software the best possible input, it will make better "guesses" as to what you are saying. You can reduce the chances of misrecognitions by using the Best Practices introduced in this chapter.

Some misrecognitions will still occur, especially with words which are not in Dragon's vocabulary. Misrecognitions should be corrected using special techniques covered in this chapter. Learn more about misrecognitions in the next section.

Can you get it to stop misrecognizing?

To a large degree, yes. If you teach the software by correcting misrecognitions, the number decreases. Eventually misrecognitions only occur when something has changed: new vocabulary, a different headset, or a stuffy nose. It's like typos—when you get better at typing, you make fewer typos. When the software understands you better, it makes fewer mistakes.

> Correct misrecognitions using the techniques in this chapter.

Is this the end for spell checkers? Doesn't the software spell everything correctly?

One huge benefit of speech recognition is that **it never misspells a word!** (It does, however, guess incorrectly—but those words are also spelled correctly.) Does this mean no more spell check? If you only dictate text, you don't need spell check—but if you do any editing or typing by hand, you probably ought to double check the spelling to be sure! (In Microsoft Word, the command for this is **Check Spelling**.)

TRUE STORIES

Marlene did everything right. She dictated warm up exercises to check her recognition, she saved her user profiles after every session, and she worked hard to learn best practices for dictating and correcting text. Unless she was frustrated, that is—then she backspaced off misrecognitions, telling herself that it didn't matter, as long as she made voice corrections sometimes. But it **did** matter. Marlene's recognition never really improved, and she grew so frustrated that she quit using the program, convinced that "it just doesn't work for me".

Special Topic:
Continuous Speech Recognition and Misrecognitions

How It Works

As a user is speaking a sentence, the software tries to match the sounds made to grammatically correct sentence structures and, using a language model, tries to put the right words in the right places. This is called "continuous speech recognition" and it **works best** with **complete phrases and sentences** which are grammatically correct.

Continuous speech recognition is different than the kind of "discrete" speech recognition used by most cell phones and other basic systems that can only understand a limited set of words (such as "call home" or "option 1").

Misrecognitions: Funny, Bizarre, Aggravating

Misrecognitions are errors in recognizing spoken language. When continuous speech recognition gets it wrong, the errors are often humorous or bizarre because they may be grammatically correct, but wildly off base.

> *For Example:* You say, "My brother likes to go to Leeds."
> On the screen you see, "My mother likes to grow weeds."

In the example above, notice how the parts of speech are consistent, but the meaning is totally different. This gives an odd kind of "Mad Libs" quality to errors: *mother* instead of *brother*, *grow* instead of *go*, *weeds* instead of *Leeds*. The nouns are replaced with nouns, the verbs with verbs, but it isn't at all the same meaning.

The software can't recognize words not already in its vocabulary, but you can **train** them. Examples may include your name, non-English words, acronyms and newer technical terms, like the e-mail scam known as "phishing".

You Teach, It Learns

The software "learns" from you; that is, the program adapts to the way you speak. It doesn't know it has made a mistake until you correct it; then it adds this knowledge to your user profile. If you don't correct misrecognitions, the software may actually get *worse* at understanding you. So, while any particular error may seem minor, it is important to correct it to get better overall accuracy.

Why shouldn't I just use the mouse and keyboard to correct errors?

The program won't learn from you and improve if you use the mouse and keyboard for corrections. It takes patience and effort to learn a new way to work with the computer, but this is why you bought this book, right? Hang in there, and soon you will be making corrections by voice faster than you ever could by hand.

> ### Corrections Made Easy
>
> This chapter presents the three levels of correction (with variations): the **Correct** command, the **Correction box**, and the **Spelling box**. After learning these methods, practice applying them quickly in order: if the first method doesn't work, go straight to the second level, and so on. This is the most efficient way to make corrections.
>
> Corrections can be made by voice alone, or voice in combination with the keyboard and/or mouse.

Making Corrections

By now you know that when the software makes a recognition error you need to make a correction. You can correct a **single word** or a **short phrase** (2–4 words). Longer phrases are best broken down into smaller units, or they will be unwieldy and hard to correct. The examples and instructions in this chapter show mostly single word corrections.

There are **three levels** of correction: using the **Correct** command to select and replace the incorrect word(s), using the Correction dialog box, and spelling out the word or phrase. Corrections can be made with **voice commands** alone, with the **keyboard**, or with the **mouse**. Each method is presented in this chapter. Words with special functions, such as **That**, are explained as well. Text or commands that are persistently difficult to dictate also can be trained following the instructions on page 60.

Many speech recognition users get frustrated or upset when what they said isn't what was typed. Don't take it personally—the computer does **not** hate you! Remember, computers are just expensive bits of plastic and metal that follow their programming instructions. You shape this process by making corrections.

Three Levels of Correction

To correct misrecognitions, begin with the methods below. Work to get these commands understood; they are important to the speech recognition method.

Level 1: The "Correct" Command—Quickest

1. **Identify** a word that needs correction
2. **Say Correct That, Correct [*word*]** or a variation
3. **Say the correct word** or phrase again
4. The correct text should replace the incorrect text
   - ✓ See page 61

Level 2: Correction Box—Most Accurate

1. Read the options in the Correction dialog box
2. If one is correct, say **Choose 3** (or the correct number) to select the option
3. The correct text should replace the incorrect text
   - ✓ See page 68

Level 3: Spell Box—For Difficult Words, Symbols, etc.

1. Say **Spell That**
2. Spell your word by voice or keyboard in the Spelling dialog box
3. Train it to your voice speaking the word if you wish
   - ✓ See page 71

Level 1: The "Correct" Command

This is the "fix it on the fly" approach, which will correct the majority of recognition errors quickly. It uses the **Correct** command, which has several variations:

- **Correct That**: corrects the last bit of speech you dictated
- **Correct [*wrong word*]**: selects the word so that you can speak the correct word again
- **Correct from [*word*] through [*word*]**: selects a range of words for correction

Correct That

Like **Scratch That**, if you say **Correct That**, the last phrase or bit of speech you have just dictated will be selected. With **Scratch That**, the text is then erased. When you say **Correct That**, the text is selected (highlighted) so that you can say the correct word to replace the misrecognized word. Practice this in Exercise 2.2.

Correct [*wrong word*]

When you finish dictating a sentence or paragraph, proofread it for misrecognitions. When you find a misrecognition, say **Correct [*wrong word*]**. When the incorrect word is selected (highlighted), say the correct word.

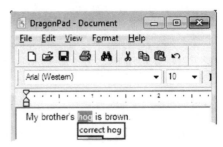

For Example:

If you say: **My brother's dog is brown.**
But you see: **My brother's <u>hog</u> is brown.**

Change *hog* to *dog* by saying **Correct *hog***. Then, when the word *hog* is selected, say *dog*. This command is also be used for short phrases (2-4) words. In this case, you would say **Correct [*wrong words*]**, pause, then say the correct phrase.

Correct from [*word*] through [*word*]

This command is used to select a range of incorrect words. It works best with phrases that aren't too long (10 words or less). Long phrases with errors should be corrected in segments.

To use this command, say **Correct from** [*first word of phrase*] **through** [*last word of phrase*]. When the phrase is selected, say the correct text again, clearly, so that Dragon can correct it.

Important Tips for Correction:

1. Do not raise your voice when you make corrections. For human listeners, this is often helpful, but not for the computer.
2. Be sure to speak clearly, but don't over-enunciate. It hinders the process.
3. If something unexpected happens (a menu opens, for example) say **Cancel** or **Escape** to undo that action.
4. Sometimes, when you make a correction, the "correction" is also wrong. Try it again—if it still is incorrect, save that misrecognized word or phrase to use with the next level of correction.
5. Occasionally, the word you want to "correct" is missing—it never got recognized when you first said it. To deal with this problem, say **Insert Before** [*word where you want to add text*] to put the cursor there. Then, say the word that was omitted.

Exercise 2.2 Use the Correct Command

DIRECTIONS: Follow the steps to correct misrecognitions in your warm up exercise (Exercise 2.1). Read the tips above before beginning.

1. Look over Exercise 2.1 for errors in recognition, including omitted words.
2. Locate one error and plan to use the **Correct** command to fix it. Turn on the microphone.
3. Say **Correct [*wrong word*]**. Pause while Dragon selects the word, then say the correct word.

Note: If Dragon "corrects" your word with another incorrect word, try it again. If it doesn't work, leave it for now. You will learn how to correct these problems with the Correction dialog box.

4. Look for a second recognition error and correct it using the **Correct [*wrong word*]**, **Correct [*wrong words*]** or **Correct That** command.
5. Correct all misrecognized words using **Correct** commands.
6. If any words you spoke were omitted, say **Insert Before [*word*]** to move the cursor, then say the omitted word. (This also works with missing punctuation.) Say, **Microphone Off** to turn off your microphone.

Review: How did it go? Did it feel strange telling the computer what to do? If so, don't worry, you will get used to it—and maybe even wonder how you did without it before! **If you had trouble** getting the command to work, try using a slightly louder voice and speak the entire command as if it were one word (no pauses). Be commanding!

What if I don't have enough errors to correct?

First of all, congratulations! If you don't have any recognition errors, things are going extremely well for you. However, if there aren't enough errors to correct, you'll need to get creative. In the warm up exercise are two possible contractions: "I'm" for "I am" and "Today's" for "Today is." These can be used for making corrections with no risk of messing up your user profile. For example, say **Correct *I am***, and when the text is selected, say ***I'm***.

What's that box under the correction I'm making?

If a list box with choices appears below your selected word when making a correction, that is the Correction dialog box, explained on page 68. You can ignore it for now.

What if I use a Correct command, and little numbers appear on the screen?

If there are multiple instances of the word you are trying to correct, Dragon will number them all. To make the correction, say the number of the word you want to correct. It is selected, and then you can say the correction as you usually would.

In the example at below, the user said **Correct *tall***.

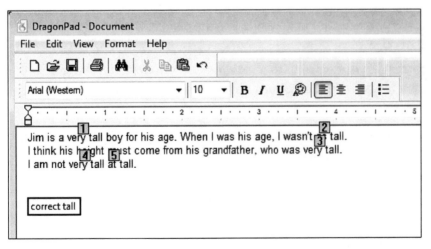

The *next* command would be to say **Choose 5**, as this is the "tall" that needs correcting, then say the correct word, **all**.

Alternate Command: The "Select" Command

The **Select** command is similar to the
Correct command above.

For Example:

If you say: **Tim is an accountant.**
But you see: **Tim is an account nut.**

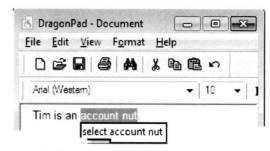

Change "account nut" to "accountant" by saying **Select** *account nut*. When it is
selected, say *accountant*. The new word or phrase will replace the incorrect one in
the text.

The **Select** command has many more functions, described later in this book.

About Exercise 2.3

The next exercise is a sample e-mail message; see the example on the next page. The
exercise uses text, punctuation, and symbols. If you have difficulty remembering how
to dictate punctuation or symbols, review the list in Chapter 1. This exercise is
designed to produce two or three recognition errors, so expect this. The point of the
exercise is to provide text to practice the **Correct** and **Select** commands, while
increasing fluency with text and symbols.

Exercise 2.3 Practice Correct and Select Commands

DIRECTIONS: Follow the steps to dictate a sample e-mail message. See the example on the
next page for reference.

1. Dictate the e-mail message on the next page into DragonPad. Don't worry
    about where the lines break, but dictate the new lines and paragraphs
    where indicated.

2. Proofread your work to locate at least two recognition errors. Check
    capitalization and punctuation as well.

3. Say **Select [*wrong word*]**, pause while the software selects the word, then
    say the correct word.

4. Look to see if the correction worked. If not, try step 3 again. (If it doesn't work after the second try, leave it for now and return to it when working with the Correction box in Exercise 2.6.)

5. Use the **Select** or **Correct** commands to correct any remaining recognition errors.

6. Save your work as "Exercise 2.3". Print if needed.

[Start Dictating]

Dear Kathy, **New Paragraph**

How are you? Robert and I were talking about you the other day, and wondering when you might visit. I meant to e-mail you sooner — so much for "seize the day" I guess! My memory is so [!&@#$] terrible these days! **New Paragraph**

Drop me an e-mail any time, or e-mail Robert. (Do you still have Robert's e-mail address?) **New Paragraph**

Best wishes, **New Line**

Sandra **Microphone Off**

[Stop Dictating]

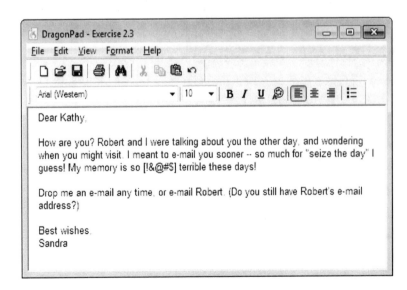

Review: How did it go? This exercise is quite a bit harder than the warm up exercise. Did you have any trouble with the dash (— or --) or brackets [ ]? Did you notice how *Robert's* and *e-mail* were automatically formatted? Dragon saves endless aggravation by automatically formatting possessives (e.g. *Jim's*), many hyphenated words, phone numbers, addresses, and more (more about this in Chapter 3).

Which is best: e-mail or email?

Either one—or the one preferred by the style guide you are using. If you prefer *email*, and Dragon types *e-mail*, correct it. Dragon will learn your preference and will adapt your user profile to reflect your preferred vocabulary. (It often takes more than one correction, so keep at it.) Note: for consistency, the spelling *e-mail* is used throughout this book.

Alternate Methods to Select Text to Correct

The keyboard (through use of a specially designated keyboard shortcut or "hot key") and the mouse provide alternate methods to select text to correct. Use these methods to select the text for correction, then dictate the correct word or phrase.

Method	Action	Pros	Cons
Keyboard Hot Key	Put the cursor in the wrong word(s) and press the **number pad minus key**, then **say** the correct word	Provides a keyboard option Improves future recognition	Requires keyboard Use If no number keypad, requires changing the hot key setting*
Mouse	**Double-click** the wrong word(s) with mouse, then **say** the right word(s)	Provides a mouse option Improves future recognition	Requires mouse use

Note: hot key settings are found in the DragonBar's Tools menu, under Options. Hot keys are explained in Chapter 8, or see the Dragon Help files.

So I can use the keyboard and mouse to correct? No speaking needed?

No. Use the mouse and keyboard ONLY to **select the words to correct.** (If you wish to—once you get used to correcting by voice, you will likely find it much faster than using the keyboard and mouse.) **Do not type the corrections,** as it does not improve your recognition; in fact, your recognition can get worse if you don't give it voice corrections.

Keyboard Hot Key

Sometimes, it can be useful to make corrections using the keyboard. For example, if you want to avoid overuse of your voice, using the correction hot key provides an option that still improves your user profile.

Exercise 2.4 Hot Key to Correct

DIRECTIONS: Follow the steps to make a correction using the keyboard hot key.

1. Locate an error in any of your exercises. Put the cursor in the wrong word.
2. Press the number keypad's minus (-) sign.
3. After the word is selected, <u>say</u> the right word.
4. The incorrect word should be replaced.

Using the Mouse for Corrections

Making corrections using the mouse in speech recognition software is different than the typical manual method. When you make speech recognition corrections using the mouse, you double-click on the incorrect word, and then **say the correct word**. In this way, you are giving a speech sample of the correct word and Dragon understands that a correction has been made. **Avoid falling into the bad habit of backspacing and typing to make corrections.** If you do that, your recognition will not improve, because the software won't know if you meant to make a correction or simply decided to type something else.

Exercise 2.5 Mouse Double-Click to Correct

DIRECTIONS: Follow the steps to correct using the mouse. (If mouse use is painful or difficult for you, skip this exercise.)

1. Locate an error in one of your exercises. Turn on your microphone.
2. Double-click with the mouse on the incorrect word.
3. **Say** the correct word.
4. The incorrect text should be replaced.

Review: What did you think of this method? The combination approach of mouse click and speaking the correct word can be a very fast way to correct—if you don't have any difficulty or pain using a mouse. Important: always speak the correction, don't type it.

Level 2: The Correction Box

Using the **Correct** or **Select** commands is quick, but sometimes it just *doesn't work*. Some reasons for this are: the word you dictate isn't in Dragon's vocabulary, the misrecognized word or phrase is not grammatically correct, you weren't speaking clearly, or, Dragon is just being persnickety!

No matter the reason, **if the first level of correction doesn't work**, here is what you do next:

1. Say either **Correct** [*wrong word(s)*] or **Select** [*wrong word(s)*].
2. The **Correction box** will appear under your highlighted text; look for the correct word or phrase in the list of choices.*
3. If the correct word is there, choose the number next to it. For the example below, you would say **Choose 1** to choose the correct text.
4. The item you chose will replace the incorrect text.

*If the Correction box doesn't appear, go to the Tools menu of the DragonBar, choose Options, then the Correction tab. Check the box next to "Select commands bring up Correction menu", click "OK".

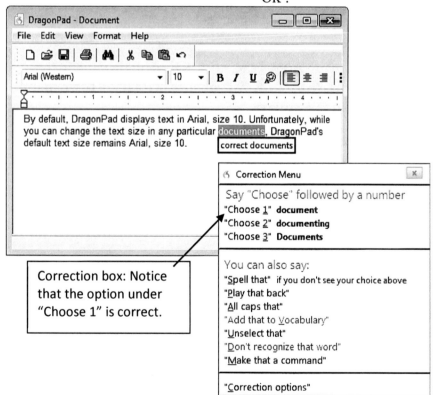

Correction box: Notice that the option under "Choose 1" is correct.

The Correction box also offers shortcuts to some useful commands, such as **Unselect That**. **Unselect That** is a command to use when something is selected that you don't want selected. Maybe it wasn't what you wanted, or perhaps you have changed your mind. Either way, **Unselect That** will cancel the selection.

Other commands in the Correction box are covered later in this text, including: **Play That Back,** which plays back your speech to you, **All Caps That,** which capitalizes the selected text, and **Spell That,** introduced below. In the Correction box you can also access the correction options, including how many choices you want to see in the box. To do this, you would choose the "Correction options" choice and select options from there.

Exercise 2.6 Use The Correction Box

DIRECTIONS: Follow the steps to make corrections from the Correction box.

1. Find an error in recognition.
2. Say **Correct [*wrong word*(s)]**.
3. The Correction box will open. Look for the correct choice, and say **Choose 3** (or the correct number). The correct text will appear in the document.

Review: Did this work well for you? What if the word you wanted wasn't in the Correction box? Take it to the last level of correction by dictating the command **Spell That** and then spelling out the word.

Do I have to speak in the Correction box?

No. If you prefer to use the mouse or keyboard, you can, and it does not negatively affect your recognition. To use the mouse, click on the correct choice. To use the keyboard, press the arrow keys to move to the correct choice, then press "Enter".

Can it Show More Choices? Or Fewer Choices?

Yes. This is set in the Options area. To get here, click on the Tools menu in the DragonBar, then choose Options. Click on the Corrections tab, and then select the number of choices you want displayed (see example at left). Click "OK" in the Options dialog box to save the changes and close the box.

Show no more than 9 choices

Level 3: Spell That

Spell That is the command to use when the first two methods don't work. By spelling it out, you are not relying on the software to guess what you want; you are going to tell it, exactly, what you want typed. Spelling is often necessary for unconventional words, like company or place names, names of people (Kathy or Cathy or Cathi or Kathie) and acronyms (SPCA, UNESCO, etc.)

Saying **Spell That**, and then pausing, opens the **Spelling dialog box**, where letters, numbers, punctuation and symbols can be dictated.

About Exercise 2.7 Spell That

When correcting any particular word is difficult, spell it out instead. In the Spelling dialog box, you speak letters (or numbers, symbols or punctuation) one at a time, until done. For phrases, say **Spacebar** to insert a space between words. If Dragon misunderstands your pronunciation of a letter (d instead of g, for example), say **Backspace** to delete just that letter. For multiple incorrect letters, say **Backspace 3** (or the correct number). You can also use the mouse and keyboard in this window.

The right word might appear in the numbered list before you have finished spelling it out—no problem! Say **Choose 5** (or the correct number) to select the number next to the correct word when you see it. If the first word needs a capital letter, look for the capitalized version in the Spelling box and choose the number next to that choice. For example, if you dictate "b-o-b" you will likely see both "bob" and "Bob" among the choices.

Exercise 2.7: Spell That

DIRECTIONS: Follow the steps to use the Spelling dialog box.

1. Open DragonPad and turn on your microphone.
2. Dictate this sentence (without quotes): "Kathie and Jon went to the Ventana Inn."
3. Say **Select [*wrong word*]** to select the first misrecognized word. Say **Spell That**. The Spelling dialog box will open.

71

4. Dictate the spelling, letter by letter, until done. Say **Backspace** if an incorrect letter is typed.

5. When you see the correct word in the list, say **Choose 1** (or the correct number) and then say **Click OK**.

6. The new word will replace the old one in your document.

7. Repeat steps 3 through 6 for each misrecognized word.

Review: How did it go? Were any steps particularly difficult? Remember, this is the type of skill that improves with practice. **Note**: If you have trouble spelling by voice, and you are able, feel free to type by hand in the Spelling box. It won't negatively affect your recognition.

 Quicker! If you select a word or short phrase, say **Spell That**, and *without pausing*, immediately dictate the spelling of the word, the Spelling dialog box *does not open* and the letters are typed directly into your document.

Buttons in the Spelling Box

Speak the names of the buttons in the Spelling box to activate them. The **Play That Back** button will play back your voice saying the word(s) selected, the **Train** button opens a window to train the item in the text field (covered soon), and the **Tell Me More About This Window** button opens the Spelling box Help area. Saying **Cancel** will close the window without saving changes, and **OK** accepts changes and closes the window. Finally, saying **Click Close** will click on the "X" icon in the window and close it.

I say a letter, and it types a different one—help!

If you still have trouble getting your letters recognized, use the radio alphabet to dictate the letter. The Radio Alphabet is one version of the **broadcast alphabet**, which assigns a word to each letter, in order to distinguish between similar-sounding letters, like "b" and "g". For example, the letter A is dictated as **Letter Alpha**. The name Ami is spelled out as **Letter Alpha, Letter Mike, Letter India**.

Will I need to spend a lot of time spelling out words?

No. This technique is only used if the first two levels don't fix the error. Always try using the **Select** or **Correct** command first, then the Correction box if needed before spelling out a misrecognized word or phrase.

What if all this correcting doesn't work and I still get the same misrecognitions?

If you find that often you have to spell out certain words, train them by using the **Improve Recognition of Word or Phrase** option in the **Audio** menu on the Dragon Bar, or click on the "Train" button in the Spelling box after the word is spelled correctly. Learn to train text or commands in Exercise 2.8.

Exercise 2.8 Train Text or Commands

DIRECTIONS: Train the software to better understand you speaking a specific command or text.

1. Open the **Audio** menu in the DragonBar by saying, **Click Audio**. If you have trouble with this, you can open the menu using the mouse, or the keyboard.

2. After the menu opens, say **Improve Recognition of Word or Phrase**.

3. The Training window will open. Type or dictate the word, phrase or command you wish to train. If it is a command, use capitalization like the text shown below. If the check box is selected, your word or phrase will be added to Dragon's vocabulary.

4. Click or say **Train** to go to the Train Words window.

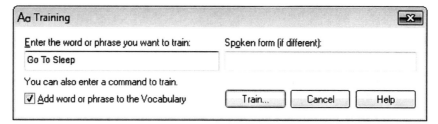

5. Say **Go** to indicate that you are ready to begin.

6. Say the word, phrase, or command. Clicking or saying **Go** each time, train the word twice more, speaking a little differently each time (faster, louder, softer, slower, etc.).

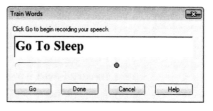

7. Say **Done** and the window will close.

8. Now test your word or command to see if it works.

Review: How did it work? If it doesn't work yet, save your user profile and try again. If it still doesn't work, try retraining it, saving your user profile, and restarting your computer.

True Stories

Sometimes the errors seem random but they may have an easy explanation. A student of mine, named Anne Benveniste, would dictate her name and see "Anne been the nasty" on the screen instead. Understandably, she found this aggravating! After following the directions in this chapter to correct her name, it improved. However, as Benveniste is not an English language word, Anne had even better recognition when she trained her last name using the technique on the previous page. Names, especially non-English names, often need to be trained.

What About Gibberish? Does It Have To Be Corrected?

Sometimes what you say gets typed as **gibberish**, which is unintentional dictation that is often both meaningless and somewhat amusing. This can happen when you have a conversation with a co-worker but your mic is on, or you cough a few times into your mic, or gremlins temporarily take over your machine (just kidding—it only feels that way)! Do you have to correct this nonsense? Fortunately, no!

To get rid of gibberish, you could park your finger on the backspace key, or say **Scratch That** over and over, but faster is to use a selective command like **Select Line**, then say **Scratch That**. (More on these commands soon!)

Example of Gibberish:

1. You are dictating when your friend asks to borrow a pen.
2. You say, "Uh, just a minute, okay?" and your microphone is still on.
3. Looking at the screen, you see, at the end of your work, this: "Uh just mind it Kay".
4. This is gibberish! To delete this unintentional dictation, say commands like:

   - **Scratch That**
   - **Select Line**, then **Scratch That**
   - **Delete Last 5 Words** (2-20 words)
   - **Delete That**

Note: Gibberish doesn't need to be corrected, because you didn't mean for it to be dictated. If you dictated some text intentionally, however, and it is incorrect, make corrections using the **Correct** command, the Correction box, or the Spelling box.

How do I move the cursor by voice?

As you learned earlier, saying **Insert Before [*word*]** moves the cursor in front of the word spoken. Here are other useful commands for moving the cursor.

Cursor Commands:

Go to Bottom	moves the cursor to the end of the text
Go to Top	moves the cursor to the top of the text
Go to End of Line	moves the cursor to the end of that line
Go to Beginning of Line	moves the cursor to the beginning of the line
Insert After [*word*]	moves the cursor to after the word spoken
Insert Before [*word*]	moves the cursor before the word spoken
Move Down 1 Line	moves the cursor down one line
Move Down [2] Lines	moves the cursor down two lines (2-20)
Move Up 1 Line	moves the cursor up one line
Move Up [6] Lines	moves the cursor up six lines (2–20)

What is this about 2–20 of something?

With certain commands, you can choose from 2–20 of the item named. For example, if you want to select the last 17 lines in a document, you can say **Select Last 17 Lines**. In this chapter, use this technique with the **Select**, **Delete** and **Move** commands. Multiple characters, words, lines, sentences, or paragraphs can be selected in this way. Some examples are: **Move Down 14 Lines, Move Right 5 Words, Select Next 2 Characters,** and **Delete Last 9 Words**.

When there is only one of the item, use commands like **Move Up 1 Line, Select Next Sentence,** and **Delete Last Paragraph**. These commands are just examples; they are discussed in-depth in dedicated sections of Chapters 2–4.

About Exercise 2.9 Move the Cursor by Voice

In this exercise, dictate a list of well-known sayings. These are sayings that students have adopted to personalize their warm up exercises as they tend to work well. Feel free to adopt any of them yourself! This is the also the first exercise to use your name. It may dictate beautifully the first time, but if your name is at all unusual (like the author's) then you can expect to correct it. You may also need to spell out your name at least once before speech recognition software consistently recognizes it correctly.

Exercise 2.9: Move the Cursor by Voice

DIRECTIONS: Open a new DragonPad document and turn on your microphone. Dictate the following text into DragonPad, including your first and last name, then follow the directions below to make corrections and move the cursor by voice.

[Start Dictating]

Today is the first day of the rest of my life. **New Line**

Those who forget the past are doomed to repeat it. **New Line**

Don't let perfect be the enemy of good. **New Line**

The only thing we have to fear is fear itself. **New Line**

Don't worry, be happy! **New Line**

(Say Your First Name and Last Name) **New Paragraph, Go to Sleep**

[Stop Dictating]

1. Turn off or sleep your mic and **look over** your work.
2. Turn on or wake up your mic and **make corrections** to the dictation, using the three levels of correction. Your name may require the Spelling box.
3. Save your corrected work as "Exercise 2.9".
4. Say **Go to Top** to move the cursor to the top of your exercise. (If "Today" is not the at the top of the document, say **Insert Before *Today*** instead.)
5. Say **Go to Bottom** to move the cursor to the end of your document.
6. Say **Insert After *perfect*** to move the cursor after the word *perfect*.
7. Say **Insert Before *first*** to move the cursor before the word *first*.
8. Say **Go to End of Line** to move the cursor to the end of the line.
9. Say **Go to beginning of Line** to move the cursor to the beginning of the line.
10. Say **Move Down 2 Lines** to move the cursor down two lines.
11. Say **Insert After *period*** to move the cursor to the end of the sentence.
12. Say **Go to Bottom**. Sleep or turn off your microphone.

Review: Are the cursor commands working for you? If you have trouble with these, practice them. If you had difficulty getting your name recognized, train it (page 60). Print your exercise if needed.

Delete Commands

Text which is deleted is permanently removed, unlike **Scratch That**, which only cuts the text. Below are useful **Delete** commands.

Delete That	Deletes permanently the last word, phrase or selection
Delete Last Word	Deletes the last word (to the left of the cursor)
Delete Last [3] Words	Deletes previous 2–20 words (left of the cursor)
Delete Last [12] Characters	Deletes previous 2–20 characters (left of the cursor)

About Exercise 2.10

This exercise uses the **Delete** commands. **Note:** the period at the end of a sentence counts as a character in a command like **Delete Last 3 Characters** and *also counts as a word* in a command like **Delete Last 5 Words**.

Exercise 2.10: Use Delete Commands

DIRECTIONS: Dictate the following text and commands (in bold), and delete as directed. Text in brackets [ ] give instructions or additional information.

[Start Dictating]

The math test was hard. [Say] **Delete That** [Text disappears]

The math test was easy. [Say] **Delete Last 6 Words** [Text disappears]

The chemistry test is today. [Say] **Delete Last 6 Characters** [*today.* disappears]

[Say] tomorrow. [Sentence reads: The chemistry test is tomorrow] **New Line**

Linda loves to take tests. [Say] **Backspace** [Replace with a question mark]

Phil loves to eat snails. [Say] **Backspace 7** [Say] pizza. **New Paragraph**

Go To Sleep

[Stop Dictating]

Review: When this exercise is finished, you will only have the following sentences left in your exercise: "The chemistry test is tomorrow. Linda loves to take tests? Phil loves to eat pizza." Save your work as "Exercise 2.10" and print if needed.

Note: Did **Backspace** work for you? If not, say **Press Backspace** instead.

 Press Right Arrow

Frequently, when you delete a word at the end of a sentence, before a period, the cursor remains on the inside of the period. To continue dictating after the period, move the cursor right over the period by saying **Press Right Arrow**. Dictate onward from there.

This is a keypress commands. Keypress commands are discussed in Chapter 3. Other keypress commands in this chapter include **Backspace** or **Press Backspace** (above), and **Escape** (which presses the Escape key).

What is THAT all about?

As you may have noticed, the word *that* has a unique meaning in speech recognition. *That* is a signifier word that means either "that which I have selected" or "the most recent unit of speech". For example, if you say **Select All**, then you say

Delete That, the *that* refers to all the text that is selected. However, if you say **Scratch That**, what gets erased is the last utterance—a word, a phrase, or maybe a whole line of text.

Can I correct the actual word, "that"?

This is a great system—until you need to correct the word *that* in your text. For example, let's say you dictate this sentence, "I like that very much" but you read it and decide that instead of the word *that*, you want to write *cooking*. Saying **Select** *that* won't work, because the command already does something else.

Instead, in this (rare) situation, use a cursor command such as **Insert After** *like* to move the cursor between the word *like* and the word *that*. Then say **Select Next Word**, then say *cooking*. That's all!

About DragonPad

Why Use DragonPad?

DragonPad, the word processing program included with Dragon NaturallySpeaking, is optimized to work with dictated speech. While its feature set is limited, it provides the basics needed for beginning speech recognition users. DragonPad is used for dictation in Chapters 1–3. Chapter 4 uses Microsoft Word, where you will be able to apply the skills you have learned to use with DragonPad.

Can I Make the Font Size Bigger?

DragonPad's default font is Arial, and the size is 10 point. The font size in any DragonPad document can be changed—the easiest way to do this is to say **Select All** and then say **Format That Size 12** (or larger). Unfortunately, however, the default font and size cannot be permanently changed. Therefore, if you wish to work in a larger font, you need to change it each time you work with DragonPad. (Font size commands are in Chapter 4.)

Speakable Menus

To speak the names of menus in DragonPad, either speak them alone (e.g. say **File**) or add the word **Click** in front of the menu name (e.g., **Click File**). Speak the names of the items within menus in this same way (e.g., **Print** or **Click Print**).

How to Re-Open a DragonPad document in DragonPad (it's not automatic!)

When you save a DragonPad document, and go to re-open it later, it may not re-open in DragonPad. This is because some programs (Microsoft Word, for example) take ownership of DragonPad files, which are saved in the rich text format (.rtf). What to do? To make sure it *does* re-open in DragonPad, open DragonPad first with the **Open** or **Start DragonPad** command. Then, from the **File** menu, choose **Open**. In the **Open** window, browse to your file and double-click it to open.

> To re-open a document in Dragon Pad, open DragonPad first, then open the document from inside DragonPad.

Can I Print by Voice?

Printing a DragonPad document using voice commands is easy. Follow the directions on the next page to print using voice commands. In later chapters, learn other ways to print (and save) by voice.

Controlling the Computer by Voice

On this page and the previous one, you can see that the menus in DragonPad and options for printing can be controlled by voice. (This is covered in more depth in Chapters 4 and 5.) These two pages are an introduction to the concept, with a program you have already used: DragonPad.

Print That

Print That is a special shortcut command which is like pressing the print button. You will learn more of these commands in the next two chapters, which can be used in many word processing programs.

Directions for Printing by Voice Using Menu Commands:

1. To print, say Click File (the File menu will open), then say Click Print.

2. When the Print window appears, look to see which printer it will go to and how many copies it will send. If all is OK, say Click OK or Click Print and your file will go to the printer. (If not, make needed changes and then choose OK.)

Directions for Printing by Voice Using Dragon's Shortcut Command:

3. If your print window is set up to send to the printer you want, you can try this shortcut printing command: **Print That**.

4. Make certain that no text is selected or only the selected text will print.

5. Say **Print That**.

6. One copy of the document will be sent to the default printer, or, if multiple printers are available, the print dialog box will open, and you can select the printer from there.

Trouble?

If you have trouble printing by voice, here are some things to check:

✓ The printer is connected to the computer and turned on.

✓ The printer driver (software) is installed properly.

✓ The DragonPad window is active. (Click into the window with the mouse to be sure.)

✓ To activate an open DragonPad window by voice, say **Switch to DragonPad**.

About Exercise 2.11

Bring together your skills in dictating text, commands, punctuation and symbols with the following letter. Remember to read aloud smoothly while dictating and try to avoid watching the screen. While this exercise incorporates a lot of new skills, many students find it goes quite well. **Tip:** housing-issues@mail.com is spoken as "housing hyphen issues at mail dot com." The word "e-mail" may be typed "e-mail" or "e-mail"; both are correct.

Exercise 2.11 Letter to Michael Franklin

DIRECTIONS: Read the text for this exercise before beginning to dictate. Say **New Paragraph** between paragraphs, say **New Line** when needed, but don't worry about line breaks. After you have finished dictating, turn off your microphone and read over your work.

[Start Dictating]

Dear Michael Franklin, **New Line**

As you know, the members of the committee to save affordable housing are concerned that you are planning to tear down your apartment buildings. These apartment buildings provide affordable housing for many families who need it. The committee would like to meet with you to discuss this issue. Would you be open to such a meeting? **New Paragraph**

You can reach me at the phone number I gave you earlier today, or you can e-mail me at: housing-issues@mail.com. **New Paragraph**

Thank you for your time and consideration in this matter. **New Paragraph**

Sincerely, **New Paragraph**

(Say Your First and Last Name) **New Paragraph**, **Go to Sleep**

[Stop Dictating]

Review: Is it getting easier? Make corrections to any recognition errors and save your work as "Exercise 2.11". Print by voice using either method given on page 80. Sign your name above your printed name—now it looks authentic. Good job!

Tips for the Ticked Off

It happens to everyone: you dictate something, and speech recognition software types something else. You select it and say the right word, but no luck. After the Correction box, the Spelling box, maybe even training the problematic text, and all of your calmest, most rational problem-solving, it still *won't work!* ARGH!

What to do (besides getting out the sledgehammer?)

First, get some perspective on the problem. If you are angry, upset or frustrated, your voice (like everyone's) tends to become louder, more forceful and different than usual. For this reason, the software *will not recognize your voice as well.* Think about it: you trained your user profile while calm, and this is how your speech recognition software thinks your voice should sound.

So, if you are frustrated or upset, **stop talking to the computer**. Turn off your microphone. Save your work (or not) and close everything. Restart the machine. Take a 5 minute break while the machine works, drink some water, walk around (helps to burn off some of that energy) and wait for the desire to throw the computer out the window to pass. Know that everyone who uses a computer sometimes wants to bash it to bits—it's going to be okay.

When you feel calmer, try again.

True Stories

Every semester, when I teach speech recognition software, I tell the students that they will want to bash the computer with a hammer at least once. Students smile politely when I say this, and I can see their thoughts, "Oh, I'm really good with computers, this won't happen to me." And, it always does. So—be patient with yourself, and know that everyone goes through a bit of aggravation before speech recognition works smoothly for them (usually by the end of Chapter 4 or sooner).

DragonBar Display Modes: How Would You Like To See Your DragonBar?

Ordinarily the DragonBar appears at the top of the screen, above other windows. While this mode works well in general, you might want to try a different display mode.

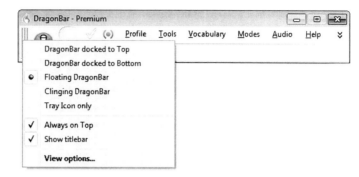

To change the display mode of the DragonBar, right-click on it and the context menu will be displayed (or use the voice commands below). From the context menu, choose one of the display modes:

- Docked to the top of the screen (default)
- Docked to the bottom of the screen (above the Taskbar)
- Floating (pictured above)
- Clinging (like a mini-toolbar at the top of the screen)
- Tray Icon (accessible only by right-clicking on the microphone icon in the Taskbar notification area)

To set other options, click the View Options item at the bottom of the menu (pictured above). This will open the Options area, which has a selection of other choices. The choices vary, depending upon which DragonBar mode you are selecting. For example, if you don't want to see messages in the notifications area, you can turn this off in certain modes.

Are there voice commands to change the DragonBar modes?

Yes. First, to activate the DragonBar (bring the focus to the DragonBar), say **Switch to DragonBar**. Commands to change the DragonBar modes are **Switch to [*name of mode*]**. For example, **Switch to Floating Mode, Switch to Docked to Top Mode, Switch to Docked to Bottom Mode, Switch to Cling Mode** or **Switch to Tray Icon Only Mode**. The alternate command is **Select [*name of mode*]**; for example, **Select Floating Mode**.

 Try changing modes by voice in Exercise 2.12 on page 88.

The DragonBar Menus

The DragonBar contains the features of the program in its menus. The DragonBar components were introduced in Chapter 1. This section points out some important items in the DragonBar menus.

The Profile Menu

The **Profile** menu contains the user profile controls, and the exit (quit) option. To open this menu, say **Click Profile**.

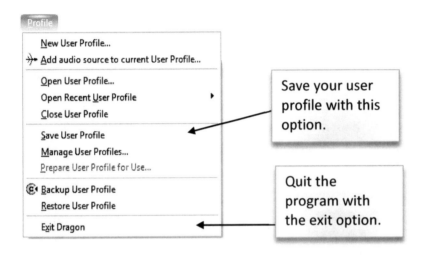

Save your user profile with this option.

Quit the program with the exit option.

The Tools Menu

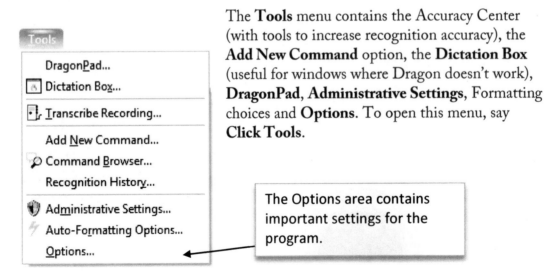

The **Tools** menu contains the Accuracy Center (with tools to increase recognition accuracy), the **Add New Command** option, the **Dictation Box** (useful for windows where Dragon doesn't work), **DragonPad**, **Administrative Settings**, Formatting choices and **Options**. To open this menu, say **Click Tools**.

The Options area contains important settings for the program.

84

The Vocabulary Menu

The **Vocabulary** menu contains options for analyzing your writing, adding a new word to the vocabulary, and importing and exporting custom vocabulary.

To open this menu, say **Click Vocabulary**.

The first option will adapt your user profile to your writing style.

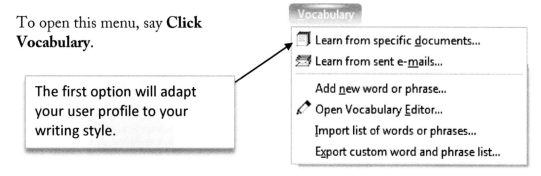

The Modes Menu

This menu contains links to the five Dragon Modes. **Modes** are used to narrow what Dragon recognizes to a limited vocabulary set, in order to make certain types of dictation easier. (Learn more about modes on page 139.)

The **Normal** mode is the one you will usually use, as it has the largest vocabulary set.

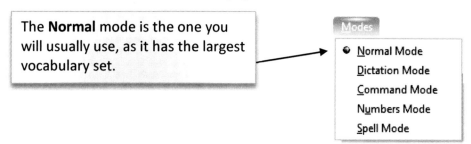

The Audio Menu

The **Audio** menu contains the playback feature and transcription options (from a mobile recording device, for example.) You can listen to your last utterance with the **Play That Back** command. The **Read That** command will read selected dictation to you using text-to-speech synthesis (computer voice). The quality of the voice that reads the text back depends on the voices installed on your computer.

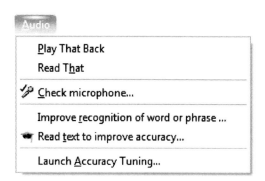

The **Audio** menu also contains a link to the microphone check feature, and the training scripts (called **Read text to improve accuracy**) which you may remember from the user profile setup process. If you want to use a new microphone, or if you need to do some additional training, these shortcuts are for you.

The **Improve recognition of word or phrase** item opens the Training window. Finally, the **Launch Accuracy Tuning** feature will adapt your user profile so that it works better. This takes some time, and it uses a lot of system resources, so run it when you don't need to use your computer for other purposes.

The Help Menu

The **Help** menu has several useful tools. The first two items help improve accuracy. The **Help Topics** item opens the **Help** menu. To open the **Help** topics quickly by voice, say **Give Me Help**. Selecting the Dragon Sidebar item will display the Sidebar. (The Sidebar is described on the next page.) The **Tutorial** is a full-featured tool designed to explain important speech recognition topics.

If you want to check for any updates to your version of Dragon, click the "Check for Updates" item. You can also visit the Dragon website through the link in the **Help** menu, register your product, and view the **About NaturallySpeaking** area (which displays your product's serial number).

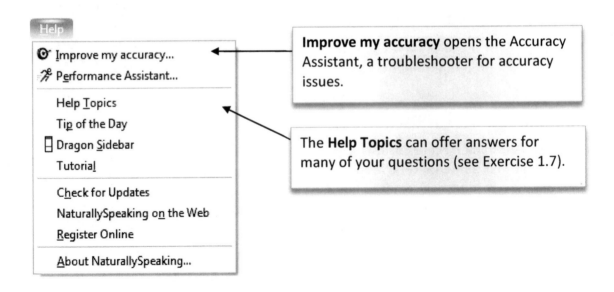

Improve my accuracy opens the Accuracy Assistant, a troubleshooter for accuracy issues.

The **Help Topics** can offer answers for many of your questions (see Exercise 1.7).

The Dragon Sidebar

The **Sidebar** displays a list of commands which change depending upon what you are doing (also called "context-specific"). In this way, Dragon tries to display the most likely commands you might need in a given situation. For example, if you are working in Microsoft Word, you would see a list of commands which can be used in Word. If you have Internet Explorer open, or DragonPad, or you are navigating the desktop, the commands list will change to show commands for these areas.

At the bottom of the sidebar is a **Dragon Tips** area with context-specific tips.

Commands for the Sidebar
Dragon Sidebar or **Open Dragon Sidebar** (makes the Sidebar active)

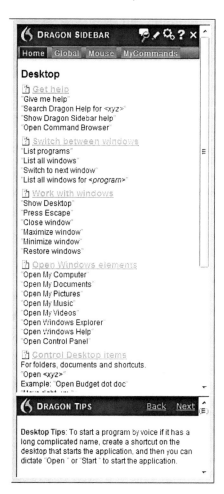

To Activate the Sidebar tabs:

 Dragon Sidebar *Home*
 Dragon Sidebar *Global*
 Dragon Sidebar *Mouse*
 Dragon Sidebar *My Commands*

To Change the Width of the Sidebar:

 Dragon Sidebar *Wider*
 Dragon Sidebar *Thinner*

To Set or Stop Auto-Hide of the Sidebar:

 Dragon Sidebar *Auto*-**Hide**
 Dragon Sidebar *Stop Hiding*

To Change the Sidebar's Position:

 Dragon Sidebar *Float*
 Dragon Sidebar *Dock Right* (default)
 Dragon Sidebar *Dock Left*
 Dragon Sidebar *Undock*

To Show or Hide Tips, Get Help or Close the Sidebar:

Dragon Sidebar *Show Tips*
Dragon Sidebar *Hide Tips*
Dragon Sidebar *Help*
Dragon Sidebar *Close*

Speakable Items in the Sidebar When Active

When the Sidebar is active, say the name of any of the links or tabs to activate that item (for example, say **My Commands** for that tab). Other commands are: **Always on Top** (sets the Sidebar on top of any other windows), **Switch to next pane** (switches between the Tips area and the main Sidebar area) and **Close Window**.

Exercise 2.12 Activate Windows by Voice

DIRECTIONS: Practice using commands to activate the DragonBar, DragonPad items, and the Dragon Sidebar.

DragonBar Commands:

1.   From the Desktop, with only the DragonBar open, turn on your microphone and say **Switch to DragonBar**. This will make the DragonBar active.

2.   Open each menu on the DragonBar, one at a time, saying **Click** in front of its name. (For example, **Click Profile**.)

3.   Minimize the DragonBar by saying **Click Minimize.** The DragonBar should be minimized (disappear from the screen, but still be open).

4.   Say **Switch to DragonBar** to bring back (restore) the DragonBar.

5.   Change the display modes of the DragonBar, using these commands: **Switch to Floating Mode, Switch to Docked to Top Mode, Switch to Cling Mode, Switch to Tray Icon Only Mode,** then **Switch to [*your preferred mode*]** to finish.

Do I need the Sidebar?

When you are working in a program with Dragon the first few times, you might like having the Sidebar open to offer commands you might not know or might not remember.

However, the Sidebar takes up quite a bit of screen real estate, even resized to its smallest size. Therefore, if you don't like clutter, and you don't need the help, close the Sidebar. You can reopen it at any time by saying **Open Dragon Sidebar**.

Exercise 2.12, Continued

Display the Sidebar and Switch Between Sidebar and DragonBar:
1. Say **Switch to Dragon Sidebar** to activate the Sidebar.
2. Say **Switch to DragonBar** to move the focus to the DragonBar.
3. Say **Switch to Dragon Sidebar** to activate the Sidebar again.

Note: The command **Switch to…** will be used to move between program windows in later chapters, such as between DragonPad and Word, or between Word and Internet Explorer.

Work with the Sidebar:
1. Display each of the Sidebar's tabs with these commands: **Dragon Sidebar Global, Dragon Sidebar Mouse, Dragon Sidebar My Commands** and **Dragon Sidebar Home.** (Also try saying **Click [*menu name*]** after the Sidebar is active, as in **Click Global, Click Mouse, Click My Commands** and **Click Home.**)
2. Change the width of the Sidebar by first saying **Dragon Sidebar Wider** (wait a few moments for it to work), and then **Dragon Sidebar Thinner.**
3. Change the Sidebar's position by saying **Dragon Sidebar Dock Left** (wait for it to move), then **Dragon Sidebar Dock Right.**

Close the Sidebar and Open DragonPad:
1. Say **Dragon Sidebar Close** or **Close Window.**
2. After the Sidebar closes, say **Start DragonPad.**

Speak DragonPad Menus:
1. When DragonPad opens, open each menu, one at a time, using the command **Click [*menu name*]**. If you have trouble, try saying **Switch to DragonPad** to make sure DragonPad is active.
2. In the **Format** menu, say **Bullet Style** to turn on bullets. (Commands are **Click Format, Click Bullet Style.)** Notice the bullet that appears in the document window.
3. Say **Undo That** to remove the bullets. (Or, say **Click Format, Bullet Style** to turn bullets off.)
4. Go to the next page to minimize, maximize and close DragonPad.

Exercise 2.12, Continued

Minimize, Maximize and Close DragonPad

1. Say **Click Minimize**. The DragonPad window should shrink to the Taskbar (it won't be visible, but it will still be open).

2. Say **Switch to DragonPad**. The DragonPad window should re-appear.

3. Say **Click Maximize**. This will cause the DragonPad window to cover most of the visible screen.

4. Say **Click Restore**. This should cause the window to be resized to its previous size (doesn't always work, but give it a try). If it doesn't work, say switch to DragonPad.

5. Say **Click Close** or **Close Window**. This will either close DragonPad, or bring up a window asking if you want to save changes. Do not save changes before closing (say **No** or **Click No**).

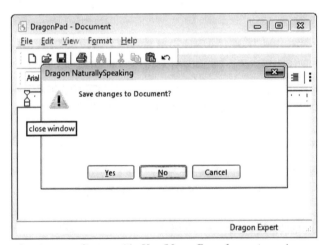

Say the text of buttons like **Yes, No** or **Cancel** to activate them.

Write and Reflect:

Open DragonPad again, and type or dictate a short paragraph answering the following questions:

1. What worked well for you when controlling windows by voice?

2. Did you find it challenging to use your voice instead of a mouse and/or keyboard?

3. Did any feature **not** work well for you?

Review: Remember to manually type any commands you wish to write about, as otherwise they will be activated, instead of written. (See the next page for details.) Proofread your text, making any needed corrections. Save your work as "Exercise 2.12". Print your work if needed.

Typing a Command as Text

When writing the assignment on the previous page, you might want to say something like, "I had trouble with the Click File command." However, if you do this, when you say "Click File", the software will usually interpret this to be a command, and Dragon will open the File menu. There is a simple solution to this problem. If you want a command to be typed as text, hold down the **Shift key** while dictating the command, and it will be typed rather than activated.

Hold down the **Shift key** on the keyboard while dictating a command to see it typed as text.

What if I have the opposite problem? What if I say "Go to Sleep" and it gets typed on my document?

Occasionally, when dictating a command, it gets typed as text. Often, saying **Scratch That** and doing it again is enough to make it work. However, you can hold down the **Control key** to tell Dragon to recognize the spoken words as a command, not text to be typed.

Hold down the **Control key** on the keyboard while dictating a command to make sure it is recognized as a command.

(Note: if you can't hold down the **Shift key** or **Control key**, you will need to use Recognition Modes commands, which are covered on page 139.)

Save User Profile and Exit the Program By Voice

Save your user profile by saying **Save User Profile** at the end of every session (if you did not set this up to run automatically upon exit).

Exit Dragon NaturallySpeaking by voice by saying **Click Profile** to click on the **Profile** menu in the DragonBar, and then say **Exit Dragon.**

Command Review

These commands are essential for success with Dragon NaturallySpeaking. Practice until you feel comfortable using them.

New commands in this chapter:

Correct That
Correct [*wrong word(s)*]
Correct From [*word*] to [*word*]
Select [*wrong word(s)*]
Unselect That
Cancel
Escape
Spell That
Choose 1 (or the correct number)
Spacebar
Press Spacebar
Backspace
Press Backspace
Backspace 3 (or the correct number)
Letter Alpha
Click [*item*] (File, Print, etc.)
Press Right Arrow
Play That Back
Read That
Go To Bottom
Go To Top
Go To End of Line
Go To Beginning of Line
Insert Before [*word*]
Insert After [*word*]
Move Down 1 Line
Move Down [3] Lines (2–20)
Move Up 1 Line

Move Up [4] Lines (2–20)
Delete That
Delete Line
Delete Last [6] Characters (2-20)
Delete Last [7] Words (2–20)
Delete Next [4] Words (2–20)
Delete Paragraph
Delete All
Select Line
Select All
Select Next [2] Characters
Select Last Character
Select Next Word
Select Last [9] Words (2–20)
Select Last [5] Lines (2-20)
Open DragonPad
Start DragonPad
Print That
Click Maximize
Click Minimize
Click Restore
Click Close *or* Close Window
Switch to DragonPad
Switch to Dragon Bar
Switch to Dragon Sidebar
Switch to [*name of DragonBar*] Mode
Open Dragon Sidebar (*more sidebar commands on page 87*)

3 CHAPTER 3
Format Text and Numbers

About Chapter 3: Review the core instructions for success with speech recognition and do the warm-up exercise. Learn the **four types of commands**, and use one type—word processing—extensively in this chapter as you learn to capitalize and format text and numbers.

Remember Core Instructions

Do this every time you use speech recognition:

1. Do a warm-up exercise
2. Take frequent sips of water
3. Take breaks regularly
4. Read the step before you do it
5. Make corrections as needed

Exercise 3.1 Warm-Up Exercise

DIRECTIONS: Start DragonPad. Dictate the following items to check your recognition. Items in **bold** are commands, and should produce an action, not be typed as text. Items in brackets [ ] give instructions, while items in parentheses ( ) are for you to customize:

[Start Dictating]

Hello computer, are you ready to work today?
New Line
I am using speech recognition software.
New Line
Dictating is much faster than typing. **New Line**
(Dictate your favorite quote here.) **New Line**
(Your First Name) (Your Last Name) **New Paragraph, Go To Sleep**

[Stop Dictating]

Make any needed corrections, then save your document as "Exercise 3.1". Keep this exercise available to use with Exercise 3.2 after reading the next section.

In This Chapter

- ✓ Quick Review: Core Instructions and Warm-Up Exercise
- ✓ Learn the Four Types of Commands
- ✓ Use Word Processing Commands
- ✓ Text Formatting
- ✓ Develop Skills in 12 Exercises
- ✓ Test Your Speed with Timed Writing Exercises
- ✓ Frequently Asked Questions
- ✓ Command Review

Four Types of Commands

There are four kinds of commands used in speech recognition: Correction, Control, Keypress, and Word Processing.

Command	Where Used	Examples
Correction	Anywhere text can be dictated	**Correct [*word*], Select [*word*], Correct That, Spell That**
Control	In programs and on the desktop	**Click File, Click Print, Click OK, Switch to DragonPad**
Keypress	Anywhere a keyboard command would work	**Press Enter, Press Right Arrow Press Spacebar, Press Escape**
Word Processing	Anywhere text could be typed or dictated	**Cap That, No Cap That Bold That, Center That**

Correction

The three levels of correction, and their associated commands, were covered in Chapter 2. These include **Correct [*word*], Correct That** and **Spell That.**

Control

Control commands are used to control applications. One way to think about them is to imagine using the mouse to accomplish an action—then think of the speech command to do the same thing. A speech command to accomplish an action a mouse could do is called a control command. One example is saying **Click File** to open the File menu in a program.

Control commands are used to control the desktop, including the Start menu, and application windows. Some Control commands save more than one mouse click: **Open DragonPad**, for example. Control commands are given throughout this book.

Keypress

Keypress commands are spoken versions of anything you can press using the keyboard. One example is saying **Press Right Arrow** to press the right arrow key or **Press Enter** to activate the Enter key. Some keyboard commands can work without the word **Press: Spacebar, Tab,** and **Backspace,** for example. Keypress commands are included throughout this book.

Word Processing

Word Processing commands are used for working within documents created by word processing programs. Some word processing programs that can work with speech recognition include DragonPad, Microsoft Word, WordPad, Notepad, and OpenOffice Writer. The category of word processing commands includes commands for editing text, dictating text and numbers, creating capitalization and other text formatting issues.

Word processing commands are used for formatting individual words, groups of words, or words and numbers.

Word Processing commands are the primary focus of this chapter. First, however, learn about using the **Select** command to select units of text—which is very helpful when you want to format text.

"Select" Commands

The **Select** commands, used for correction in Chapter 2, are used also to **select amounts of text** to delete, move, format, and more. While these are control commands, they are frequently paired with word processing commands, as demonstrated in this chapter.

These commands are used to select specific amounts of text:

Select Line	Selects the entire line of text
Select Last [2] Lines	Selects the last number of lines of text (2–20)*
Select Sentence	Selects the sentence closest to the cursor
Select Last [3] Sentences	Selects the last number of sentences (2–20)
Select Paragraph	Selects the paragraph closest to the cursor
Select Last [4] Paragraphs	Selects the last number paragraphs (2–20)
Select All	Selects all the text in the document
Select Last Word	Selects the last word (to the left of the cursor)
Select Last [6] Words	Selects the last number of words (2–20)
Select Last Character	Selects the last character (left of the cursor)
Select Last [5] Characters	Selects the last number of characters (2–20)

The last 2–20 characters, words, lines, sentences, or paragraphs can be selected.

What if what I want to select is ahead of the cursor, not behind it?

To select the next character, word, line, sentence, or paragraph, substitute the word *next* for the word *last* in the commands above. Use commands like **Select <u>Next</u> 3 Words** and **Select <u>Next</u> 12 Lines.**

Exercise 3.2 Select Commands

DIRECTIONS: Follow the steps below to save your "Exercise 3.1" as "Exercise 3.2". Work with the new "Exercise 3.2", using the **Select** commands to select text and delete it.

1. Open Dragon Pad.
2. From DragonPad's **File** menu, choose **Open**. Browse to your "Exercise 3.1" and open it.
3. Go to the **File** menu and choose **Save As**. In the window that opens, save Exercise 3.1 as "Exercise 3.2". (This will keep you from making changes to Exercise 3.1.)
4. Turn on or wake up your microphone.
5. Say **Go To Top** to put the cursor at the beginning of the document.
6. Say **Select Line**. When the line is selected, say **Delete That**.
7. Say **Insert After** *typing*.
8. Say **Select Last 2 Words**. When the words are selected, say **Delete That**. (If an extra space remains, say **Backspace** to remove it.)
9. Say **Move Down 1 Line**.
10. Select the sentence by saying **Select Line**.
11. Say **Delete That**.
12. Say **Microphone Off**.
13. You should have 3 lines of text remaining (see example).
14. Save "Exercise 3.2" and print if required.

15. Close DragonPad.

Review: How did this go? While DragonPad is low on features, it is designed to work well with Dragon's word processing commands.

Word Processing Commands

Word processing commands are used for formatting individual words, blocks of text, numbers, and alphanumeric formats (dates, addresses). The next section describes commands for formatting **individual words** properly: controlling capitalization, creating compound words, hyphenating words and creating strikethroughs.

Text Formatting: Individual Words

Function	Description	Examples
Capitalization	Capitalize the first letter of a word or a whole word	**Cap [*word*], Cap That** **All Cap That** **All Caps On, All Caps Off**
	Remove capitalization	**No Caps On, No Caps Off**
Compound Words	Join two words together, remove spacing between words	**Compound That** **No Space On, No Space Off**
Hyphenation	Add a hyphen between two words	**Hyphen, Hyphenate That**
Strikethrough	Strike through text	**Format That Strikethrough**

Creating Capitalization

English uses capital letters for several purposes: proper nouns, at the beginning of a sentence, for titles, and for holidays. Speech recognition software has really improved at knowing which words to capitalize. For most proper nouns, you may not have to use the **Cap** command at all. Therefore, some of these examples may seem a bit far-fetched!

About Exercise 3.3

This exercise, which continues for the next few pages, has a combination of instructions and sentences to dictate. Text to be dictated is indented and in larger type than the instructions. As capitalization can be created using any of several methods, they are presented here, one at a time, with examples for you to try. After you have tried the various methods, feel free to stick with the single method or methods which works best for you. Note: remember to correct misrecognitions before capitalization—this is part of the axiom to always correct misrecognitions before applying formatting.

Exercise 3.3 Capitalization

DIRECTIONS: Dictate the following sentences into a new DragonPad document. Do not dictate these instructions and explanations, just the sentences with capitalization. Say **New Line** between sentences.

Automatic Capitalization

[Start Dictating]

> Dr. Roberts has visited India, Japan, and Russia. **New Line**
> Rachel and Michael's anniversary is in November. **New Line, Go to Sleep**

[Stop Dictating]

Notice how Dragon will capitalize many proper nouns without you commanding it. However, sometimes you have to dictate commands to capitalize words or phrases, as seen below.

The *Cap* Command—Before Dictating the Word

DIRECTIONS: Dictate the following sentences with proper nouns, using the **Cap** command before the word to be capitalized. It is most effective to pause briefly before saying **Cap**, to help the software understand that you are dictating a **Cap** command. Say **New Line** after each sentence.

[Start Dictating]

> My dog is named **Cap** Sandy. **New Line**
> He won the **Cap** Dog of the **Cap** Week award. **New Line**
> My mother's dog, **Cap** Fluffy, is a **Cap** Poodle. **New Line**
> They don't like music by **Cap** Green **Cap** Day. **New Line, Go to Sleep**

[Stop Dictating]

Exercise 3.3, Continued

If you find that the word **Cap** is typed rather than used as a command, remember to pause before dictating it, and to use a commanding tone—a little bit louder and firmer than usual.

The *Cap That* Command—After Dictation

DIRECTIONS: Dictate these sentences <u>without</u> using the **Cap** command. Make any needed corrections to recognition, then select the word that needs a capital letter, and say **Cap That**. Text in brackets [ ] give instructions or additional information. Note: The cursor will be in the middle of the sentence after capitalization, so when finished say either **Go To End of Line,** then **New Line** or **Insert After** *period* to move to the end of the sentence.

[Start Dictating]

> The mayor of Freedom, California, visited Liberty, Kansas last week.
> > [Say, **Select** *Freedom*, then **Cap That**]
> > [Say, **Select** *Liberty*, then **Cap That**]

> When Nurse Johnson talks, people listen.
> > [Say, **Select** *Nurse*, then **Cap That**]

> Did you see that great magic show by Mickey Magic?
> > [Say, **Select** *Magic*, then **Cap That**]

[Stop Dictating]

Using Caps On and Caps Off

DIRECTIONS: The **Caps On** command puts a capital letter at the beginning of each word you speak, until you turn it off. This Sentence Is An Example. Use **Caps Off** at the end of the word or phrase to return to standard capitalization. For best recognition, give a brief pause after saying one of these commands before dictating the text to be typed.

[Start Dictating]

> **Caps On** Monster Trucks Meet Godzilla **Caps Off** is a terrible movie.
> My favorite book of all time is **Caps On** To Kill a Mockingbird. **Caps Off**

[Stop Dictating]

Exercise 3.3, Continued

Your finished sentences should look like this:

> Monster Trucks Meet Godzilla is a terrible movie.
> My favorite book of all time is To Kill a Mockingbird.

Acronyms and Abbreviations: *All Caps On* and *All Caps Off*

DIRECTIONS: Dragon has gotten very good at capitalizing common acronyms and abbreviations. Dictate the following, and notice how "all caps" will be on automatically.

[Start Dictating]

> It is important to save your work ASAP. Most computers have several USB jacks. However, if you don't have a USB drive, use a blank CD or a DVD.

[Stop Dictating]

DIRECTIONS: If an acronym is not common, however, it is better to dictate commands for **All Caps On** and **All Caps Off**.

[Start Dictating]

> The **All Caps On** ACHIEVE **All Caps Off** program taught office skills.
> The **All Caps On** METRO BUS STOP **All Caps Off** sign was new.

[Stop Dictating]

DIRECTIONS: Add emphasis to a sentence by making a word all capitals. Dictate the following sentence first, then select the word "are" and say **All Cap That**.

[Start Dictating]

> I haven't seen you for years! How ARE you?

[Stop Dictating]

Tip: What if you need to REMOVE caps? Select the word(s) and say **No Cap That**.

Review: How did this work for you? Probably by now you are getting the hang of selecting, then formatting, a single word or short phrase. You will use these skills in the exercises to follow. Save your work as "Exercise 3.3". Print if desired.

Exercise 3.4 Creating Compound Words, Hyphenation and Strikethrough

The **Compound That** command is used after dictating two words that need to be joined. The **Compound That** command also adds the new compound word to your vocabulary, so it is less likely that you will need to compound it again in the future. Use commands like **New Line, Go To Bottom**, and **Go To Sleep** as appropriate.

DIRECTIONS: Dictate the two sentences below, then select the words and say **Compound That**.

[Start Dictating]

> Yesterday, I received an e-mail from AnneMarie Smith.
>> [Say **Select *Anne Marie***, then **Compound That**]

[Stop Dictating]

DIRECTIONS: As software products and company names have become compound, the need to dictate them has become more frequent. Try the ones in the exercise below.

[Start Dictating]

> Have you ever used TextAloud?
>> [Say **Select *text aloud***, then **Cap That**, then **Compound That**.]

> It comes from NextUp, which is owned by AT&T.
>> [Say **Select *next up***, then **Cap That**, then **Compound That**.]

[Stop Dictating]

Tip: An alternate command to **Compound That** is **No Space That**, which removes the spaces between selected words.

Exercise 3.4, Continued

Hyphenation

When you need a hyphenated word, you can speak the hyphen in the middle, or select the two words and say **Hyphenate That**.

DIRECTIONS: Try the sentences below.

[Start Dictating]

> Is this an open entry class? [Say, **Select *open entry*, Hyphenate That]**
> No, but it is late **hyphen** starting.

[Stop Dictating]

The finished sentences should look like this:
> Is this an open-entry class? No, but it is late-starting.

Strikethrough

DIRECTIONS: Dictate the sentences below. To show some text with a strikethrough, select the text and say **Format That Strikethrough**. The alternate command is **Format That Strikeout**.

[Start Dictating]

> This was a ~~really~~ very difficult day. [Say, **Select *really*, Format That Strikethrough]**
> Tomorrow will be a much better ~~kind of~~ day. [Say, **Select *kind of*, Format That Strikethrough]**

[Stop Dictating]

The finished sentences should look like this:
This was a ~~really~~ very difficult day. Tomorrow will be a much better ~~kind of~~ day.

Review: Save your work as "Exercise 3.4". Print as needed. To get a new document for the next exercise, go to the File menu and click "New". To do this by voice, say **Click File**, **Click New**.

Add Emphasis to Text: Bold, Italics, Underline

Making text bold, italicized, or underlined are frequent needs in a document and there are several commands for each to choose from. Try them all and then use the ones you prefer. Remember always to dictate text and make corrections before applying formatting for best results.

Text Formatting	Description	Commands	Keypress Commands
Bold	Makes text bold	**Bold That** **Format That Bold** **Bold [*word*]** **Bold from [*word*] to [*word*]** **Bold [*word*] through[*word*]**	**Press Ctrl + B**
Italics	Makes text italicized	**Italicize That** **Format That Italics** **Italicize [*word*]** **Italicize from [*word*] to [*word*]** **Italicize [*word*] through[*word*]**	**Press Ctrl + I**
Underline	Makes text underlined	**Underline That** **Format That Underlined** **Underline [*word*]** **Underline from [*word*] to [*word*]** **Underline [*word*] through[*word*]**	**Press Ctrl + U**
Bold Italics	Makes text bold and italicized	**Format That Bold Italics**	**Press Ctrl + B** **Press Ctrl + I**
Remove Formatting	Removes formatting	**Restore That** **Format That Plain Text**	---

About Exercise 3.5

This exercise, like the previous one, has a combination of sentences to dictate, and instructions in brackets [ ]. Read the directions and examples before beginning.

Exercise 3.5 Bold, Italics, Underline, Bold Italics and Text Alignment

DIRECTIONS: Get a new DragonPad document. Read about how to add bold formatting below, then follow the directions to create bold text.

Bold

One-Step Bold:

To apply bold in one step, use the following commands:

Bold [*word*]	Bolds a single word or short phrase
Bold [*word*] **through** [*word*]	Bolds a longer range of words, such as a paragraph

Select and Bold:

Select text, then say **Bold That**.

DIRECTIONS: Dictate the following text, make any corrections to recognition, then add bold as indicated to get the paragraph below.

[Start Dictating]

> **Sometimes** you want to add **emphasis** to words by making the letters **darker and slightly larger**. This feature, called bold, is frequently used for **headings** and titles.

[Stop Dictating]

1. Say, **Bold** *emphasis*
2. Say, **Bold** *darker* **through** *larger*
3. Say, **Bold** *headings and titles*.

Exercise 3.5, Continued

4. Say, **Select *sometimes*, Bold That**.

Your text should now look like the text in the example on the previous page.

Italics

Italics also are used to add emphasis to selected text, and to indicate major works (films, book titles, etc.).

One-Step Italics:

To apply italics in one step, use the following commands:

Italicize [*word*]	Makes italics a single word
Italicize [*word*] through [*word*]	Makes italics a range of words

Select and Italicize:

Select text first, then say **Italicize That**.

DIRECTIONS: Dictate the following text, add italics as indicated, to get the paragraph below.

[Start Dictating]

> My coworker *loves* to read business books. I recommended several to her recently, including *How to Get a Raise* and *Business Communication for Beginners.*

[Stop Dictating]

1. Say, **Italicize *loves***
2. Say, **Italicize *How* through *Raise***
3. Say, **Select *Business Communication for Beginners*, Italicize That**

Trouble?

Sometimes, people find it hard to say "italicize". If you have trouble with this, select the text you wish to see italicized, then use the keypress command instead by saying **Press Ctrl+ I** (spoken as "press control eye"). See the chart on page 103.

Exercise 3.5, Continued

Underline

Text can be underlined in one step, or selected and then underlined. Try both methods below.

One-Step Underline:

To apply underlines in one step, use the following commands:

Underline [*word*]	Underlines a single word
Underline [*word*] through [*word*]	Underlines a range of words

Select and Underline:

Select text, say **Underline That**.

DIRECTIONS: Dictate the following text, then add underlines to get the sentences below.

[Start Dictating]

> My aunt <u>won a trip</u> to Europe. I hope she takes <u>me</u> with her. I <u>need a vacation</u>!

[Stop Dictating]

1. Say, **Underline *me***
2. Say, **Select *won a trip*, Underline That**
3. Say, **Underline *need* through *vacation***

True Stories:

Katie is a very patient person, but bold text tested her calm demeanor. She dictated a few Bold commands, and after that, they just wouldn't turn off. Everything she dictated afterwards was bold. She said **Delete That** and did it again. Then, she selected the text and used the **Format That Plain Text** command (usually the best choice). No success! Finally, she closed her document and re-opened it, which worked. Remember: dictate all of the text you want to see typed, then go back selectively and add formatting.

Exercise 3.5, Continued

Bold Italics

To add bold and italics to text at the same time, select the text and say **Format That Bold Italics.**

DIRECTIONS: Make the previous sentence in your exercise bold and italicized.

> Say, **Select *I need a vacation***, then say **Format That Bold Italics**.
> (Now it ***really*** looks like you need a vacation!)

Review: Look over your work, and make any needed corrections. Save your work as "Exercise 3.5" and print if needed.

Tip: To *remove* any formatting you no longer want, select the word or range of words and use the command **Format That Plain** or **Format That Regular.** An alternate command is **Restore That.**

Text Formatting: Alignment

When formatting text, alignment is also a consideration. For example, an academic paper might have a title which is centered. Your name on a test might need to be aligned to the right side of the page. Most pages of text are left-aligned. Text aligned to both the left and right is called "justified".

Text Formatting	Description	Commands	Keypress Commands
Left Align	Aligns the text left; used in most paragraphs	Left Align That Format That Left Aligned	**Press Ctrl + L**
Center	Center aligns text; used for titles, headings	Center That Format That Centered	**Press Ctrl + E**
Right Align	Aligns the text right; various uses	Right Align That Format That Right Aligned	**Press Ctrl + R**
Justify	Aligns text to the left and right; newspaper columns	Justify That	**Press Ctrl + J**

Exercise 3.6 Text Alignment

DIRECTIONS: Dictate the passage below without formatting, make any needed corrections to recognition, then format as directed in the steps below.

[Start Dictating]

Preamble to the Constitution

We the People of the United States of America, in order to form a more perfect union, establish justice, insure domestic tranquility, provide for the common defense, promote the general welfare and secure the blessings of liberty, to ourselves and our posterity, do ordain and establish this constitution for the United States of America.

Adopted in 1787

[Stop Dictating]

1. Review the paragraph carefully. Correct any recognition errors, capitalization mistakes and punctuation misplacement.
2. Save your work as "Exercise 3.6" before continuing. If any strange mistakes occur as you work through the next steps, say **Undo That**.
3. Say, **Select *Preamble to the Constitution***
4. Say, **Center That, Bold That**
5. Say, **Insert Before *Adopted*, Select Line, Right Align That, Italicize That**
6. Say, **New Paragraph.** Notice how the cursor remains on the right side.
7. Turn off italics now by saying **Press Control I** (sounds like "eye").
8. Say, **Left Align That**. The cursor should now appear left aligned, as usual.
9. Say, **New Paragraph.** Put your microphone to sleep or turn it off.
10. Compare your work to the finished example that on the next page.
11. Make any needed changes and save your work as "Exercise 3.6".

Review: How did all of this work for you? You are probably still seeing some errors in recognition—this is normal. Save your work as "Exercise 3.6" and print if desired. Close the document.

Finished Example:

Preamble to the Constitution

We the People of the United States of America, in order to form a more perfect union, establish justice, insure domestic tranquility, provide for the common defense, promote the general welfare and secure the blessings of liberty, to ourselves and our posterity, do ordain and establish this constitution for the United States of America.

Adopted in 1787

Justify

What about the Justify Command?

The Justify command wasn't practiced in the previous exercise because DragonPad doesn't support it. Therefore, if you want to try justifying text, you should try it in a full-featured word processor, like Microsoft Word.

What is Justify used for?

Justify is used mainly for newspaper columns, sidebars, and in long quotes. Below is an example of justified text. The main drawback is that it adds spaces between words in order to get the left and right alignment, and that can be a bit choppy to read.

> Here is some justified text. It looks nice for a block quote, because both edges are straight, not "ragged". The drawback is the extra spaces between words, which can look choppy and odd.

Cut, Copy, and Paste

Cutting, copying, and pasting text are essential tasks, and ones you will use frequently. You can cut, copy, and paste within the same document or between documents. Also, you can copy text from a webpage or e-mail and paste it into a document.

This is possible because of a temporary storage area inside the hard drive called the clipboard. When you copy text, it is moved to the clipboard until you paste it. It is best to get in the habit of pasting text you copy quickly, as the clipboard is just a temporary storage area, and information you paste there isn't saved.

Commands to Cut Text

To cut text means to <u>remove</u> it from its current location and copy it to the clipboard (for pasting elsewhere). Commands for this are the following:

Cut [*word*]
Cut [*word*] through [*word*]
Cut That

Commands to Copy Text

To copy text means to <u>leave it</u> in its current location and make a copy of it on the clipboard (for pasting elsewhere). Commands for this are the following:

Copy [*word*]
Copy [*word*] through [*word*]
Copy That

Command to Paste Text

To paste text means to take text that has been cut or copied from the clipboard and "paste" it into a document. Use this command to paste:

Paste That   Pastes the text from the clipboard into your document

Exercise 3.7 Cut and Paste

DIRECTIONS: Read this exercise carefully before beginning so that you know what to expect. Get a new DragonPad document. Dictate the two paragraphs below, make any needed corrections, and save as "Exercise 3.7". Then, cut and paste as directed. Compare your paragraph to the sample below, making any needed changes.

[Start Dictating]

After all, as Mark Twain said, "The coldest winter I ever spent was a summer in San Francisco." **New Paragraph**

When you come to visit us in San Francisco this summer, be prepared for cool weather. Especially along the coast, it can get quite foggy, and the evenings are often chilly and damp. Our summer weather is not like your weather in New Orleans at all. **New Paragraph**

[Stop Dictating]

1. Put your microphone to sleep and look over your text. Make any needed corrections.
2. Say, **Insert Before** *After* (or say **Go To Top**).
3. Say, **Select Paragraph**. This will select the first paragraph.
4. Say, **Cut That**. (The text will be cut, and placed on the clipboard.)
5. Say, **Go To Bottom**. (If needed, say **New Line** to get space between paragraphs.)
6. Say, **Paste That**. The Mark Twain paragraph should now appear at the bottom of the passage, instead of at the top.
7. Say, **Insert Before** *Our*. Say, **Select from** *Our* **through** *period* to select the sentence, including punctuation.
8. Say, **Cut That**.
9. Say, **Go To Top**.
10. Say, **Paste That**. Say **Spacebar** to add a space after the period, if needed. Now compare your text to the finished example on the next page.

Finished Example:

> Our summer weather is not like your weather in New Orleans at all. When you come to visit us this summer in San Francisco, be prepared for cool weather. Especially along the coast, it can get quite foggy, and the evenings are often chilly and damp.
>
> After all, as Mark Twain said, "The coldest winter I ever spent was a summer in San Francisco."

Review: How did that go? Was it pretty easy, or did it present some challenges? If you want to challenge yourself further, select a sentence, and say **Copy That**. Then, go to another place in the document and say **Paste That**. Save your work, and print if needed.

Note: Copying and pasting text by voice is especially useful when you are moving text from one document to another, in which case the commands go like this: **Select [*text*], Copy That, Switch to [*document name*], Paste That.** This technique is practiced in Chapter 4.

Can I Use These Commands to Consolidate My Work in One Document?

Yes, absolutely. The exercises in this chapter work best when you use a new DragonPad document for each one. However, since most of them do not take a full page, printing each one individually might use more paper than you would prefer.

To consolidate the exercises for printing, open an exercise you wish to move, say **Select All** to select all of the text, then say **Copy That**, to copy the text to the clipboard. Next, open the place where you wish to copy the text, and get the cursor where you want to put the text. When you are ready, say **Paste That**, and your exercise text will be pasted into the spot you chose.

Tip: If you are new to copying and pasting text, make sure you have saved copies of the work you are moving. Also, make a habit of having both items open before

beginning—both the document you wish to copy from, and the location you wish to paste the text into. Or, for a less stressful option, practice with some unimportant text until you are good at copying and pasting. Finally, remember that if something seems to have gone wrong, the first thing to do is say **Undo That**.

Dictating Numbers

Numbers are dictated alone, or as part of a phrase involving other characters and words (dates, for example). Dictating numbers is not difficult once you know a few basic commands and techniques.

In the chart below is a handy guide to number formats and commands. The items in parentheses are the pronunciations for the numbers shown, such as 18, which is spoken as ("eighteen") and not ("one eight"). Read the chart below, then practice these in the next section of this chapter.

Numbers	Description	Examples
0–9	Single digit numbers	**Numeral 3, Numeral 7**
10–99	Two digit numbers	**18 ("eighteen")**
100–999	Three digit numbers	**320 ("three hundred twenty")**
1000–9999	Four digit numbers	**2632 ("two thousand six hundred thirty-two")**
Larger Numbers	Ten thousands, hundred thousands, millions, billions, trillions	**17,300,002 ("seventeen million, three hundred thousand, and two")**
Money	Dollars and cents	**$26.32 ("twenty-six dollars thirty-two cents")**
Time	AM and PM	**2:30 PM ("two thirty pm")**
Dates	Month, Day, Year	**July 22, 2012 ("July twenty-second, twenty twelve")**
Phone numbers	With area code or without	**800-555-1212**
Addresses	Street, City, State, Zip	**1285 Main St., San Jose, CA 95076**

Number Formatting Commands

Numbers can be dictated as words ("six") or as numerals ("6"). Speech recognition software will often format your number based on the context in which you are working. However, when you need to change the format of a number, say **Correct [number]** and then choose the other number format from the list.

Number formats in this section include times, dates, phone numbers, numbers formatted with hyphens or commas, and currency formats. Help with automatic formatting is available at the end of this chapter. Help with region-specific settings is available in Dragon's Help file.

About Exercise 3.8 Numbers

This exercise is several pages long—it is one of the longer exercises in this book. Get a new DragonPad document and save it as "Exercise 3.8" before beginning. To do this by voice, say "**Cap *Exercise* Numeral *three point eight***". Below, begin by dictating plain numbers and numbers in specific formats, such as dates, times, money, and addresses.

Exercise 3.8 Numbers

DIRECTIONS: Get a new DragonPad document and save it as "Exericise 3.8" before you begin dictating below. Dictate the numbers given, following the examples. If a number is misrecognized, say **Correct That** and make the correction. Do not dictate the instructions.

Numbers 1–9

Dragon NaturallySpeaking writes numbers 1–10 as words (six, not 6) when in a sentence, unless you format it as a numeral using the command **Numeral [ ]**.

For Example:	8	Say, **Numeral eight**
	0	Say, **Numeral zero**

Exercise 3.8, Continued

DIRECTIONS: Practice dictating numbers 1-10. For the number 1, say **Numeral 1**. Give a brief pause and say **Spacebar** or **Press Spacebar** between each one.

[Start Dictating]

> 1 2 3 4 5 6 7 8 9 **New Paragraph**

[Stop Dictating]

DIRECTIONS: Now try sentences that use numbers 1–10. Notice that the numbers will be spelled out as words. (If they are not, correct them.)

[Start Dictating]

> Emily invited seven girls to sleep at her house. **New Line**
> Her mother said she could invite two or three friends. **New Paragraph**

[Stop Dictating]

DIRECTIONS: Now try sentences that use both formats. Say **Numeral [ ]** to format as number; (in the sentence below, say **Cap *Chapter Numeral 5*** and ***question Numeral 9***).

[Start Dictating]

> For three weeks, I have been meaning to read Chapter 5 in the textbook. Are there two correct answers for question 9?
> **New Paragraph**

[Stop Dictating]

Luckily, only numbers 1–9 have this issue. Larger numbers are much easier to work with!

Note: If you prefer Dragon to always format numbers 1-9 as numerals, you can set up this option in the Auto-Format dialog box, discussed at the end of this chapter.

Exercise 3.8, Continued

Numbers 10–99

DIRECTIONS: Numbers 10–99 are dictated exactly the way you usually say them. Dictate these numbers between 10–99 (say **Space**, **Spacebar** or **Press Spacebar** to put a space between each one):

[Start Dictating]

18 27 36 45 54 63 72 81 90 99 **New Paragraph**

[Stop Dictating]

DIRECTIONS: Dictate the following sentences that have numbers 11–99 in them.

[Start Dictating]

My lotto numbers are 12, 16, 19, 23, and 34. **New Line**
The winning numbers were 22, 31, 15, 26, and 39. **New Paragraph**

[Stop Dictating]

Numbers 100–999

Three digit numbers (hundreds) can be dictated as three separate numbers, as one number followed by a two-digit number, or as a hundred followed by a two-digit number. For example, the number 247 can be dictated as "two four seven" as "two forty-seven" or as "two hundred forty-seven".

DIRECTIONS: Dictate these three digit numbers. Say **Tab Key** or **Press Tab** to get tabs between them:

[Start Dictating]

| 326 | 742 | 289 | 519 | 208 | **New Line** |
| 452 | 178 | 834 | 367 | 720 | **New Paragraph** |

[Stop Dictating]

Exercise 3.8, Continued

Numbers 1000–9999

Four digit numbers, when dictated in the ways they are usually spoken, appear without a comma. For example, if you say "two thousand four hundred sixty seven" you will see 2467 typed.

DIRECTIONS: Dictate these four digit numbers. Say **Tab** or **Tab Key** or **Press Tab** to get tabs between each one.

[Start Dictating]

1280   1642   2500   3750   4999   5771   6212   7250   8001
New Paragraph

[Stop Dictating]

Roman Numerals

Roman numerals are dictated in this way **Roman Numeral [ ].**
For example, the command **Roman Numeral 2014** will appear as
MMXIV.

DIRECTIONS: Dictate these roman numerals. Say **New Line** after each:

[Start Dictating]

IX	(Say, **Roman Numeral** *nine*)
XLIII	(Say, **Roman Numeral** *forty-three*)
DLXVII	(Say, **Roman Numeral** *five hundred sixty-seven*)
MMXCV	(Say, **Roman Numeral** *two thousand ninety-five*)
	New Paragraph

[Stop Dictating]

Exercise 3.8, Continued

What About Larger Numbers?

Tens of thousands, millions, billions and trillions, etc. are dictated by saying them outright.

For Example:	26,480,000	Say, **twenty-six million, four hundred and eighty thousand**
For Example:	4,220,133	Say, **four million, two hundred twenty thousand, one hundred thirty-three**

DIRECTIONS: Dictate these numbers. Say **New Line** after each.

[Start Dictating]

> 3,265,842
> 45,731,990
> 14,280
> 7389
> 3,524
> 17,000,000,000,045 (Say, **seventeen trillion forty-five**) **New Paragraph**

[Stop Dictating]

Review: How did the numbers work for you? Did you remember to say **New Line**? This was a long exercise—be proud of yourself for hanging in there! Look over your work, and make any needed corrections. Save as "Exercise 3.8" and print if desired.

Important Note: The **New Line** command will not appear in exercises from this point forward. (You probably noticed it missing from the last two segments of Exercise 3.8.) If you see that the next item begins on a new line (as with a list of telephone numbers), give the **New Line** command. If you need to add a new line later, remember that you can say **Insert Before** [*word you want to move*] and then say **New Line**.

Formatted Numbers

Dates, telephone numbers, postal addresses, money and time all use numbers in special formats. These number formats are applied automatically once you know how to dictate them. At the end of the next exercise is more information about controlling formatted numbers.

The instructions can seem a little cryptic. Try what you see printed in the following pages, and if it doesn't work the first time, try it again more quickly or slowly. Be patient, and soon you will be able to get these commands to work for you.

Exercise 3.9 Dates, Telephone Numbers, Addresses, Money and Time

Dictate numbers in specific formats in this exercise.

Dates

Dates are dictated with this formula: Month Day Year. Commas will be inserted for you.

DIRECTIONS: Get a new DragonPad document. Dictate these dates. Say **New Line** after each.

[Start Dictating]

July 4, 1787	(Say, *July 4 1787* or *July 4th 1787*)
March 5, 1880	
November 8, 1971	
October 28, 2005	(Say, *two thousand and five*)
April 21, 2030	(Say, *twenty thirty or two thousand and thirty*)
June 1st	(in DragonPad it looks like June 1, in Microsoft Word it looks like June 1st)
The 1980s	(Say, *the nineteen eighties*)
10/19/14	(Say, *ten slash nineteen slash fourteen*)
	New Paragraph

[Stop Dictating]

Exercise 3.9, Continued

Telephone Numbers

Telephone numbers can be dictated quickly and easily if you speak the number in a smooth, continuous way, especially if you use the area code.

Quick way: continuously, without pausing, dictate the number with the area code.

> *For Example*:   800-475-5262   (Say, *8004755262*)

To dictate quickly, and to include parentheses around the area code, say **left paren** and **right paren** and then continue dictating the number, as in the example below.

> *For Example:*   (831) 475-5262   (Say, **left paren 831 right paren 475 5262**)

DIRECTIONS: Dictate the telephone numbers below. Say **New Line** after each.

[Start Dictating]

> 510-728-9372
> 202-456-1111   [*This is the White House phone number*]
> (310) 440-7300
> (831) 377-6379
> 1 (800) 662-3535   (Say **Numeral 1** before the number)
> **New Paragraph**

[Stop Dictating]

Trouble?

If you find that telephone numbers you are dictating aren't being typed as numerals, you can set an option in the Auto-Format dialog box which allows numbers to be spoken more slowly and less fluently and still be recognized as formatted numbers. See the end of this chapter for more information.

Exercise 3.9, Continued

Postal Addresses

To dictate a postal address, try to dictate it as you would a telephone number—that is, smoothly and continuously. If you do this, the address will likely be formatted properly. It is worth practicing addresses to master the technique.

If you aren't successful at dictating addresses using the faster technique, do it the more deliberate way: line by line, with pauses between each element. E-mail addresses are covered in a later chapter.

DIRECTIONS: Dictate the following address as smoothly and continuously as you can. Say **New Line** at the end of each line.

[Start Dictating]

To Dictate This Address:	Say This:
Jim Smith	Jim Smith
27 Penny Lane	Twenty-seven Penny Lane
Watsonville, CA 95076	Watsonville California 95076

[Stop Dictating]

DIRECTIONS: Dictate your home or work address as smoothly and continuously as you can.

[Start Dictating]

> Your Name
> Your Street Address
> Your City State Zip Code

[Stop Dictating]

Is it easier or harder to do one you have memorized? If you want to try another address, dictate a relative or friend's address, or a business address you know well.

Exercise 3.9, Continued

Dictating Money

U.S. currency (actually, all currency based on dollars and cents) is dictated the way it is spoken. For example, $37.25 is dictated "thirty seven dollars and twenty five cents." Whole dollars are dictated very easily; for $72, say "seventy two dollars."

Currency not in dollars and cents is dictated with the name of the currency unit as well. For example, to dictate Euros, Pounds or Yen, speak the name and it will be typed: €58 is spoken as "fifty-eight euros", £29.99 is spoken as "twenty-nine point nine nine pound sterling", and ¥322 is spoken as "three hundred twenty-two yen".

DIRECTIONS: Dictate these amounts (say **Tab Key** to tab between items, and **New Line** as needed):

[Start Dictating]

$12	$4.25
$13.75	$288.09
$41,163	$.99 (say, **ninety-nine cents**)

[Stop Dictating]

Note: if you want to dictate "99 ¢" say "**ninety-nine Cent Sign**".

DIRECTIONS: Dictate these sentences with numbers and currency. Make corrections if needed. Do not worry about line breaks, but do say **New Paragraph** after the first paragraph and the last paragraph.

[Start Dictating]

The ad said that if I was one of the first 100 callers and gave them $29.99, I would win a free trip to Hawaii in June.

Luckily, before I called the Bogus Hawaiian Holidays telephone number of 800-555-1234, I found out it was a scam that has made over $802,500 since January 12!

[Stop Dictating]

Exercise 3.9, Continued

Note: The previous segment uses formatted numbers in sentences. How did it go for you? It can take a little while to get used to dictating in this way, but don't worry—you will get more practice soon.

Talking About Time

The time of day is dictated as it is normally spoken, for the most part. Dragon NaturallySpeaking types the colon if you say "am" or "pm" while dictating the time. If you do not use "am" or "pm," you might need to add the colon with the colon command.

DIRECTIONS: Dictate times of day, saying **New Line** between each item.

[Start Dictating]

> 9:30   (Say, **nine colon thirty**)
>
> 3:15 PM
>
> 10:25 AM
>
> 11:02 PM
>
> 12:00   (Say, **twelve colon zero zero**)

[Stop Dictating]

Review: How did this work for you? You may notice "am" and "pm" written as "AM" and "PM". At the end of this chapter is information about how to change the number, date and time formats, if you wish to do so. Save your work as "Exercise 3.9" and print if needed. Close your DragonPad document.

About Exercise 3.10 Create a Flyer with Formatting

In the exercise on the next page, put your best practices to the test. Dictate the text in the flyer first, make corrections, then save it. (It may look strange to see so much unformatted text if you are used to formatting by hand.) Go back and add formatting such as bold, underlining and centering. Remember **New Line** and **New Paragraph**.

Exercise 3.10: Create a Flyer with Formatting

DIRECTIONS: Create the flyer below for a school open house by voice. Dictate text first, make corrections, then add formatting. Say **Tab** or **Press Tab** after dictating the times on the left. Review commands for capitalization, text alignment, bold, and punctuation if needed. It is acceptable if "PM" is formatted "pm". Optional: To make the centered headings size 14, as pictured below, say **Select *Woodland* through *15*,** then **Format That Size 14**.

[Start Dictating]

Woodland School
Open House
March 15

You are invited to the Woodland School Open House!

Events:

6:15 PM	Potluck dinner, hosted by Mrs. Foster's sixth grade class
7:15 PM	Presentation by Susan Miyamoto, Principal
7:30 PM	Play by Mr. Miller's third grade class, "Spring Is Here"
8:15 PM	Visit the classrooms.

Refreshments provided in every room!

If you would like to help us with this wonderful event, call our volunteer coordinator at 479-3642.

[Stop Dictating]

Review: Look over your work after dictating. Notice the formatting that will need to be added, and any misrecognitions. Fix misrecognitions first. Save your work as "Exercise 3.11". Add formatting using commands you have already practiced. Save again, and print as needed.

Exercise 3.11: Professional Letter

DIRECTIONS: Dictate and correct the text, then save it as "Exercise 3.11". Add bold, italics, and underlining as shown. Say **Select All**, then say **Format That Size 12.** Save the document again, and print if desired.

[Start Dictating]

(Today's Date)

Oswald Greene
Transcription Pros
324 Main St.
Greendale, CA 95327

Dear Mr. Greene,

I am writing to you today regarding the transcriptionist position posted on September 5. While I am new to the field of transcription, I have six years of experience in proofreading for the **Greendale Times**, and two years of experience using speech recognition software.

Transcriptionists must be able to work quickly with a high degree of accuracy. In my last 10 timed dictation tests, I have an <u>average</u> speed of 132 words per minute. Depending on the type of documents being dictated, my speed varies from 95 to 154 words per minute, with *less than* two errors per minute.

I would like to be considered for the position. Please call me at 708-465-7291 or reply by e-mail. I can also be reached at the address below.

Thank you very much for your time and consideration.

Sincerely,

Lee Gregory
290 Elm St.
West Greendale, CA 95329

[Stop Dictating]

Review: This exercise is challenging, because it asks you to use skills from Chapters 1-3 to dictate a letter composed of complex sentences—much more difficult than dictating a list of punctuation or numbers. If this was easy for you, then you are prepared for the challenges of the next chapter!

About Exercise 3.12

Timed writing exercises are a quick tool to measure speed and accuracy. After you complete the two timed writing passages, compare your scores to your work on Exercise 1.6, the first timed writing exercise.

Exercise 3.12 Timed Writing II

DIRECTIONS: Use the tips below to complete the timed writings.

1. Read the entire passage *carefully* before you dictate it. Practice any difficult words.

2. Do not look at the screen as you dictate—keep your eyes on the printed word you are speaking. If you reach the end of the passage but you still have time left on your timer, say **New Line**, then start dictating the passage again.

3. Dictate the text first, then use the remaining time to make corrections or begin dictating the passage again.

4. Do not let yourself get distracted. If you do get interrupted, don't count that attempt—just start again.

5. Set a timer for one minute. Turn on your microphone. When you are ready, turn on the timer and begin speaking. When the timer rings, turn off your microphone immediately.

Timed Writing II	Words per line	Total Words
People who are good at typing on a keyboard might feel that speech	13	13
recognition software is just too much trouble to use. However, for	11	24
those who claim that speech recognition is too much trouble, a	11	35
timed writing exercise often leads them to reconsider. If the average	11	46
good typist can enter text at 40 to 60 words per minute, and the	14	60
average person dictating text can enter text at 80 to 120 words per	13	73
minute, then the person using speech recognition can work twice as	11	84
fast!	1	85

Total words minus errors = adjusted words per minute

Review: How did your errors compare to your first timed writing? Because this passage includes numbers, there is often a higher error rate. Of course, the best way to get good at timed writings is to practice. Save your work as "Exercise 3.12 TW2" and print. Count the number of total words per minute, and the number of errors (it helps to underline or highlight these), then write this information on the exercise. Keep this exercise for reference, or turn in to your instructor.

Exercise 3.12, Continued: Timed Writing III

 DIRECTIONS: Follow the tips from the previous page as you complete this slightly longer timed writing.

Timed Writing III	Words per line	Total Words
Mrs. Smith's kindergarten class took a field trip to a bakery last	12	12
week. The children saw several bakers working in the production	10	22
room. One was adding cinnamon and sugar to the dough, rolling it	12	34
up and slicing it to make cinnamon rolls. Another was adding flour	12	46
into a giant mixer to make bread dough. The real excitement,	11	57
however, came as the children went to the cake decorating room,	11	68
where two pastry chefs piped icing to make swirls, dots and other	12	80
fanciful creations onto a line of waiting cakes. A final highlight came	12	92
when the children were each presented with lovely pale butter	10	102
cookies with colored sprinkles on top.	6	108

Total words minus errors = adjusted words per minute

Review: How did it go? Even people comfortable dictating to a computer can get nervous when a timer is involved. The best way to get good at timed writings is to practice. Save your work as "Exercise 3.12 TW3" and print. Count the number of total words per minute, and the number of errors (it helps to underline or highlight these), then write this information on the exercise. Keep this exercise for reference, or turn in to your instructor.

Save your updates to your user profile by saying **Save User Profile**.

Auto-Formatting Options

How does Dragon know to format numbers, dates, times, etc.?

In the **Tools** menu of the DragonBar, the **Auto-Formatting** item opens up a window like the one pictured on this page. Here you can select or de-select many kinds of auto-formatting.

If you have a favorite way of formatting dates, you can choose it from the "Dates as Spoken" list. This can save a lot of time if you tend to stick to one type of date format.

If you prefer for numbers 0-9 to be written as numerals, change it in the "Numbers, if greater than or equal to [ ] list box.

If you need more time to dictate phone numbers, addresses, or other number formats, check the box next to "Allow pauses in formatted phrases". This is helpful for people who have difficulty getting the auto-formatting to work due to speaking slowly or haltingly.

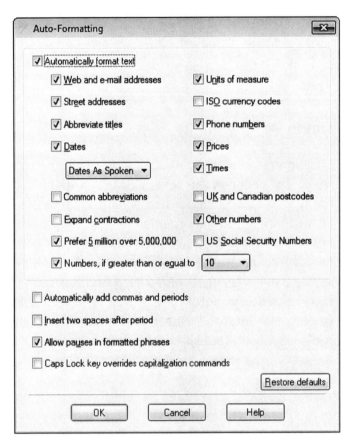

To reset the **Auto-Formatting** area to the default settings, check the "Restore defaults" button, Click "OK", and Dragon will return to the original specifications for formatting. For more information, see the Dragon **Help** file for specifics on each item.

Command Review

New commands in this lesson:

Selecting:
Select Line
Select Last [2] Lines
Select Last [3]
   Sentences
Select Paragraph
Select Last [4]
   Paragraphs
Select All
Select Last Word
Select Last 6 Words
Select Last Character
Select Last [5]
Characters

Capitalization/Spacing:
Cap [*word*]
Cap That
Caps On
Caps Off
All Caps On
All Caps Off
No Cap That
No Caps On
No Caps Off
No Space On
No Space Off
Compound That
Hyphenate That
Format That
   Strikethrough
Format That Strikeout

Numbers:
Numeral [6]
Roman Numeral [20]

Bold, Italics, Underline:
Bold That
Format That Bold
Bold [*word*]
Bold from [*word*] to
   [*word*]
Bold [*word*] through
   [*word*]
Press Ctrl + B
Italicize That
Format That Italics
Italicize [*word*]
Italicize from [*word*] to
   [word]
Italicize [*word*]
   through[*word*]
Press Ctrl + I
Underline That
Format That
Underlined
Underline [*word*]
Underline from [*word*]
   to [word]
Underline [*word*]
   through[*word*]
Press Ctrl + U
Format That Bold
   Italics

Alignment:
Left Align That
Format That Left
   Aligned
Press Ctrl + L
Center That
Format That Centered
Press Ctrl + E
Right Align That
Format That Right
   Aligned
Press Ctrl + R
Justify That
Press Ctrl + J

Editing:
Cut [*word*]
Cut [*word*] through
   [*word*]
Cut That
Copy [*word*]
Copy [*word*] through
   [*word*]
Copy That
Paste That

Miscellaneous
Make That Size [14]
Format That Plain
Format That Regular
Restore That

4 CHAPTER 4
Dictate in Windows and Programs

In this chapter you will move beyond the basic skills of the first three chapters (training a user profile, learning to make corrections, and formatting text) and use your skills to navigate the desktop and work in non-native Dragon programs, such as Microsoft Word.

Remember Core Instructions

Every time you use speech recognition, do this:

1. Do a warm-up exercise
2. Take frequent sips of water
3. Take breaks regularly
4. Read the step before you do it
5. Make corrections as needed

Exercise 4.1 Warm-Up Exercise

DIRECTIONS: Dictate the following into DragonPad to check your recognition. Say **New Line** and **New Paragraph** as appropriate. Items in brackets [ ] give instructions, while items in parentheses ( ) are for you to customize:

[Start Dictating]

> Hello computer, are you ready to work today?
> I am using speech recognition software.
> Dictating is much faster than typing.
> (Dictate your favorite quote here.)
> (Your First Name) (Your Last Name)

[Stop Dictating]

Correct any recognition errors and save your document as "Exercise 4.1". Close DragonPad.

In This Chapter

- ✓ Core Instructions
- ✓ Warm-Up Exercise
- ✓ Navigating the Desktop and Program Windows
- ✓ MouseGrid
- ✓ Recognition Modes
- ✓ Working with Microsoft Word
- ✓ Working with OpenOffice
- ✓ Text and Graphics Commands
- ✓ Practice skills in 11 Exercises
- ✓ Frequently Asked Questions
- ✓ Command Review

Navigating the Desktop

To start or open items on the desktop, use the command **Start** or **Open**; for example, you can say **Start Internet Explorer, Start Recycle Bin,** and **Start Computer**. However, to open up the Start menu, use the command **Click Start** or **Start Menu**.

About Exercise 4.2 The Start Menu

The Start menu, accessed from the Taskbar (usually in the lower left-hand corner of the desktop), provides shortcuts to programs and locations in the computer. Windows 7 and Windows Vista make it even easier to find documents, drives, and programs in the computer by using the search box in the Start menu. In the exercise below, begin by opening the Start menu by voice.

Then, use the search box to start (open) programs simply by speaking their names. Note that your Start menu may look different than the sample below; adapt this exercise where needed to work for you.

Exercise 4.2 The Start Menu

DIRECTIONS: Follow the steps below to work with the Start menu by voice.

1. Say **Click Start** to open the Start menu. Wait a few seconds for it to open.
2. Notice how the Start menu has a search box above the start button with a blinking cursor, and two columns with lists of items. The left column contains program shortcuts and the right column contains links to locations within the computer.
3. Say **Paint** and the word "paint" should appear in the search box. (If not, say **Scratch That** and try it again. If you still get the wrong word, say **Correct That**, and dictate the correct word.) Note: it does not need to be capitalized.
4. When you see the word Paint in the search box, say **Press Enter** and the Paint program will open. (This may take up to 10 seconds. On the other hand, it may happen automatically, without saying **Press Enter**.)

Exercise 4.2, Continued

5. Look at the Paint program window to confirm that your command worked.
6. Say **Click Close** to close the Paint program.
7. Say **Click Start** to open the Start menu again. Look at the right side of the Start menu and decide on a link to speak.
8. Open the item by saying its name with or without the word **Click** in front of it. For example, if you have a Computer icon, say either **Computer** or **Click Computer**. The window you named will open.
9. Say **Click Close** to close the window that you just opened.
10. Say **Click Start** to open the Start menu again. Look at the left column of the Start menu, and notice the All Programs item. (This will display a list of installed programs.)
11. Say **All Programs** or **Click All Programs**, and the All Programs item opens.
12. Choose a program from the list. Say the name of the program with or without the word **Click** in front of it. The program should open.
13. Say **Click Close** or **Close Window** to close the program window you just opened.
14. If the Start menu needs to be closed, say **Press Escape**, or say **Click Start** again, and it will close.

Review: This exercise often goes smoothly, but it can get hung up when a command doesn't work, or a program window won't close. Be patient, and if you need to, jump in with the mouse or keyboard to fix a step and move on to the next step. With practice, you will be able to speak items and have the actions work the first time (usually!).

Searching the Computer

The Search box in the Start menu can be used even when the Start menu is closed. To search the computer for something using the Search feature, use this command: **Search the Computer for [*something*]**.

Here are some examples to try if you wish: **Search the Computer for [*pictures*]**, **Search the Computer for [*documents*]**, **Search the Computer for [*Microsoft Word*]**, **Search the Computer for [*Brenda Jones*]**. In each case the Search returns a list of results which are, or contain, the search word or words. So, if you lose items in your computer, this is a quick command to find them again!

Sometimes when you use a Search command, a Dragon Keyword Edit window appears (see example at left). When this happens, check that the word in the window is the one you want (correct it if it is not) and then say **Search** to continue. Note: if

you do not want to see this window again, say Do not display this window again, and the checkbox next to that option will be checked, and the window will not appear again unless you change this option in the Options area.

The other method to search the computer, practiced in Exercise 4.2, is to open the Start menu, wait for the cursor to appear in the Search box, then speak the search terms. Say **Press Enter** to activate the search box.

Switching Between Windows and the Desktop

Often, when using a computer, one needs to switch between several open windows, or between the desktop and open windows. Say **List All Windows** to get a window like the one at left. Then, say the number of the desired item.

To move between open items and the desktop, use these commands:

Say This Command...	To Perform This Action...
List All Windows	Opens a window to list the open windows; say number desired *(see example above)*
List All Windows *for Microsoft Word*	Opens a windows to list the open Word windows; say number desired
Switch to *Desktop*	Puts the focus on the desktop
Switch to *Microsoft Word**	Switches to the first open Word window
Switch to *Next Window*	Switches to the next window
Switch to *Previous Window*	Switches to the previous window
Press Alt Tab	Switches to the next window

*Program or file names can also be used (i.e., **Switch to** *Midterm Report*)

Working in Program Windows

When you open a window, whether it's a program window like Paint, or a Windows Explorer window which displays folders and drives, some items will be "speakable" and some will be "non-speakable". Also, some windows are "supported" by Dragon NaturallySpeaking, and some are "unsupported".

Learn about these terms below.

Speakable Items

Commands you can say in windows include the names of menus, names of tabs, and the names of items in Windows that are links or buttons. Choices in dialog boxes can usually be spoken.

Commands to move around a window include: **Press Tab, Press Shift Tab, Move Up, Move Down, Page Up, Page Down, Move Left, Move Right, Press Enter, Press Escape, Press Cancel, Open List,** and **Close List.**

If you aren't sure that an item in a window is speakable, try saying it. If something unexpected occurs, say **Cancel, Escape** or **Undo That** as needed.

Non-Speakable Items

Some items in windows usually can't be spoken. These include some names of individual items (files or icons) in a window, toolbar icons (pictures), and **anything which is not currently visible on the screen.**

A special feature, called MouseGrid, makes it possible to click anywhere on the screen, and this is especially useful for non-speakable items. MouseGrid is introduced in the next section of this chapter.

Super-Quick Commands

To **start** any program quickly, get to the desktop and say:
Start [*program*]

For Example:
- **Start *Microsoft Word***
- **Start *WordPad***
- **Start *Paint***
- **Start *Internet Explorer***
- **Start *Calculator***

To **shut down**, logoff, or restart the computer, close any open programs (except Dragon) and say:

- **Shut Down the Computer,**
- **Restart the Computer** *or*
- **Logoff the Computer.**

Supported vs. Non-supported Programs

Some programs are "supported" by Dragon, and others are "unsupported". Supported programs work well with Dragon. Most Microsoft programs are supported, but not all. Dragon calls unsupported program windows "non-standard windows" which means that fewer Dragon commands will work.

That said, it is worth a try to see what works. For example, **Close Window** often works better than **Click Close** in non-standard windows. So, if the primary command doesn't work, use an alternate command or a keypress command. (The keypress command to close an open window is **Press Alt F4.**)

MouseGrid

MouseGrid is a way to click the mouse by voice, by narrowing in on the item using a numbered grid. This is helpful when you can't get regular methods to work, or when you find an element hard to dictate (such as a toolbar icon).

Here is how it works:

1. Say **MouseGrid** to bring up the grid, then hone in on your target by saying the number in the grids until the numbered square is where you want the mouse pointer to be. Then say **Click, Double-click,** or **Right-click,** depending upon the desired action.
2. To undo your last MouseGrid action, say **Undo That.**
3. To close MouseGrid at any time when it is displayed, say **Cancel.**
4. To place the MouseGrid over a window only (not the whole screen) say **MouseGrid Window.**

For Example: MouseGrid, 5, Click (clicks the center of the screen)

MouseGrid 7, 7, 7, Click

MouseGrid 2, 4, 3, Double-Click

MouseGrid 5, 7, Right-Click

MouseGrid Window, 3, Click

MouseGrid 3, Mark. MouseGrid 7, 2, Drag

Exercise 4.3 MouseGrid

DIRECTIONS: Turn on your microphone and practice MouseGrid.

1. Get to where you can see the Taskbar and the Desktop. Locate the Start button.
2. Say, **MouseGrid**, and wait for the grid to appear. (If it doesn't work in 10 seconds, say it again.)
3. When the numbered grid appears, say **7**; the grid will shrink to the lower left corner of the screen.
4. Say the number closest to the Start button again, probably **7**.
5. Say **7** a third time and the grid will have focused on the Start button.

Recycle Bin

6. Say **Click**, and a mouse click occurs over the Start button, which opens the Start menu.
7. Say **Press Escape** to close the Start menu. (Alternately, you could click on a blank area of the desktop with the command **Mousegrid, 5, Click**.)
8. Now double-click on the Taskbar clock using MouseGrid. The commands are usually **MouseGrid 9, 9, 9, Click**. Depending upon your version of Windows, a window might open with the date or a calendar; if so, say **Press Escape** or **Click Close** to close it.
9. Turn off or sleep your mic. Read the following information and continue with Exercise 4.3 below.

Mark and Drag

Mouse Grid can also be used to "click and hold" an item so that it can be moved to a different spot on your desktop. The commands for this are **Mark,** then **Drag.**

1. Get to where you can see the Taskbar and the Desktop. Choose an icon (for example, the Recycle Bin) to move to another location on the desktop.
2. Say **MouseGrid**. Say the numbers you need until the grid is over the icon.
3. Say **Mark**, and the mouse clicks and holds on the icon.
4. Now, select the location where the icon will be moved to. Say **MouseGrid** and the numbers needed until the grid is over the new location.
5. Say **Drag**, and the icon should appear in the new location. (For example, to move the icon to the center of the screen, the command would be **MouseGrid, 5, 5, 5, Drag**.)
6. Now, give MouseGrid **Mark** and **Drag** commands to return the icon to its original location—you can do it!

Review: Did you have any problems with MouseGrid? Can you imagine where you might use this in the future?

 # QUESTION TIME!

What if I accidentally say the wrong number? Can I go back a grid?

If you say the wrong number in the grid, say **Undo That**, and MouseGrid moves back one step. However, if this doesn't solve the problem, say **Cancel** to close MouseGrid. Then, say **MouseGrid** and try it again.

Sometimes I just need to click on the desktop—how do I do this?

MouseGrid works well for a quick desktop click or a click inside a window to make it active. Say **MouseGrid, 5, Click** to click in the center of the screen, or customize the command as needed.

MouseGrid didn't put the pointer on the tiny icon I need it on—help!

If you need to move the mouse just a little bit, here's how: Say **Mouse Up 10**. This command works with the following variations: **Mouse Down 1–10, Mouse Right 1–10**, and **Mouse Left 1–10**. This isn't practical for moving the mouse over long distances, but it's handy when you just need to move the mouse pointer a tiny bit.

Can I move the mouse pointer by voice, more than a tiny bit?

To move the mouse by voice, use the **Mouse Drag [*direction*]** command. This command starts the mouse moving in a direction, until you tell it to **Stop**. There are four **Mouse Drag** commands: **Mouse Drag Right, Mouse Drag Left, Mouse Drag Up** and **Mouse Drag Down**.

Can I click the mouse by voice?

Yes. Say **Mouse Click** for a single left click, **Mouse Right-click** or **Mouse Double-Click** for those types of mouse clicks. More on mouse actions is found in the Dragon Help files.

So, it sounds like you are saying that I can pretty much do everything by voice, if I am patient, and learn and practice the commands?

Yes, if you want to, and especially if you need to, you can have a hands-free computer experience. Only a few items will be out of your reach, and Dragon is improving with those difficult items (gaming, picture editing, and so on) in each new version.

Recognition Modes

Have you ever dictated a command and it was typed as text instead? Or, have you ever dictated some text which was interpreted as a command? These situations are frustrating and can be avoided if you understand Dragon's recognition modes.

Recognition modes, or just *modes*, narrow the vocabulary that Dragon uses when matching your dictation to text or commands. There are five modes, each with specific advantages. Until now you've been using the most general mode, called the "Normal" mode. (It might be better called the "everything" mode.)

Mode	What it Recognizes	Used For...
Normal	Dictation, commands, numbers, spelling (all)	General use
Dictation	Words, punctuation, limited commands	Text dictation with no risk of command actions
Command	Commands only	Commanding without any text being typed
Numbers	Numbers, commands, and punctuation	Dictating numbers, spreadsheets
Spell	Letters, numbers, commands, and punctuation	Internet or e-mail addresses, alphanumeric input/data entry

Switching Recognition Modes

To switch to another recognition mode, say the mode you want in either of these command forms: **Switch to [*name of*] Mode,** or **[*name of*] Mode On.** Examples of valid commands are: **Switch to Dictation Mode, Switch to Numbers Mode, Spell Mode On,** and **Command Mode On.** Another way to switch modes is to speak or click on the desired mode from the list in the DragonBar's Modes menu. Commands to do this are: **Click Modes, Normal Mode.**

Changing recognition modes is useful when dictating without looking at the screen (use Dictation mode), dictating numbers in Excel (Numbers mode) and e-mail and web addresses (Spell mode).

Finally, occasionally it is desirable to switch modes for just a moment. As you may recall from Chapter 2, if you are having trouble getting a command recognized, press and hold the **Control** (Ctrl) key while speaking the troublesome command to force the Command mode. Conversely, if some dictated text is activated as a command, press the **Shift** key to force dictation mode. When you let go of the key, Dragon returns to Normal mode.

Microsoft Office and The Ribbon

Dragon NaturallySpeaking works with many Microsoft Office programs, including Microsoft Word, Excel, PowerPoint, Outlook, and InfoPath. Check the help files in your edition of Dragon NaturallySpeaking to determine which Microsoft Office programs it supports and to see the latest list of commands for each program. Microsoft Office 2007 and higher use the ribbon interface, which organizes program options in groups within tabs. To move between tabs, speak their names, with or without the word **Click**.

Microsoft Word 2010 places the save, print, and exit features in a File tab. To activate it, say **Click File Tab**. In Word 2007, these features are accessed by the Office button. To do this by voice, say **Click Office Button**. The Application menu, new to the ribbon in Microsoft programs like Paint and WordPad, is used for save, print and exit. To activate the Application Menu, just say **Click Application Menu**. Many items can be spoken directly—but not all, so try them and see. If something unexpected happens, say **Undo That** (or **Press Ctrl Z**).

Working with Microsoft Word

Microsoft Word is an enormously popular word processing program—and for good reason. It works well, and it is loaded with useful features; for example, users can run spelling and grammar checks in their documents, create bulleted and numbered lists, and format text in many ways that cannot be done with DragonPad or other basic word processing programs. Microsoft Word has advanced features as well, such as mail merge, macros, and features to support long documents.

Learning the features of Microsoft Word fills semester-length courses, and if you have never used Microsoft Word (or, just "Word") before, you may want to plan to learn more about what this program can do. In this chapter, you will learn how to use some of Word's most popular features quickly and easily with Dragon NaturallySpeaking.

> Good news! Nearly all commands used so far also work in Microsoft Word!

140

Do DragonPad commands work in Word?

Yes. Word processing commands used in Chapter 3 with DragonPad also work in Word. Commands for bold, italics, underlining, capitalization, and numbers all work well. Commands for correction, from Chapter 2, also work in the same way. In addition, a new set of commands is available, specific to Word, called Natural Language Commands. (More on this below.)

What about the Ribbon? Can I speak any of those items?

Yes. Dragon supports the ribbon interface, and in the Exercise 4.5, you learn how to speak the ribbon "tabs". You can also say the names of items in the tabs—the trick is knowing what those icons are called and how to speak those commands. Practice speaking items in the ribbon is also found in Exercise 4.5.

CAUTION! While text is selected in Microsoft Word, don't clear your throat or make other sounds. Dragon NaturallySpeaking may *interpret such sounds as speech* and replace a selection with new text. If this happens, say **Undo That** right away to reverse it.

About Natural Language Commands

Natural Language Commands are designed to imitate what people normally would say if they were telling an assistant to make changes in a document. (Go ahead, picture it: you are the boss standing over your assistant, pointing to the computer screen where he or she is ready to revise your document. You tell the assistant what to do, and it is done!) Some examples are: **Make That Dark Blue** and **Move This Line Down 2 Paragraphs**.

You can use either the Natural Language Commands given, or you can use the tried-and-true standard Dragon commands you have learned in previous chapters. For example, the standard Dragon commands for the Natural Language Command **Make This Paragraph Bold** would be **Select Paragraph, Bold That**. Unfortunately, Dragon doesn't provide a list of Natural Language Commands because there are too many variations—thousands, in fact! They recommend just saying what you want Word to do, and see if it works. If you try this, and the results aren't what you wanted, quickly say **Undo That**.

So, I should just make up commands?

Here's where it gets interesting—since there isn't a single list of Natural Language Commands, you do have to "try it and see". To make this easier, this chapter covers commands for the most popular Word features, and ideas about how to make your own commands, following certain command formats. (Author's note: My students and I have discovered many useful undocumented commands over the years—many are in this book.) For even more detailed information about command structures, see the discussion of the Command Browser on page 203.

About Exercise 4.4

In this exercise, use the tried-and-true warm-up exercise to see how your recognition is in Microsoft Word. (Hint: expect more errors at first.) Make corrections, then use Word-specific commands to format text in headings and save. Finally, practice moving the cursor and activating the ribbon tabs by voice.

Tip: Be ready to turn your microphone off (or asleep) when you aren't actually dictating, to avoid extra sounds which might cause problems. The number keypad plus key is very useful for this purpose. The hands-free version is to say **Go to Sleep** as soon as you finish dictating.

Exercise 4.4 Dictate Into Microsoft Word

DIRECTIONS: Open Microsoft Word, dictate the warm-up exercise, make corrections, apply formatting, and save it as Exercise 4.4. Practice moving the cursor around in the document and creating headings.

1. Open Microsoft Word. How you do this varies depending upon your computer setup. Often, you say **Click Start** to open the Start menu, then the Microsoft Word item by speaking the entire name as it appears ("Microsoft Word 2010" or "Microsoft Word 2007").

2. If a new, blank document does not automatically appear when you open Microsoft Word, say **Create New File** or **Open a New Document**.

3. Dictate the sentences of the warm-up exercise as you normally would, adding punctuation and **New Line** as needed:

[Start Dictating]

Hello computer, are you ready to work today?
I am using speech recognition software.

Exercise 4.4, Continued

> Dictating is much faster than typing.
> (Dictate your favorite quote or saying here.)
> (Dictate your first and last name)

[Stop Dictating]

Make Corrections and Save

4. Make corrections to misrecognitions using the commands you learned in Chapter 2. If anything unexpected occurs, say **Undo That**.

5. Say **Save Changes** to open the "Save As" dialog box.

6. Use the mouse and keyboard to work through this window, or say **Exercise Numeral 4.4, Cap That** in the File Name field and, if the location is correct, say **Click Save**. (If the save location isn't correct, try speaking the name of the location you wish to save in, provided you can see it in the box. If not, use the mouse and keyboard, or MouseGrid, to select the correct location.)

Insert Text and Format Headings

7. Say **Go To Top**. The insertion point will move in front of the word "Hello". Or, if you prefer, say **Insert Before** *Hello*.

8. Say **Exercise Numeral 4.4** to see "exercise 4.4" appear at the top of the document.

9. Say **New Line** to move the rest of the text on that line down one line. Now "Exercise 4.4" will be on its own line, and the warm-up sentences will begin on the next line.

10. Say **Insert Before** *Exercise* to move the insertion point to this position. Say **Cap That** and the word "Exercise" becomes capitalized.

11. Say **Select Line** to select this line. In the next step, format this text as a heading.

12. Say **Set Style Heading 1** to format this text as a heading level 1. It should look different than the sentences below it; it might be a different font, or color, or both. This will depend upon the settings in your Word document.

13. Say **Go to Bottom** to move the insertion point to the end of the document. If this is the line with your name, you are ready for the next step. If not, say **Insert After [*your last name*]** to move the insertion point to the correct line.

14. Say **Select Line** to select your name.

15. Say **Set Style Heading 3** to format your name as a Heading Level 3.

Exercise 4.4, Continued

16. Again, this should look different from the sentences, and from the Heading 1 at the top of the document. See the completed example below.

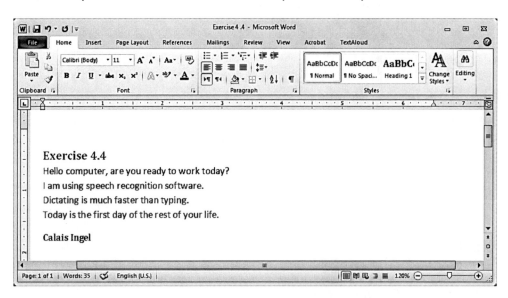

17. Say **Save Changes** to update your document with your changes.

Review: How was your first dictation into Microsoft Word? Did you have any trouble moving the cursor with commands like **Go to Top, Go to Bottom, and Insert After [*word*]**? While Exercise 4.4 provides practice moving the cursor, you can do these tasks more quickly in the future. For example, to select your name, as in step 11 and 12, you could say **Select [*your name*]** instead of the three commands used.

What if I want to change the name of a document, or where it is saved?

To change the name, the storage location, or even the file type of a document, say **Save Document As.** When the "Save As…" dialog box opens, make the needed changes, then say **Click Save.**

What are all those commands to save a document about?

When saving a Word document, you have many command choices. When a document has not been saved previously, these commands will all open the "Save As" dialog box, where you can set the location for the save, dictate the file name into the File Name text box, and say **Click Save** to activate the Save button.

If the document has been saved and named previously, these commands will update the save, adding the latest unsaved material to the file.

- ❖ **Click Save** is a control command which "clicks" a Save icon, if one is visible.
- ❖ **Save That** also sends a "save" command to the software. (Make certain no text is selected in your document or it won't work properly.)
- ❖ **Press Ctrl S** is the keypress command which sends a "save" command to the software.
- ❖ **Save Changes** is a Natural Language Command version of the "save" command.

About Exercise 4.5 Formatting Text Using the Ribbon

This exercise uses the Microsoft Word ribbon. If you have trouble getting a command recognized, say **Switch to Command Mode**, say the command again, then say **Switch to Normal Mode**.

Exercise 4.5 Formatting Text Using the Ribbon

DIRECTIONS: Get a new Word document and try the ribbon commands. Dictate the text below, make corrections, and save your work. Finally, format it using the ribbon commands given.

1. Open a new Microsoft Word document. (If the Word program is still open, and you only need to open a new document, say **Open a New Document.**)
2. Dictate **your name** into the document. Say **New Line**.
3. Dictate **Exercise Numeral 4.5**. Say **Cap That** if needed. Say **New Paragraph**.
4. Speak your way through the tabs on the ribbon by using these commands:
   Click Insert, Click Page Layout, Click References, Click Mailings, Click Review, Click View, Click Home and **Click File Tab.**

Skip "Click"

Commands for the tabs do not always require the word **Click**. The **File Tab** command <u>does</u> require the word **Tab**, but the other tabs work better without it.

5. Now try the commands (in this order) without the word click: **Insert, Page Layout, References, Mailings, Review, View, File Tab** and **Home**. (If you have trouble getting these to work, see the tip in the **Review** below.)
6. Dictate the text below into your document.

Exercise 4.5, Continued

[Start Dictating]

Computer Maintenance **Cap That, New Line**
Computers make it easier to do many kinds of work, but owning and maintaining a computer can be costly and time-consuming. Not only do computers need regular maintenance, they also need updates to important software, such as anti-virus and anti-spyware software. If a computer you own works more slowly than it used to, it may be time for some maintenance. In fact, establishing a regular maintenance schedule (rather than waiting for a problem) is a good idea. **New Paragraph**

Upgrade Memory and Back Up Files **Cap That, New Line**
Upgrading the memory in a computer can help it to run faster and keep it from crashing. Also, remember to back up your documents, photos, and any other files you would not want to lose if your hard drive were to crash. Using an external hard drive for this purpose is a good idea. Some people also like to back up to online storage, such as Microsoft's Sky Drive or a service like Dropbox. **New Paragraph**

[Stop Dictating]

1. Make corrections to any misrecognition using the **Correct [*word*]** command. When Dragon numbers multiple instances of a word, say the number next to your selection.
2. Make any needed corrections to capitalization using the **Select [*word*], Cap That** commands.
3. Correct any other errors before continuing, using commands you know.
4. Say **Save Changes** and save your document as "Exercise 4.5".

Use Features in the Ribbon: Heading Styles

5. Say **Click Home** (if needed) to activate the Home tab. Notice the Styles group toward the right side of the Home tab.
6. Say **Select *Computer Maintenance*** and say **Set Style Heading Two**. Notice the focus in the Styles group on the Heading 2 style.

Exercise 4.5, Continued

7.   Say **Select *Upgrade Memory and Back Up Files*** and say **Set Style Heading Two**. Both headings should now be set as Heading 2 styles.

Set Line Spacing and Remove Extra Space After Text

8.   Say **Insert Before [*your first name*]**. Say **Select Next 2 Lines** to select your name and Exercise 4.5.

9.   Say **Line and Paragraph Spacing**. This will open the Line and Paragraph Spacing item in the Home tab's Paragraph group.

10. When the item is open, notice that the line spacing may not be set at single spaced (1.0). Say **1.0** ("one point oh") to select this option. The menu closes.

11. There is still some space between the two lines, due to hidden spacing after each line. Get rid of this by saying **Line and Paragraph Spacing** to re-open this item, then **Remove Space After Paragraph**. The two lines should look single-spaced.

12. With the paragraph selected, say **Bold** or **Bold That** and the first two lines should be bold. Notice the Bold icon is illuminated.

Increase Indent, then Decrease Indent

13. Say **Select All**. When the text is selected, say **Increase Indent**. (This activates the "Increase Indent" button.) The text should move to the right up to 5 spaces.

14. If the text has become de-selected, say **Select All** again; otherwise, just say **Decrease Indent** to remove the indenting you added in the previous step.

Add Formatting, then Clear Formatting

15. Select the last paragraph. To do this, put the cursor in the first paragraph (using a command like **Insert Before *Upgrading***) and say **Select Paragraph**.

16. Make this paragraph bold, italicized, and underlined by giving commands— one at a time, waiting for each to work—to activate those buttons in the Font group: **Bold, Underline** and **Italics** (or, **Press Control I**). Looks pretty ugly, doesn't it?

17. Remove the formatting by saying (**Select Paragraph** if needed first), **Clear Formatting**. This command activates the Clear Formatting button in the Font group. **Clear Formatting** removes all formatting from a selection.

18. Say **Go to Bottom**, then **New Paragraph** to move the cursor out of the text area. Say **Save Changes** to update your save of Exercise 4.5.

19. Close your Microsoft Word document with the command **Close Document**. You will need a new document for the next exercise, but not yet.

Review: How was that? Were you able to navigate the tabs and get the commands to work without problems? If you have difficulty getting commands to work, try saying **Switch to Command Mode** before giving them, then say **Switch to Normal Mode** after working with the ribbon.

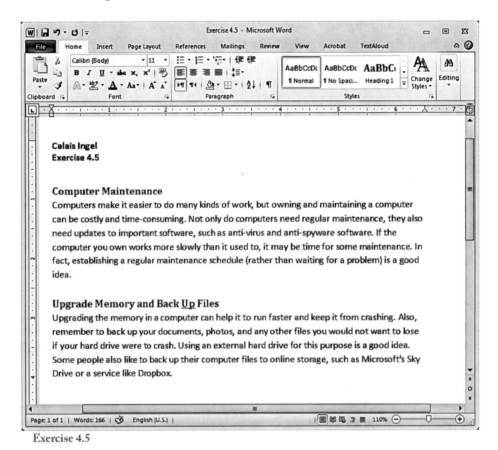

Exercise 4.5

How do I know what commands I can say to use the ribbon icons and items?

To figure out ribbon icons you can command by voice, hover the mouse over an item in the ribbon to find out what it is called. (The little captions that appear when you hover the mouse over an icon in the ribbon are called Screen Tips. If your screen tips don't appear, turn the feature on in the Word Options area.) Then, say the name of the item to activate it. You may want to select some text first, so see the action applied to text.

In the next section are shortcut commands for font size, style and color, and line spacing. Practice these commands in the exercises that follow.

Changing Font Size, Style and Color

The approach you take to changing font features depends on what you want to do. While you may not need all of these commands, it can be helpful to see the range of options available by voice.

To Change the Font Type Only

To change the font type (also called *font face*) only, you first select the text, then dictate the command: **Format That [*Font Name*]** or **Make That [*Font Name*]**.

> *For Example*: **Select All, Format That Arial**
> *For Example*: **Select Paragraph, Make That Times New Roman**

Important: This only works with a few fonts: Arial, Times New Roman, Courier New, Palatino and Garamond. *(Dragon does not publish a list of the fonts you can dictate—if you have success with any others, please let the author know!)*

So, I can't use any other fonts?

Of course you can! Feel free to use any font you have installed in Word. To choose a font not in the paragraph above, select the desired text and say **Click Font** (puts the focus in the font box of the Font group), **Open List**, then **Move Up [*number*]** or **Move Down [*number*]** the list 1–20 until the focus is on the font you want. Say **Press Enter** to select the font item.

Are there other hands-free methods?

Yes. Keypress commands are useful here. Say **Press Ctrl D** to open the Font dialog box and speak the choices you want there. Helpful commands in dialog boxes are **Tab, Open List, Close List, Press Enter**, and arrow commands.

To Change the Font Size Only

To change the font size only, select the text, then say: **Format That Size [*number*]**.

> *For Example*: **Select All, Format That Size 12**
> *For Example*: **Select Paragraph, Format That Size 14**

To Change The Font Size A Little Bit

If you only want to make your current font a little bigger or smaller (to make it more readable, for example), select the text and use these commands to change the size by a point or two:

> *For Example*: **Make That Bigger**
> *For Example*: **Make That Smaller**

To Change the Font Type and Size Together

To change the font type and size, you first select the text, then dictate this specific command: **Format That [*Font Name*] [*number*] Points**.

> *For Example*: **Format That Courier 12 Points**
> *For Example*: **Format That Times 12 Points**

To Change The Font Color

To change the color of text, select the text, say **Make That [*color*]** and say one of the following color options: blue, dark blue, red, dark red, green, dark green, yellow, dark yellow, gray, dark gray, light gray, white, and black.

> *For Example*: **Make That Dark Red**
> *For Example*: **Make That Blue**

Setting The Font and Size Before Dictating

When you want to set up a font for a document before dictating, use these commands, beginning with **Set Font**:

> *For Example*: **Set Font Arial**
> *For Example*: **Set Font Palatino 12 Points**

While the **Format That** command is used more frequently with text already on the screen (whether dictated or typed), the **Set Font** command is often used to set a choice ahead of dictating or typing. However, use the one you prefer.

150

Changing Line Spacing

Sometimes you need single spacing, but other times double is better. (If you need triple spacing or 1.5 spacing you need to use the ribbon.) To change the spacing, select the text, then use these commands:

> *For Example*: **Double Space That**
> *For Example*: **Single Space That**

About Exercise 4.6: Fonts, Sizes and Spacing

In this exercise, practice the font commands to create a flyer for a yard sale. Use the **Insert [ ] blank lines** command to move the cursor down the page before dictating text.

Exercise 4.6: Fonts, Sizes and Spacing

DIRECTIONS: follow the steps to create the yard sale flyer pictured on the next page.

1. Get a new Microsoft Word document. Say **Insert 9 Blank Lines** to move the cursor down the page. Dictate the flyer text, saying **New Line** and **New Paragraph** where needed.

[Start Dictating]

> Community Yard Sale!
> Saturday June 12th
> 9 AM to 6 PM
> 352 Brook Way
>
> Books, toys, clothes, household items, and much more!
>
> Proceeds benefit the neighborhood garden

[Stop Dictating]

1. Make any needed corrections to recognition.
2. Select text and say **Cap That** as needed to add capitalization to match the sample text.
3. Say **Save Changes** and save your work as "Exercise 4.6".

Exercise 4.6, Continued

4. Say **Select All, Center That** to center the text.

Format Each Line: Font, Size and More

5. Say **Insert Before** *Community*, **Select Line.**
6. Say **Format That Arial 36 Points**, [pause] **Bold.**
7. Say **Select** *Saturday, June 12*[th]. Say **Format That Arial 24 Points.**
8. Say **Select** *9 AM to 6 PM*. Say **Format That Courier 18 Points, Bold.**
9. Say **Select** *352 Brook Way*. Say **Format That Times 16 Points.**
10. Say **Insert Before** *Books*, **Select Line.** Say **Format That Garamond 16 Points.**
11. Say **Insert Before** *Proceeds*, **Select Line.** Say **Format That Palatino 12 Points.**
12. With the last line of text selected, say **Make That Dark Green.** The text color should change to dark green.
13. Say **Select from** *Community* **through** *Garden*. Say **Line and Paragraph Spacing**, then say **1.5** ("one point five"). Each line should have more spacing.

Review and Save Your Work

14. Look over your document and compare it to the example below. Make any needed changes.
15. Say **Save Changes** to update your saved work.

Review: Did you have any difficulty pairing commands, such as formatting font face, size, and making the line bold? Practicing these helps with fluency.

Exercise 4.6 Sample

Community Yard Sale!

Saturday, June 12th

9 AM to 6 PM

352 Brook Way

Books, toys, clothes, household items, and much more!

Proceeds benefit the neighborhood garden

What if I just need to add some space in my Word document?

Use the **Insert** command, as you did at the beginning of the last exercise. To add spaces, lines or paragraphs in a Word document, just say **Insert** followed by what you want to add.

Examples:	**Insert Paragraph**
	Insert 8 Blank Lines

Creating Bulleted or Numbered Lists

Bullets or numbers are useful for visually displaying itemized lists. When you get to the first item to be bulleted or numbered, speak the text and then say **Bullet That** or **Number That**. Bulleting or numbering will continue until you say **Bullets Off** or **Numbers Off**.

Alternately, you can dictate all the items in a list, then select the text and say **Format That Bullet Style** or **Make That Numbered**. Practice this in Exercise 4.7, after reading about tables below.

List Style	Description	Commands
Bulleted List	Creates a bulleted list	**Format That Bullet Style**
		Bullet That/Unbullet That
Numbered List	Creates a numbered list	**Make That Numbered, Number That, Numbers off, Unnumber That**

Working With Tables

Tables are wonderful for organizing information visually. While tables can be added by voice by first speaking **Click Insert** to open the Insert tab, then the **Table** item, then the item in the list you need (such as **Insert Table**), there is no need to do this.

Dragon NaturallySpeaking has special table commands that make it quick and easy to add tables to your documents. Table commands are executed at the location of the insertion point, **so always check first** to see where the insertion point is before giving a table command.

Table Function	Description	Commands
Insert a Table	Inserts a table at the cursor's location	**Add a Table** (opens dialog box) **Add a 3 by 3 Table** (rows by columns)
Delete a Table	Deletes a table	Move the cursor to the table, then say **Delete This Table**
Add Rows	Adds rows	**Add a Row, Add 5 Rows**
Add Columns	Adds columns	**Add a Column, Add 5 Column**
Delete a row or column	Deletes the row or column which contains the cursor	**Delete This Row, Delete This Column**
Move cursor in a table	Moves the cursor up, down, left or right by cell	**Tab, Press Shift Tab,** **Press Up (or Down) Arrow** **Press Left (or Right) Arrow**
	Move up, down, left or right a number of rows or columns	**Move Left (or Right) 3 Rows** **Move Up (or Down) 1 Row (or Columns)**

For Example: You say, **Add a 3 by 2 Table**. You should see this appear:

For Example: You say, **Add 2 Rows**. It would now look like this:

For Example: You say, **Delete a Row**. It would now look like this:

What if I want a different table style?

When a table is active (the insertion point is inside of it) say **Design** (or **Click Design**), and the **Design Tab** opens. Say **Table Styles**, (or **Click Table Styles**) and the Table Styles group opens. In the Table Styles group, use commands like **Move Down 4** and **Move Right 2** to choose a table style. Say **Press Enter**, and that style is selected. Your table will now have the new table style. (The style below is called "Light Grid".) Note: You may have noticed many different table styles in this book. Tables can be varied in nearly endless ways!

Add A Table command: Opens the Insert Table dialog box

Another way to make a table is to say **Add A Table**, and the Insert Table dialog box opens. Notice that the "Number of columns item" is selected in the example below; this means that if you say a number, using the **Numeral** command (for example, **Numeral 5**), it goes in this field automatically.

To move to the "number of rows" item, say **Number of rows**, and the field becomes selected. Say the number that you want using the **Numeral** command. If you want AutoFit behavior, speak the name text next to the round radio button you wish to select.

When you have made all the choices you wish in this window, say **OK** and the table appears in your document where the insertion point is located.

You are now ready to dictate into the cells, make corrections, and format text using the commands you have learned so far. To move between cells, say **Press Tab Key** or dictate an arrow movement, as in **Press Right Arrow, Press Down Arrow, Press Left Arrow, Press Up Arrow**. Try this in Exercise 4.7.

Exercise 4.7 Lists and Tables

DIRECTIONS: Get a new Microsoft Word document and follow the steps below. Read this entire exercise before beginning so you will know how your finished work should look and what to expect.

1. Dictate the text and commands below and make any needed corrections.

[Start Dictating]

Travel to South America! **Cap That, New Paragraph**
There are many countries in South America that can make for a unique vacation. Tours are offered to: **New Line**
- Bolivia *[pause]* **Bullet That,** *[pause]* **New Line**
- Argentina **New Line**
- Peru **New Line**
- Brazil **New Line**
- Ecuador **New Line**
Unbullet That, New Line

Here are some exciting places you can visit: **New Paragraph**

[Stop Dictating]

2. Say, **Add a 3 by 4 Table** (table appears). Dictate the text and commands below, saying **Tab Key** between each cell (the first three are marked for you):

[Start Dictating]

Country **Tab Key**	Largest City **Tab Key**	Official Language **Tab Key**
Argentina	Buenos Aires	Spanish
Peru	Lima	Spanish
Brazil	São Paulo	Portuguese **Move Down 1 Line** [exits table], **New Line**

We look forward to serving you! **Go to Sleep**

[Stop Dictating]

Exercise 4.7, Continued

3. Correct misrecognitions. Select text and capitalize as needed.
4. Save your work as "Exercise 4.7". Make the changes in steps 5-12.
5. Say **Insert Before** *Travel*, **Select Line, Format That Courier 18 Points, Center That.**
6. Say **Insert Before** *There*, **Select Next 7 Lines, Format That Times 14 Points.**
7. Say **Insert Before** *Here*, **Select Line, Format That Times 12 Points, Italicize That.**
8. Say **Bold** *Country*, **Bold** *Largest City*, **Bold** *Official Language*. (Or say, **Insert before** *Country*, **Select Row, Bold That.**)
9. Say **Select Table** (all table text is selected), **Format That Arial 12 Points.**
10. Say **Insert Before** *We*, **Select Line, Format That Times 12 Points.**
11. Say **Go To Bottom**. Say **Save Changes** to update your exercise. Close Word.

Review: How did it go? This exercise is fairly complex--If it was challenging, practice your skills further in the remaining exercises in this chapter. By the end of this chapter, you should begin to feel comfortable dictating into Word.

Exercise 4.7 Example

```
       Travel   to   South   America!
```

There are many countries in South America that can make for a unique vacation. Tours are offered to:

- Bolivia
- Argentina
- Peru
- Brazil
- Ecuador

Here are some exciting places you can visit:

Country	Largest City	Official Language
Argentina	Buenos Aires	Spanish
Peru	Lima	Spanish
Brazil	São Paulo	Portuguese

We look forward to serving you!

Help! Mine didn't look quite like that! What's up?

Your settings in Microsoft Word may be different. For example, there are many bullet styles: circles, squares, check marks, and so on. Don't worry, as long as you have the bulleted list, the table, and most of the formatting—these are what matters.

Spelling and Grammar Check

When you use Dragon to dictate, you **don't have spelling errors.** However, if you use the combination voice/keyboard method, or if your Dragon has run amok, you may have some incorrect words or phrases. The spelling and grammar checker can proofread your document to catch these errors, allowing you to make changes. **Always save your work before a spelling and grammar check,** and **always begin with the cursor at the top of the document.**

To run the spelling and grammar check, say **Go to Top,** then **Check Spelling.** To work in the Spelling and Grammar dialog box, speak the name of items in the box. For example: **Suggestions, Ignore Once, Undo, Edit, Change.** To move around in the suggestions list, use **Move Up [number]** or **Move Down [number]** commands.

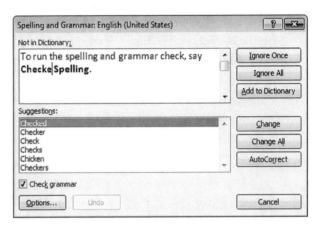

For Example:

1. Say **Go to Top** to move the insertion point to the top of the page.
2. Say **Check Spelling.**
3. Make necessary changes to your document from the Suggestions list. To move to the Suggestions list, say Suggestions.
4. To move down the Suggestions list, say **Move Down [number].**
5. When the focus is on the correct word, say **Change.**
6. If problems occur, say **Cancel,** then re-open the Spelling window again.

If you like, try this now with one of your exercises. (If you don't have any spelling errors in the document, you should create one by hand—so that you have something to fix!)

What about printing a document?

There are many commands for printing a Word document and you will need to experiment to see how they work with your computer and printer setup, as results do vary!

- ✓ **Click Print** is a control command that "clicks" a Print icon, if one is visible.
- ✓ **Print That** send a "print" command to the software, this command was introduced on page 80. (If you want to print a selection of text, select the text you want printed first, and say **Print That** or **Print Selection**.)
- ✓ **Press Ctrl P** usually opens the Print dialog box in any Windows program.
- ✓ **Print the Document** is a Natural Language version of the "print" command.

Help! I Just Want It All To Go Away!

What if you want to delete all of the text in a document? This might happen, for example, if you decide you want to start over completely. To delete the entire document, dictate this command: **Delete The Entire Document**. However, don't say this unless you really mean it!

Create Custom Commands

The MyCommands Editor allow you to create custom commands. Some examples of useful custom commands are:

- a signature line
- an address command that types your entire address with formatting
- a phone number command
- a password command where you say "type my password" and it types a password, thus avoiding the possibility of anyone overhearing you dictate your actual password

Note: The MyCommands Editor does not create macros. If you need macros (little scripts that simplify or automate certain tasks), you need to use Dragon NaturallySpeaking Professional.

To Create A Custom Command

Say **Add New Command,** or in the **Tools** menu of the Dragon Bar, choose **Add New Command**. This opens up the MyCommands Editor window. Follow the steps on the next page to create a new command for your work (or other) address.

Exercise 4.8: MyCommands Editor

DIRECTIONS: Follow the steps to create a custom command. See the example pictured below. (If you don't have, or don't want to use, a work address, feel free to use another address or make one up.)

1. From the desktop, say **Add A Command**.
2. In the "MyCommand Name" text field, say (or type) **Type my work address**.
3. In the "Description" box, say (or type) **types my work address with formatting**. (Note: Write this command down somewhere so you don't forget the exact wording. Try putting it on page 170 with the other chapter commands.)
4. Under "Availability", check that "Global" is selected. This makes the command available in the maximum number of locations.
5. In the "Content" box, dictate or type your work address (or use a home address, if you prefer).

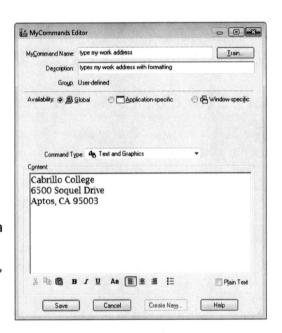

Plain Text, or Formatted?

6. In the example to the right, the "Plain Text" box was not checked. Checking this box will make the text match the font and size that are in the document you paste the command into.
7. If you want your content to have a specific font and size, select the text, then click on the font button, represented by the "Aa" symbol. Set options in the font window that opens.

Train and Save Your Command

8. Say **Train** to click the **Train** button in the upper right-hand corner of the window. Train the command name at least three times. Say **Done** to click the Done button. The window will close.
9. Say **Save** to choose the Save button in the MyCommands Editor window. The command will be saved, and the My Commands Editor window closes.
10. Custom commands can work best after you save your speech profile, so say **Save User Profile** before continuing.

Exercise 4.8, Continued

Test Your Command

1. Open a new document in either DragonPad or Microsoft Word.
2. When you have a new document open, dictate your command. Wait at least 10 seconds for it to work before you dictate the command a second time. If it doesn't work, say **Switch to Command Mode** to turn on command mode and dictate the command again.

Trouble?

The most common reason dictating the command doesn't work is that it was dictated incorrectly (even one word different will keep it from working, unlike many other Dragon commands). Be sure to write down custom commands somewhere that you will think of to refer to them again, such as the Commands Review at the end of this chapter. Another cause of problems is not opening a document window to try the new command in—it only works when there is a document ready to accept the dictation.

About Exercise 4.9

Use the commands from the last exercise, such as **Add A Command**, to create two more custom commands. This exercise does not give step-by-step command guidance—now is your chance to see what you have learned, and practice anything you may have forgotten! (Of course, you can always refer to the last few pages if needed.)

Exercise 4.9: Create Phone Number and E-mail Commands

DIRECTIONS: Read the entire exercise before beginning. Follow the steps below to create phone number and e-mail commands.

1. Say **Add A Command**. Fill in the fields to create a custom command for your phone number. Refer to the steps in the previous exercise as needed.
2. Name the command **Type My Phone Number**.
3. Make the font of your phone number Times New Roman, size 16.
4. Train and save your new command. Save your user profile.
5. Test the command in a document window.

Exercise 4.9, Continued

6. Now, make a custom command for your e-mail address.
7. Name the command **Type My E-mail Address**.
8. Make the size 12, and the font any font except Arial or Times New Roman.
9. Open a new Dragon Pad or Word document and dictate your three new commands (address, phone number, and e-mail address). The font and size changes should be noticeable.
10. Dictate a sentence or two describing how the process worked for you. Start a new paragraph, then dictate the date and Exercise 4.9.

Review: Save your work as "Exercise 4.9" and print if needed.

 ## QUESTION TIME!

Why name custom commands "Type My [something]"?

It is a good idea to name your custom commands **Type My [*something*]** because, first, if you say, for example, **My Phone Number** (with no command phrase in front of it), there is a good chance that this will be typed into your document as **my phone number**. Second, if you want to edit the command, it helps to be consistent and start them with the same word, so that they will all be grouped together. Finally, if you start with the same phrase for every custom command you make, such as **Type My,** it will be easier to remember their structure later when you need them.

What if I want to go back in and edit the command I made?

This is possible, but not especially easy. If you want to change a command you made (for example, you have a new phone number) the easiest way is to create a new command, with a new name (such as **"type my home number"** or **"type my cell"**).

However, you can view your custom commands in the Command Browser, and delete any that aren't useful for you. Then you are free to create a new command with the same name. For more information on commands, see the Dragon Help file.

Can you use this command to insert a graphic?

Actually, you can also create a custom command to insert a small bitmap image (a picture). This is often used for signatures. If you have a graphic you would like to incorporate into a command, follow the process above, but instead of typing text in the Content area, paste in the image you wish to use.

162

Exercise 4.10: Create a Contact List

DIRECTIONS: Open a new Word document. Follow the steps to create the contact list shown. **Note:** This exercise can be difficult because it does not give every commands to use! If you have difficulty remembering the commands you need, look back over the chapter. (Hint: capitalization commands are very helpful here.)

1. Dictate the first three lines in this document without formatting.
2. Say **Add a 4 by 8 Table.** Dictate the table text as shown.
3. Make corrections and save as "Exercise 4.10".
4. Return to your document and make the formatting changes shown. The two headings are in Arial, size 16, centered, and the first heading is bold.
5. "We watch and protect" is Arial, size 10, italics. To add quotes around the phrase, try this neat trick: Say **Select Line**, then **Quote That.**
6. Bold the table's header row text. All of the text in the table is Arial, size 12.

[Start Dictating]

Valley Birdwatchers
Member Contact List
"We watch and protect"

Name	Street Address	City	Phone Number
Emily Larson	7580 Everett Dr.	Scotts Valley	438-1756
Georgia Tyler	88 Maple Ln., Apt. 4	Riverside	728-5259
Alice Lee	23 Acacia Ave.	Scotts Valley	325-1590
Mark Andrews	2360 Orchard St.	Sun Valley	522- 8890
Nena Van Adam	56 Redwood Rd.	Mountain View	216-4825
Luis Hernandez	112 Freedom Blvd.	Riverside	728-0358
Karen Parker	17 Oceanview Lane	Mountain View	219-3771

[Stop Dictating]

Review: How did it go? Did you say *apartment numeral 4* to get "Apt. 4"? Are you making fewer corrections than you did when working in earlier chapters? If so, great! If not, use tools in Chapter 5 to improve your recognition. Save changes before closing the document.

What about other word processing programs, like OpenOffice Writer?

 OpenOffice Writer, by Sun Microsystems, is a free word processor which is part of the OpenOffice suite. OpenOffice Writer is designed like Microsoft Word 2003, using menus and toolbars instead of the Ribbon interface.

Benefits

OpenOffice Writer is supported by Dragon beginning with version 11. OpenOffice Writer works with nearly all of the word processing commands you have used so far. OpenOffice Writer is a full-featured word processor, with features such as spell-checking and advanced page layout options. Dictating into it works well, and the menus can be commanded by voice. Then there is the real selling point: it is a free download from openoffice.org.

Drawbacks

Some advanced features available in Microsoft Word aren't available, or aren't supported, in OpenOffice Writer. Dictating into tables and forms are two such features. Also, if you need to create a mail merge, or work with layout in a complex way, Microsoft Word is still the better choice. For more information about support for specific versions of OpenOffice Writer, see the Dragon Help files.

How about Google Docs? Or Other Word Processors?

 Google Docs accepts dictation quite well, and some of the commands work as well. However, Google revises Google Docs frequently, and the situation may be different as you read this. The best advice? Give it a try and see how it goes!

Any other tips?

If you are using a word processor, and you aren't sure what commands will work, dictate keypress commands for the greatest likelihood of success (say **Ctrl S** instead of **Save That**, for example) and use the Dictation Box, presented in Chapter 5, at the first sign of trouble.

Can I speak the accessibility features in Word?

For more accessibility in Microsoft Word, use the **Alt** command. Say **Press Alt**, and the tabs will be lettered (for example, the File tab is lettered "F"). Say **Press F**, and the File tab opens. Say **Press Alt** again, and each icon is given a one or two letter combination to speak (for example, **Press N** will open a new document). While most items can be spoken, some might not work for you, or you might not know the command. This provides an alternative.

Dictating Your Own Writing

After learning how to dictate printed text, the next step is to learn to dictate your own compositions. Whether you're writing an instant message, e-mail, a report, or a novel, the technique is the same. **A lot of people find that at first this is more difficult** than they expect. There are several good reasons for this.

First, most of us are **not used to composing out loud**, and it feels a bit strange to hear our voices speak in the way that we write (which is very different than the casual style of conversational speech). Second, we've become accustomed to composing our writing at the decreased speed with which we can type or handwrite; that is, it takes time to become accustomed to the faster rate with which we can write using speech recognition software.

Finally, dictating our thoughts and then seeing them appear on paper can be distracting—**especially when there are misrecognitions**. Seeing misrecognitions in the middle of a paragraph leads some writers to lose focus on what they were saying, as their attention shifts to the misrecognitions and away from the composition.

You may have all of these problems at first, or none of them. All of these issues resolve with practice, and the process goes most smoothly if you follow the recommendations below.

Recommendations for Dictating Original Work

1. Begin by reading aloud something you have written, preferably something which is grammatically correct and representative of your writing style or what you frequently need to write. For example, if you are a poet, go ahead and read in your poetry, as it represents your writing style, but also read some memos, reports, or even e-mail that you have written, to build your skill in dictating the types of writing you do.

2. Remember to make corrections, and don't take it personally. If you have a lot of "um" and "uh" to correct, train yourself to avoid these filler words.

3. Begin by composing short, easy writing without a lot of formatting. For example, a good place to begin would be a paragraph about your favorite

weekend activities, or a reflection on the best day of summer (or winter, spring or fall) you have ever had.

4. Use the Accuracy Center tools to adapt to your writing style. For more information, see page 195.

5. Remember the best practices: dictate text first, then make corrections. If you find misrecognitions distracting, don't look at the screen while dictating. **Switch to dictation mode if you are dictating without looking**—it keeps most commands from activating.

6. **Longer documents can pose special problems**. When dictating into a 20–50 page document, recognition may slow down a bit. If that document grows to over 100 pages, recognition may take several more seconds, and there may be more errors. The solution is to try to keep documents below the number of pages where slowdowns occur (how many pages cause slowdowns varies by computer and individual documents). Making each section or chapter a new document and combining them before printing or publishing works well.

7. Finally, **be patient with yourself**. Dictating original work takes time, and sometimes something that seems like it should be easy just doesn't work at first. Because your voice quality varies more when dictating your own compositions, your recognition may not be as good at first. It really will improve.

Exercise 4.11: Your Writing Style

DIRECTIONS: Complete the short writing exercises below, dictating the text given and filling in the blanks with your own composition. After you have dictated the three practice pieces, make corrections to recognition and save your work as "Exercise 4.12".

[Start Dictating]

1. About My Week

Today is (day of week). Tomorrow will be (day of week). Here are three things that I did last weekend: first, I _____. Second, I _____. Finally, I _____. **New Paragraph**

2. About Traveling

Some people like to travel, and I (am/am not) one of them. There are several reasons that I (like/dislike) traveling. (Write two or three sentences here explaining your preference for or against traveling.) **New Paragraph**

3. Sample E-mail

Dear (friend, relative, or colleague's name),

(Dictate a practice e-mail message to a friend or relative. Dictate at least four sentences.)

From,

(Your Name)

[Stop Dictating]

Review: How did it go dictating your own words? Did you have more recognition errors than usual, or about the same? Learn more about how to dictate e-mail messages in Chapter 5.

More Word Commands In the Command Browser

The command browser, discussed on page 203, shows many variations of commands that can be used with Microsoft Word. A few examples to pique your curiosity are **Create Index, Insert Page Numbers** and **Add A Special Character.** Your custom commands are listed here as well.

True Stories

From the author: I was asked to demonstrate to a community group how Dragon works. Just for fun, I trained a new user profile, and then made several Custom Commands ahead of time. When it was time for the presentation, I said, "Hi computer, how are you today?" and the DragonPad document typed, "I'm working well, how are you?" I had a faux "conversation" with the computer in this way. The crowd was awed. I didn't tell them that I created a command called **Hi computer how are you today** and put the answer in the Content box!

Now, imagine what you could do with this feature....

You Are a Dictator! (The best kind, of course!)

The end of Chapter 4 marks a transition in your speech recognition skills. At this point, you can dictate text and commands, make corrections, use menus and speakable items in windows, navigate the desktop by voice, and use the Dragon Help file or this book when you need more ideas about how to complete a task. If you have been successful with Chapter 4 exercises by voice, then you have certainly learned the speech recognition methods and best practices detailed in this book.

The hardest part is over! Whether you ultimately decide to dictate with Dragon NaturallySpeaking, Windows Speech Recognition, another speech recognition program, or a combination of programs, you have all of the basic skills needed to be successful.

You are now ready to learn advanced techniques for improving recognition, formulating commands and setting options; in addition, you are prepared to apply your skills in more challenging applications, such as web browsers and e-mail clients.

Congratulations!

Command Review

New commands in this chapter:

Navigating the Desktop
Press [*item*] (Spacebar, Tab Key, etc.)
Click Start
Start Menu
Start Recycle Bin
Start My Documents
Click Computer
Click All Programs

Working in Program Windows
Press Tab
Press Shift Tab
Press Escape
Open List
Close List
Click Application Tab

Using MouseGrid
MouseGrid
MouseGrid Window

Recognition Modes
Switch to ___ Mode
___ Mode On

Microsoft Word
Click File Tab
Click Office Button
Click [*name of tab*]
Click [*name of item*]
Undo That
Delete the Entire Document

Move Commands
Move This Line Down 2 Paragraphs

Move This Paragraph to the End of
  the Document
Move Up [ ] Lines
Move Down [ ] Lines
Move Up a Paragraph
Move Right a Character
Go to End of Document
Go to Previous Paragraph
Go to Beginning of Line
Insert Paragraph
Insert 8 Blank Lines
Page Up
Page Down

Save Commands
Click Save
Save That
Press Ctrl S
Save Changes

Print Commands
Click Print
Print That
Press Ctrl P
Print the Document

Spelling
Check Spelling

Bullet Style and Numbering
Bullet That
Unbullet That
Format That Bullet Style
Make That Numbered

Number That
Numbers Off
Unnumber That

Line Spacing
Double Space That
Single Space That

Font Name, Size and Style
Make This Paragraph Bold
Open a Document
Format That [*font name*]
Make That [*font name*]
Press Ctrl Shift F
Format That Size [*number*]
Format That Arial 12 Points
Make That Bigger
Make That Smaller
Set Font Arial 12 Points
Make That Blue

Switch To Commands
Switch to [*Program or Item name*]
Switch to Next Window
Switch to Previous Window

Table Commands
Add a Table
Add a 3 by 4 Table
Add a Row
Add 5 Rows
Add a Column
Add 2 Columns
Delete This Row
Delete This Column
Delete This Table

Custom Commands (MyCommands Editor)
Add New Command
Train

Write your custom commands here:

_____
_____
_____
_____
_____
_____

5 CHAPTER 5
Internet Skills and Improving Recognition

Many of us spend significant amounts of time working in web browsers, e-mail programs, and other Internet applications. From social networking sites to online banking, the Internet is central to our computer experience. Navigate web pages, perform searches, and use your favorite web pages—faster and by voice. First, two useful tools for working with the Internet: the screen shot and the Dictation box. Then, learn to use the Internet by voice. Finally, leverage the power of the Accuracy Center and the Command Browser to improve your recognition and help you work more efficiently.

In This Chapter

- ✓ Warm-Up Exercise
- ✓ Screen Shot
- ✓ Dictation Box
- ✓ Navigate Web Browsers
- ✓ Search the Web
- ✓ E-mail Commands
- ✓ The Vocabulary Editor
- ✓ The Accuracy Center
- ✓ The Command Browser
- ✓ 14 Exercises
- ✓ Frequently Asked Questions
- ✓ Command Review

Exercise 5.1: Warm-Up Exercise

DIRECTIONS: Dictate the following into DragonPad or Microsoft Word to check your recognition. Say **New Line** and **New Paragraph** as needed. Items in brackets [ ] give instructions, while items in parentheses ( ) are for you to customize:

[Start Dictating]

> Hello computer, are you ready to work today?
> I am using speech recognition software.
> Dictating is much faster than typing.
> (Dictate your favorite quote here.)
> (Your First Name) (Your Last Name)

[Stop Dictating]

Review: Make any needed corrections and save your document as "Exercise 5.1". Close the word processing program you used (DragonPad or Word).

Next, learn two important skills: how to capture a picture of the screen with a screen shot and how to dictate to non-standard windows with the Dictation Box.

Take a Picture of the Screen: Screen Shot

Have you ever wished you could take a picture of what was on your screen and save it? Maybe you'd like to save a web page as it appeared on a certain day, or capture an error message so that you can ask someone for help, or you need to document your work. Well, you can! It's called a **screen shot** (or screen capture).

The **Print Screen button** (located in the upper right-hand corner of the keyboard next to the Scroll Lock and Pause/Break keys) takes a picture of the viewable area of the screen. It's as if you were standing in front of the screen with a camera: it captures everything. This Windows feature has been around for a long time, but many people don't know how to use it. For one thing, the name "Print Screen" is a bit misleading because it doesn't print the screen. What actually happens is that a picture of the screen is sent to the clipboard—and you don't see that it worked until it is pasted somewhere.

About Exercise 5.2

In the next exercise, use the keypress command **Press Print Screen** to take a picture of the whole screen. Then, open Microsoft Word and use the **Paste That** command to paste the screen shot into a document. Finally, add some text to the Word document below the screen shot, and save it as "Exercise 5.2".

Exercise 5.2: Screen Shot

DIRECTIONS: Follow the steps below to take a picture of the desktop and paste it into Microsoft Word. It is helpful to read this exercise before doing it.

1. Begin at the desktop. Turn on your microphone.
2. Say **Press Print Screen** and watch for the Results box. If you see the command appear (even briefly) in the Results box, you can be reasonably confident that a picture of your desktop has been placed on the clipboard. (If you don't see it, try the next step to see if it worked anyway.)
3. Say **Start Microsoft Word,** and wait 10 seconds for Word to open. If it does not open, open it from the Start menu. (If you don't have Microsoft Word, you can use DragonPad, but the image quality will be less than ideal.)
4. Say **Paste That**. The picture of the desktop should appear in the document.

Exercise 5.2, Continued

5. If the image seems too big, and you are able, resize it manually.

6. Say **New Paragraph** and the cursor moves below the picture, giving you room to dictate text.

7. Dictate your name and "Exercise 5.2" on the page. Save as "Exercise 5.2" using a command like **Save That** (or **Save Changes**).

8. Close Microsoft Word (or DragonPad) with commands like **Press Alt F4** or **File Tab, Exit** or **Close Window**).

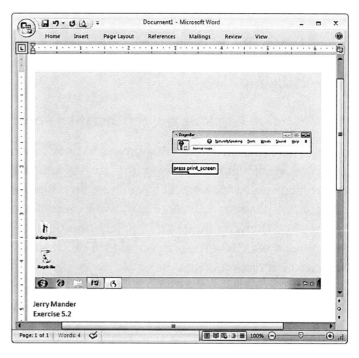

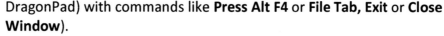

Review: If you don't see the Results box, then you just have to hope that the screen shot worked without visual confirmation. It usually does work. Screen shots are very handy; you may be able to imagine many uses for them. (If needed, you can also manually press the Print Screen key on the keyboard to take a screen shot.)

Do I have to paste into Microsoft Word?

No, you can paste into DragonPad, WordPad, Paint, or any other program installed on your computer that can handle images and text (not Notepad). It is certainly preferable that you choose a program with which you are familiar, and which is compatible with Dragon NaturallySpeaking.

What if I don't want a picture of the whole screen—just a single window?

To take a screen shot of the **active window**, say **Press Alt Print Screen** or, manually, press the **Alt** key on the keyboard and the **Print Screen** key at the same time. Unfortunately, the **Press Alt Print Screen** command can be tricky to get to work by voice, but it is worth a try.

The Dictation Box

The Dictation Box is a text window, optimized to work with Dragon NaturallySpeaking, which facilitates dictation, correction, and formatting of text in "non-standard windows".

Non-Standard Windows and the Dictation Box

There are many word processing programs, web browsers (programs for using the Internet), e-mail programs, instant messaging programs, and so on, that don't accept dictation as well as one would like. These are called "non-standard windows" by Dragon. In the past, the way to work with these difficulties was to dictate into DragonPad then copy and paste the text into the non-standard window. This can be laborious, however, and a Dragon feature called the **Dictation Box** makes it easy to work around this problem.

Using the Dictation Box to Edit Text

The Dictation Box is opened by saying **Show Dictation Box** or by clicking the "Dictation Box" item in the DragonBar's Tools menu. Text is dictated into the window. Make any needed corrections, then format the text as needed. To paste it, say **Transfer** to move it into the non-standard window at the location of the

insertion point. Also, if you dictate into a non-standard window and then discover that you need to make some changes, you can paste the text into the Dictation Box to fix it by voice there.

Changing Settings for the Dictation Box

The Dictation Box has settings that can be changed. You can view all of the settings in the Settings area of the Dictation Box and learn about the more esoteric ones in the Dragon Help file. The most frequently requested item is a larger font size, as the default in the Dictation Box is on the smaller side—10 point Arial. Practice changing Dictation Box settings in the next exercise.

Important: If you **don't have a program open** where the Dictation Box could work, the *Dictation Box won't open*. For example, if the focus is on the desktop, and you say **Dictation Box,** nothing will happen.

Exercise 5.3 uses the Notepad program as the word processor for practicing the Dictation Box. As you do this, imagine using it in a form field on a webpage.

Exercise 5.3 Dictation Box

DIRECTIONS: Use Notepad to practice dictating, transferring and editing text, as well as to change settings in the Dictation Box.

1. From the desktop, say **Start Notepad**, a basic word processor available in all Windows versions. (Or, go to the Start menu, say **Notepad** in the search box and say **Press Enter**.)

2. Check to see that there is a blinking insertion point in the Notepad window. This is where your text will be pasted.

3. Say **Show Dictation Box**. The Dictation box opens.

4. Dictate two simple sentences (see example). Make any needed corrections using corrections command like **Correct [*word*]**. When the text is correct, go to the next step.

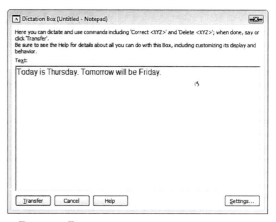

Dictation Box

5. Say **Transfer**.

6. The text will be pasted into the Notepad window and the Dictation Box will close.

7. Notepad remains open, with your sentences visible. Now select the sentences and transfer to the Dictation Box.

8. Say **Select All** to select your sentences in Notepad.

9. Say **Show Dictation Box**.

10. The Dictation Box appears and your text is automatically copied into it.

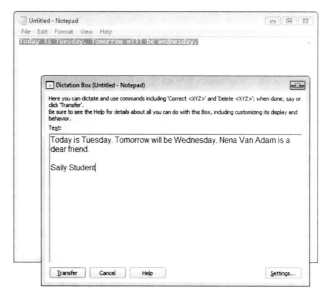

Notepad and Dictation Box, Step 12

Exercise 5.3, Continued

11. Say **Go To Bottom** to move the insertion point. Add a sentence to your text in the Dictation Box. Make the sentences have at least one name that will be new to your Dragon vocabulary: for example, "My aunt is Esmeralda Frankel" or "My speech recognition book was written by Calais Ingel." (**Why?** You will use this exercise again in Exercise 5.13 when you add new vocabulary to your user profile.)

12. Say **New Paragraph**, then dictate your name. Make corrections as needed.

13. Say **Transfer** to move the edited text back into Notepad. The Dictation Box will close.

14. Dictate a short reflection (1-3 sentences) into your Notepad document about how this process worked for you—was anything confusing, or did it go pretty smoothly?

15. Say **Click File, Save** (or **Press Control S**), and save your work as "Exercise 5.3". Leave Notepad open.

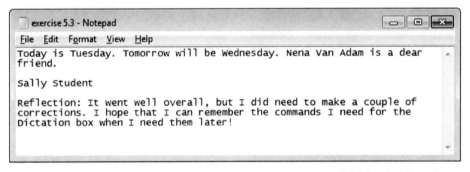

16. Next, change the Dictation Box's font settings. Say **Show Dictation Box**.

17. Say **Settings** to open the Settings area.

18. Say **Change Font** to open the Font dialog box (pictured at right).

19. Speak or click on the font style and size you prefer. (For example, to change the font size, say **Size**, then say **12**.) Check that the change has occurred, then say or click "OK".

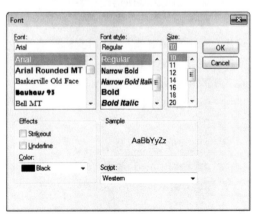

20. The Font box closes.

21. The Dictation Box should now show text in your preferred font style and size.

Exercise 5.3, Continued

22. Test this by saying a sample sentence, such as **This is a sentence**.
23. Say **Delete That** to remove the test sentence you just dictated. Say **Cancel** to close the Dictation Box without transferring text. The Dictation Box closes.
24. Say **Close Window** to close Notepad. If Notepad asks if you want to save changes, do so.

Review: Note that changing the font size and style of text in the Dictation Box does not affect how it looks after it is pasted into a word processing program or a text field. That is determined by the program you paste the text into.

Does this mean that Notepad is "non-standard"?

Actually, no. Windows word processing programs, such as Notepad, WordPad, Works, and Microsoft Word, all work as standard windows. Exercise 5.3 uses Notepad because everyone with the Windows operating system already has Notepad preinstalled.

Using Dragon with the Internet

Using speech recognition with the Internet can be quick and easy—or it can be difficult and frustrating. How it goes depends upon several factors, including the type and version of web browser used, the type of web page, and if you are using all the speech recognition techniques learned so far.

Many Dragon commands you have already used will work with web pages, especially commands to move the cursor, and the keypress commands. Switching to a different mode, such as Spell Mode, helps with web and e-mail addresses. MouseGrid, from Chapter 4, is helpful for items that are difficult to activate by voice.

About Browsers and Versions: Internet Explorer and Mozilla Firefox

Dragon NaturallySpeaking works best with Internet Explorer (IE) and some versions of Mozilla Firefox. Currently, Dragon has limited functionality with Google Chrome and most other browsers; experiment with your browser of choice to see if the situation has improved. Also, the most recent version of a browser isn't always the one that is most compatible with Dragon NaturallySpeaking. Add-ons can make a difference as well. Check your Dragon Help files for more specific information.

Because it is the most compatible with Dragon NaturallySpeaking, and has the most commands available, Internet Explorer is the browser primarily used in this chapter.

In the next several pages, learn to view pages, scroll, click text and image links, dictate into the Address Bar, use navigation buttons, save a page as a Favorite, use shortcut commands to search for web pages, save and print web pages and more.

Viewing Pages and Scrolling

Most web pages are more than one screen long, and only links which are visible can be spoken. To move up and down through pages, use the following commands:

Move Down the Page	Move Up the Page
Start Scrolling Down	Start Scrolling Up
Speed Up/Slow Down	Speed Up/Slow Down
Stop Scrolling (stops)	Stop Scrolling (stops)
Page Down	Page Up
Move Down [1-20] Lines	Move Up [1-20] Lines
Go to Bottom	Go to Top

About Exercise 5.4: Moving Up and Down Web Pages

In this exercise, you will learn the various ways to move up and down pages. You can only speak a link or image you can **currently see** on the screen, so knowing how to move the pages up and down is essential. **Note:** If your home page doesn't scroll, manually go to one that does, such as the Library of Congress site at loc.gov.

Exercise 5.4: Moving Up and Down Web Pages

DIRECTIONS: Study the commands in the table above, then follow the steps below to move up and down web pages.

1. Say **Start Internet Explorer** from the Desktop to open the program. (Or start it from the Start menu.)
2. Wait while the home page loads. Say **Click Maximize** if page is not full-size.
3. To begin moving down the page, say **Start Scrolling Down**.
4. Say **Stop Scrolling** to stop the scrolling. Say **Start Scrolling Down** again to continue. To see it scroll faster, say **Speed Up**. To slow it, say **Slow Down**.

Exercise 5.4, Continued

5. After the page reaches the bottom, say **Start Scrolling Up** to start moving <u>up</u> the page. **Speed Up** and **Slow Down** also work while scrolling up to increase or decrease scrolling speed.

6. Now move up and down the page using the **Move Down 10 Lines** command until you are at the bottom, and then use the **Move Up 10 Lines** command until you are at the top. (Vary the number of lines [2–20] as desired.)

7. Some pages won't scroll (bad code!) but you can make them move with **Page Up** and **Page Down** commands. Try these commands now, repeating them until you get to the bottom and back up to the top of the web page.

8. A quick way to move to the very top or bottom of a page is with **Go to Top** and **Go to Bottom** commands. Try these commands now. Turn off your mic when finished.

Review: This exercise presents many choices for scrolling up and down pages. Use the commands for moving up and down pages that you prefer. The variety of commands Is given in case you find that your preferred method doesn't work on a particular page. **Page Up** and **Page Down** tend to work on difficult pages, or try the **Move Up/Down [*number*] Lines** command.

Getting Around: Clicking Text and Image Links

Links (also called "hyperlinks") are areas of text or images you can click to go to the web page they are associated with. Speak the words in a text link to select it. A red arrow may appear under a link to indicate that it has been selected. Multiple links or images are numbered with arrows; say the number that corresponds to the link to select it.

Command	Action
Click [*Name of Link*]	Selects the spoken link
Click Link *	Numbers the visible links; say the desired number
Click Image	Numbers the visible images; say desired number
Choose [1]	Chooses a numbered item

An alternate command for **Click Link is **Click Text**.*

Exercise 5.5: Click Links

DIRECTIONS: Follow the steps below to click text and image links.

1. In the webpage you have open, say the name of a link (the text of the link itself). You may see a red arrow before it loads the page (or maybe not). If nothing happens in 5 seconds, try again.

2. On the new page that opens, pause while the page loads, then say **Click Link**. A numbered list of links should appear. If nothing happens in 5 seconds, try again.

3. Choose a link by saying its number, as in **Choose 17**.

4. If your page has images, say **Click Image**. A numbered list of images appears.

5. Choose one by saying its number, as in **Choose 3**. If it doesn't work in 5 seconds, say **OK** to activate the selection.

6. If your page doesn't have images that are links, go to one that does, such as myloc.gov or npr.org.

7. Try this several times until you are familiar with the process.

Review: It is not always necessary to say "Click" when speaking the name of a link. For example, if the link says "About Us", you could say **Click *About Us*** or just ***About Us***. See which one works best for you and use that method. Put your mic to sleep while you read the next section on how to dictate an address into the address bar.

The Address Bar and URLs

Often, you can't click a link to get to a particular website—you have to enter the address into the address bar. (The address bar is where the website address is located. Another term for web address is URL.) Web addresses usually start with "http://www". To dictate this, one says *h t t p colon slash slash w w w dot.* However, most web browsers will add this on for you, so they don't need to be dictated.

Web addresses are easy to dictate when the name is one word, or only letters: for example: **npr.org, irs.gov, amazon.com, google.com, facebook.com** and **soap.com**.

For web addresses which don't dictate well into the address bar, use either of these two methods once the insertion point is in the Address bar: 1) say **Show Dictation Box** and dictate (and if needed, correct) the address there before transferring it into the Address bar; or, 2) say **Switch to Spell Mode**, spell out the address (including punctuation) and then say **Switch to Normal Mode** and say **Go There**.

Dictating into the address bar can be frustrating and tricky; read the commands below, and then try them out with the exercise that follows. You may decide to type into the Address bar, if you are able, as it is quicker for difficult-to-dictate addresses.

Command	Action
Go to Address *or* **Address** *or* **Go to Address Bar**	Selects the URL in the Address bar
Switch to Spell Mode	For spelling out URLs, dictate this command, then spell out the address
Switch to Normal Mode	Returns to Dragon's Normal Dictation Mode
Delete Last Character *or* **Backspace**	In the Address bar, use these commands to delete an unwanted character(s)
Show Dictation Box	Use to show the dictation box to dictate difficult addresses
Go There *or* **Click Go**	Clicks the Go button

Exercise 5.6: Dictate a Web Address

DIRECTIONS: Open Internet Explorer and follow the instructions to enter an address into the address bar.

Spell Out an Address

1. Say **Go to Address** (or alternate command from the list above).
2. The address bar will be selected.
3. Say **Switch to Spell Mode** and then spell out the address for **http://www.bbc.co.uk** (say **Dot** or **Press Period** for the dots).
4. Say **Switch to Normal Mode** when you are done, in order to leave spell mode.
5. Say **Go There** to go to the website address you just entered.

Now, try easier ones!

1. Say **Go to Address**. The address bar will be highlighted.
2. Say **google dot com**. (Note: don't dictate the "http://www".)
3. Say **Go There**. The Google page should load.
4. Say **Go to Address** again. Pause, then say **amazon dot com**, (correct if needed), then say **Go There**.
5. Try one more: say **Go to Address, yahoo.com, Go There**.

Review: If this worked easily for you, great! If not, an alternate command for **Go to Address** is **Press Alt D**, and an alternate command for **Go There** is **Press Enter**.

Trouble? Use the Combination Method
Web and e-mail addresses are one place where you may decide to type manually. Do this by saying **Go to Address.** When the address is highlighted, type in addresses that would otherwise have to be spelled out. (If the address is a word that will be easy to dictate, such as twitter.com, it is faster to dictate it.) When the address is entered, say **Go There** and the page will load.

Basic Navigation

Navigating among pages requires going back to a previous page, going forward a page, going to a new page, refreshing the current page, or going to the home page. Use the following commands:

Command	Sample Icon	Action
Back *or* **Go Back**		Clicks the Back button to go back one page
Forward *or* **Go Forward**		Clicks the Forward button to go forward one page
Go, Click Go *or* **Go There**		Clicks the Go button to load the page
Refresh Page *or* **Press F5**		Clicks the Refresh button to reload the page
Home *or* **Go Home**		Clicks the Home button to load the home page

Exercise 5.7 Speak the Navigation Buttons

DIRECTIONS: Follow the steps below to use the navigation buttons.

1. From the home page, say the name of a link. In a few seconds the new page should load into the browser window. (If not, try another link by speaking its name.)
2. Say **Back** or **Go Back.** You should be returned to the home page.
3. Say **Forward** or **Go Forward.** The second page will reload.

Exercise 5.7, Continued

4. Say **Home** or **Go Home.** The home page will reload.
5. Say **Refresh Page,** which will cause the page to load again.
6. Say **Home** or **Go Home** to return to the home page. Put your microphone to sleep and read the next section before continuing.

Review: Turn off your microphone when you pause while working with the Internet (to read a page, for example). Get into this habit and save yourself the extra effort of undoing mistakes from unintentional dictation (especially if you like to comment aloud when you read an interesting article on a web page!).

Favorites or Bookmarks Menu

The Favorites menu is where you can store a list of web addresses you want to remember—and avoid typing or dictating in the future. Mozilla Firefox calls these Bookmarks. (Make sure the menu bar is displayed in your browser before beginning. If you don't see menus with names such as File, View, Tools, Favorites or Bookmarks (and so on), go to your browser's help to find out how to display them.)

Exercise 5.8 Favorites List

DIRECTIONS: Follow the steps below to add a site to the Favorites list in Internet Explorer.

1. Open Internet Explorer. Make sure you are on a website that is **not** your home page. Say **Click Favorites** to open the menu.
2. Say **Add To Favorites** and a dialog box will open to ask if you want to save the web page as a favorite.
3. Say **Add** to click the button to add to the list of Favorites.
4. Say **Click Favorites**. You will now see the link in the list of Favorites.
5. Say **Go Home**. The home page will load.
6. Say **Click Favorites** and move down by lines (for example, say **Move Down 6 Lines**) until you get to the list item for the site; then say **Press Enter** and the page will load.

Review: Some browsers, such as Internet Explorer 9, let you pin website links to the Start menu (or taskbar). For more information on pinning web sites to the Start menu, and using Dragon with these items, see the Dragon Help files. If you would like to do this exercise with Firefox, use the **Add to Bookmarks** command instead.

Shortcuts for Web Searches: Cool Tricks and Serious Time-Savers!

Searching the web is usually done by going to a search box in a browser window or on a search engine site, such as Google, Bing, or Yahoo, and then entering text and saying **Press Enter**. However, Dragon has helpful shortcuts for some popular types of searches that can save a lot of time. In fact, **you don't even need to have your web browser open**—Dragon will open your default browser and take it from there.

Web Sites to Search by Name

Here is a list web sites that can be used with the command at right:

- About
- AltaVista
- Amazon
- Answers
- AOL
- Ask
- Bing
- Creative Commons
- eBay
- Facebook
- Google
- IRS
- MSN
- MySpace
- Twitter
- Wikipedia
- Yahoo
- YouTube

Search The Web for [*item*]

This command is used to begin a search using your default search engine and your default web browser (default = the one set as primary). This brings up a page of results for you to select from.

For Example:

> **Search the Web for *Movies in Santa Cruz***
> **Search the Web for *Zucchini Recipes***
> **Search the Web for *Antique Rugs***

Search Certain Web Sites by Name

Dragon will recognize certain popular web sites within searches. For example, if you want to know if amazon.com has books on Julia Child, you can say **Search Amazon for *Julia Child***. The web browser will open with the results page of a search of amazon.com for "Julia Child".

For Example:

> **Search Yahoo for *Movies in Boston***
> **Search Wikipedia for *Carrot Cake Recipes***
> **Search YouTube for *Israeli Folk Dances***

See the list at left for web sites to search by name. Dragon adds to this list from time to time—check the Dragon Help file for more information.

Are You Feeling Lucky? Find A Website...

If you want to find a website on a certain topic, but don't want to sift through search results, the **Find A Website** command is for you. It goes to Google, does the search with your search words, and chooses the "I'm Feeling Lucky" button on the Google page.

I'm Feeling Lucky

This has the effect of opening a page that is likely to be about your subject (although maybe not the exact site you wanted).

To try the **Find A Website on [*topic*]** command, use these types of commands:

For Example:

Find a Website on *New Zealand*
Find a Website on *microphone headsets*
Find a Website on *car repair*

Specify Your Media or Category

To find something in a specific media or category, use a specific search. For example, to search only photos for a picture of F.D.R., say **Search Photos for *Franklin Delano Roosevelt*.**

However, if you want to find places with this president's name, say **Search Places for *Franklin Delano Roosevelt*.** The default web browser opens with search results from your default search engine.

For Example:

Search Maps for *Paris*
Search Video for *Penguins*
Search Events for *Ukulele Performances*

See the list above for the categories that can be searched specifically. This can save quite a bit of time!

> **Specify Your Media or Category**
>
> The following categories can be spoken in commands:
>
> - Images
> - Pictures
> - Photos
> - Videos
> - Movies
> - News
> - Events
> - Products
> - Shops
> - Maps
> - Places

185

About Exercise 5.9 Search the Web

Before beginning the next exercise, make sure that your web browser is closed. Dragon needs to be open, and the focus should be on the desktop. (If you are looking at the desktop, you are probably ready to start.)

While this exercise works best with Internet Explorer, Mozilla Firefox will work as well. Google Chrome and other browsers (Safari, Opera, etc.) may not work at all with these commands.

Exercise 5.9: Search The Web

DIRECTIONS: Follow the steps to search the web from your desktop.

Search the Web

1. With your web browser closed, turn on your microphone and say: **Search the Web for *Dragon NaturallySpeaking***.
2. Wait while the browser loads and the search is executed. This may take several seconds or longer. (Be patient.)

Look at Results and Close the Browser

3. Look at the results you get. (Is one of them nuance.com, the company that owns Dragon NaturallySpeaking?)
4. Close the browser with the command **Close Window**. Wait while the browser closes. (Note: some versions of browsers hang at this point. If yours does, then say **Press Alt F4** or close it by hand in the future.)

Search A Specific Website

5. From the desktop, try this command: **Search Amazon for *Dragon NaturallySpeaking***. Notice that the amazon.com site opens and that it shows Dragon results.

Find a Website (Feeling Lucky?)

6. Now try this command: **Find a Website on *Dragon NaturallySpeaking***. This should take you to a page that in some way deals with Dragon.

Search a Specific Category

7. Finally, say **Search Images for *Dragon NaturallySpeaking***. Wait while the search occurs, and look at the images which appear in the results.
8. Close the browser when you are done.

Review: What did you think of searching in this way? This method can be very quick—provided your computer responds promptly. In the next section, learn the nitty-gritty of working by voice in web pages: how to speak buttons, boxes, and fields.

Using Buttons and Boxes

There are many kinds of buttons, boxes, and fields on web pages. **Radio buttons, check boxes, text fields, and search boxes** are the most common. The following is a list of commands to use with these web page elements. After you have read the list, try these commands in Exercise 5.10.

Tip: Try speaking the labels for text fields. For example, if the label next to the text field says "First Name" try saying this and see if the cursor moves into the field associated with this label. If not, use the commands that follow.

Command	Action
Click Text Field *or* **Click Edit Box**	Moves to the first text field on the page and numbers them
Choose [3]	Say desired number of a numbered item to select it
Press Tab Key	Move to the next element on the page, such as a text field
Click Check Box	Numbers the check boxes on a page
Click Radio Button	Numbers the radio buttons on a page
Click List *or* **Click List Box**	Numbers the list boxes on a page
Show Choices *or* **Open List**	Opens up the list in list boxes (To choose an item in a list, say the name of the item. Or, say **Move Down/Up [*number*]** until you get to the item you want; say **Enter** to activate the choice.)
Hide Choices *or* **Close List**	Closes the list in list boxes

About Exercise 5.10

This is an exercise designed to be useful to those who want a hands-free computer experience. If you do use the mouse occasionally (the Combination Method), you might choose to skip this exercise. Then again—why not see how it goes?

Exercise 5.10: Use Buttons, Boxes and Lists

DIRECTIONS: Follow the steps to practice boxes, buttons and lists.

1. Go to a website you visit often. Look for forms and lists. If you don't know a website with a form, try going to **gmail.com** and choose the "Create an account" button. You should see a form with text fields, check boxes and lists. (Don't worry, you don't have to create an account in order to try out these commands—just close the page when you are done.)

2. Say the label of the first text field (for example, *First Name*) or say **Click Text Field.** If the text fields are numbered, say the number of the one you want. Dictate the information that goes in this box. Use correction commands if needed. If you have problems with recognition, use the Dictation Box.

3. Say **Press Tab** to move to the next text field, or say the name of the text field (i.e., *Last Name*). Dictate into this text field.

4. Now look for a checkbox. Say **Click Check Box**. The check boxes should be numbered—say the number next to the one you want and it will be checked, or unchecked (or vice versa). Try this a few times. See example pictured at right.

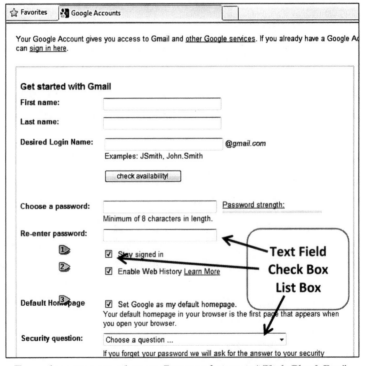

5. Look for a list box. List boxes have lists of choices in them. Say **Show Choices** or **Open List** to open the list box. (The "Security question" list box is pictured above.)

Form elements on a web page: Command given is "Click Check Box"

Exercise 5.10, Continued

6. Show the choices again, and choose one by saying it or using the **Move Up** or **Move Down** commands to get to the item. (For example, **Move Down 6**.)

7. Say **Press Enter** to select the item and close the box. Say **Click Radio Button** if there are radio buttons on your page. Speak the number of the one you want to choose.

8. When you have tried these form elements, close your browser window without saving. A good command for this is **Close Window**.

Review: This exercise can be a bit difficult to carry out, as each web page is a bit different. How did it work for you—did you get one or two elements to work? More than two? When you next encounter a web form, consider trying these commands and see how it works for you!

Will it hurt my speech recognition if I use just some of the web commands, like search, but not use others—and use the mouse or keyboard instead at other times?

No.

Tabs In Internet Explorer and Firefox

Tabs in Internet Explorer

Tabs are a useful way of displaying another browser window within the same web browsing program. It is very quick and convenient to switch between two tabs. Internet Explorer and Mozilla Firefox have different commands for tabs. They are:

To Do This...	In Internet Explorer	In Firefox
Open a new tab	Open New Tab	Add A New Tab
Close a tab	Close Tab	Close Tab
Switch to the next tab	Switch To The Next Tab	Go To The Next Tab
Switch to the previous tab	Switch to the Previous Tab	Go To The Previous Tab
View the 3rd tab	View the 3rd Tab [1–8]	----

Exercise 5.11: Use Tabs

DIRECTIONS: Use the tab commands to open, close and move among tabs.

1. Open either Internet Explorer or Mozilla Firefox. After the home page loads, give the command for a new tab (**Open New Tab** or **Add A New Tab**). A new tab opens.

2. Give the command to open a new tab twice more. You should now have four tabs in total.

3. Cycle between the tabs using the command to switch to the next tab and then to switch to the previous tab (see table above). After you have cycled through all of the tabs at least once, go to the next step.

4. Say **Close Tab** to close the tab you are on. This will close the tab and move the focus onto another tab. Close that one the same way. Continue until only one tab remains.

5. Turn off your microphone and read about printing and saving web pages.

Review: Once you get used to using tabs you may wonder how you ever did without them!

Printing a Web Page

To print a web page, use some of the print commands you are familiar with; say **Click File**, then say **Print** (if the browser has menus displayed), say **Print That** or say **Press Control P**. (The keypress command is the most reliable.)

Watch the page range: don't choose ALL in the print window, or you might print more pages than you think! Instead, specify a number of pages or highlight a selection and print that selection only (see directions below).

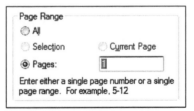

Choose " Pages: 1"for only 1 page

Saving a Web Page

To save a webpage, follow the same techniques as for saving a document: say **Click File, Save As** (if the browser has menus displayed) or say **Press Control S**.

Tips for Web Pages

Don't be shy about switching among modes: for example, **command mode** for most of your browsing; **spell mode** for entering e-mail addresses or web addresses, and

dictation mode for longer text entries. Remember that **MouseGrid** is also handy for clicking on items as needed.

Exercise 5.12 Find and Print a Single Web Page

DIRECTIONS: Read the entire exercise before beginning. You will print a web page as part of this exercise; before beginning ensure that you have a connection to a printer and that the printer is ready.

1. With the browser closed, give a search command based on those in this chapter. Note on some scratch paper what your search command was.
2. Practice the commands and skills you have learned in this chapter by choosing a link to go to, then continue moving through pages until you find something of interest to you (i.e.: a sports team page, a news article, this week's movie listings, a recipe, etc.).
3. Say **Print That, Press Control P,** or **File, Print** and choose just the currently displayed page (look for a radio button in the Print dialog box that says "current page") before you say **OK** and print.
4. Close the web browser after your page prints. Look over your printout.

Document Your Work

Open the word processor of your choice and answer the following questions:
1. Was your search result closely linked to the command you gave in Step 1?
2. Did you print a single page (or a selection)?
3. How did the other web commands work for you (Exercises 5.4-5.11)?
4. Was this easy for you, or did you need to look back through this chapter for commands?
5. Is there anything you would do differently next time?

Review: Save your work as "Exercise 5.12". Print and staple to your web page printout if you are turning in this assignment.

What about other browser features?

Browsers have many other features than the ones listed here. To access these, speak the name of the menu where they exist, and then the feature itself. For example, to delete the browsing history in Internet Explorer, say **Click Tools** to open the Tools menu (if displayed), then say **Delete Browsing History** to open up that item. Speak selections from there.

If the item you want is on a toolbar only (not in a menu), you may need to use MouseGrid to select it by voice. If the feature can be accessed by speaking a keypress command, that is often the fastest choice. (For example, in most web browsers, **Press Control F** will open the Find dialog box, where you can search a web page for a certain word or phrase.)

Desktop E-mail Programs

Several desktop e-mail programs (e.g., Microsoft Outlook, Outlook Express, Mozilla Thunderbird, Windows Mail, Windows Live Mail, Lotus Notes) are supported by Dragon NaturallySpeaking, depending upon the version of the e-mail program and the version of Dragon that you are using. To find out which ones work with your version of Dragon, search Dragon's Help file. In the Help area you can also find out more commands for each e-mail program. Then, test the commands and see what works for you.

E-mail Command	Action
Start Mail	Starts (opens) your default mail program
Check for Mail	Checks for new messages
Open Mail	Opens a selected e-mail message
New Mail *or* **Write Mail** *or* **Write E-mail**	Write an e-mail message
Reply *or* **Reply to Mail**	Replies to the sender of the current message
Reply to All	Replies to the sender and all recipients of the current message
Forward Mail	Forwards the current message
Send Mail *or* **Send E-mail**	Send the current e-mail message
Send an e-mail to *Name*	Open a new e-mail message addressed to someone (from the address book)
Send an e-mail about *subject*	Open a new e-mail message with specific text in the subject line
Delete Mail *or* **Delete E-mail**	Delete a selected e-mail message
Print Mail *or* **Print E-mail**	Print a selected e-mail message
Close Mail	Closes the current e-mail message.
Click [*name of link or button***]**	Activate a link or button by name
Go to [*name of***] Field [***To, CC, BCC, Subject, Body, First, Next, Previous, Last, etc.***]**	Move to a particular field by name

What about Internet-based e-mail?

If you use internet-based e-mail, like Gmail, Hotmail, Windows Live, or Yahoo, you can use the Internet commands in this chapter to get to the e-mail site and navigate around within it. Use word processing and correction commands within the e-mail window. If you have any trouble getting this to work, use the Dictation Box to dictate your e-mail messages, then transfer them into the message window. To click on icons, use MouseGrid.

It is as though you are working with a combination of two different programs—web pages (and their commands) and a word processor (and its commands) within the same window. It can be challenging, but once you have some practice doing it, it's not prohibitively difficult.

Gmail Commands (In Basic HTML View)

If you are using Gmail in Internet Explorer or Firefox, Dragon has some special commands you can use. These work best in Basic HTML view: **Click** *Compose Mail,* **Move to** *Next Field,* **Move to** *Text Field,* **Click** *Send,* **Click** *Reply,* **Click** *Forward,* **Click [***name of***] Folder, Click** *Report Spam,* **Click**  *Archive* and **Click** *Refresh.* With a message selected, you can say: **Click** *Delete,* **Click** *Move To,* **Click** *Labels* and **Click** *More Actions.* Also, the **Click Link** command will number the links in the page, giving you access to many more items than the direct commands given above.

Does speech recognition work on social networking sites, like Facebook or Twitter?

Dragon 11.5 offers new commands for posting to Facebook and Twitter—and the programs do not even need to be open. To post a status update to Facebook, say **Post to Facebook**, and the window pictured at right appears. The first time you do this, a window opens asking you to log on. After you put in your Facebook logon information, another window appears asking for permission for Dragon NaturallySpeaking to have access to some of your Facebook information. Read this page, and if you accept the terms, click **Allow**. (This only works if you already have a Facebook account.) Finally, if you have some text in a word processor that you would like to post, select the text, then say **Post That to Facebook**. The text will be copied in the "Post to Facebook" window for you. Say **OK** to complete the post.

Facebook can also be searched by name when it is closed (for example, **Search Facebook for [*someone or something*]**. Internet commands for scrolling through pages, activating links, and selecting text fields (when you want to comment on someone's post) given in this chapter work on Facebook.

To send a tweet from your Twitter account, say **Post to Twitter,** then dictate the message, or select the desired text and say **Tweet That** (see example at left). You will

need a Twitter account for this to work, and it will need to be set up the first time you post. Only one Twitter account and one Facebook account can be supported by Dragon. Note: voice corrections can be made in the Facebook and Twitter posting windows.

Select text, say Tweet That

Other types of online social networking, such as instant messaging, blogging and chat programs usually work with speech recognition, although not always smoothly. For example, some windows are difficult to navigate by voice, but once the cursor is in the text box, dictation and correction work just fine.

If you are worried about accidentally posting something with recognition errors, use the Dictation Box instead of dictating directly into the text box online. The first time you use a new site with speech recognition, pay attention to what works and doesn't, then try alternate commands or methods until you find the method that works best.

How come some sites work better than others?

Web pages utilize many different kinds of coding (programming) to make them look and act the way that they do. Some of these, like HTML, tend to work pretty well with speech recognition software. Others, designed with programs like Flash, hardly work at all. In general, the more animated and flashy a webpage is, the more likely it is that there will be problems—especially with animated advertising.

While universal design principles and accessibility standards are well developed and are followed by many web designers, just as many others don't follow the standards. Ultimately, you just have to try it and see if it works. Note: If the webpage belongs to the U.S. federal government or any U.S. government-funded entity, then it is required to be accessible under federal law (Section 508 of the Rehabilitation Act). For more information, visit section508.gov. Many other countries have similar regulations. To test a website for accessibility, try a site like wave.webaim.org.

In the rest of this chapter, learn about Dragon tools to help increase your recognition, make your Dragon run better or help you find commands.

The Accuracy Center

The Accuracy Center collects together in one place all of the tools that help you improve accuracy. These tools customize your vocabulary (the set of words Dragon recognizes you saying), adjust the program options, work with the speech recognition and accuracy and acoustics, and help you access and learn commands.

Open the Accuracy Center by selecting the **Improve My Accuracy** option in the **Help** menu in the DragonBar or dictate the command **Start Accuracy Center**. To use the items in the Accuracy Center, speak the name of the item you wish to open.

If you aren't sure which item you need, say the first item with the **Click** command: **Click *Which tool to use first.*** Alternatively, you can say **Click Link**, and the links on the page will be numbered. Say **Choose 1** (or the correct number) for the link you wish to activate.

Note: Click Link works in all Accuracy Center windows, and can be quicker than speaking the long link text.

On the next page begins Exercise 5.13, which is several pages long. This exercise gives a description of each item in the Accuracy Center. The exercise is designed to give a guided tour of the Accuracy Center at the same time.

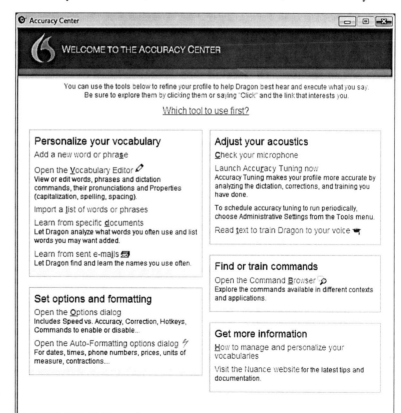

The Accuracy Center

Exercise 5.13

DIRECTIONS: Follow the steps to learn the options in the Accuracy Center. This exercise, which is seven pages long, gives a guided tour of the Accuracy Center, after which you will write a short paragraph reflecting upon the tools you learn about here.

1. Open the Accuracy Center by saying **Start Accuracy Center**.
2. Read over the Accuracy Center window. Each of areas and its links is designed to help increase your accuracy or fix difficulties you may have with recognition in Dragon NaturallySpeaking.

Which Tool To Use First?

Saying **Click *Which Tool to Use First*** opens up a window called the Accuracy Assistant. It describes common recognition problems such as, "When I speak, nothing happens". Identify the difficulty you are having and Dragon will direct you to the tools that can help.

1. **Choose a link** to speak in the Accuracy Assistant window. There are three ways to activate links: 1) Speak its name, 2) say **Click Link** and then **Choose [*correct number*]**, or 3) say **Alt [*underlined letter*]**, where the letter you say is the one underlined in the phrase you are choosing. (For example, in the first phrase, "When I speak, nothing happens" the underlined letter is W, so the command would be **Press Alt W** to activate that link.)

2. Activate the link using one of the three methods above. (When you find a method you prefer, feel free to stick with it!)
3. Notice the suggestions given in the window that opens. After you have read the window, activate the **Go Back** link (with any of the three methods in Step 3) and try another link.

Exercise 5.13, Continued

4. After you have tried at least **two links** in the Accuracy Assistant, you are ready to move on. Make a note of any new or useful information, then say **Click Exit** (or an alternate command) to return to the Accuracy Assistant.

Personalize Your Vocabulary: Add a New Word or Phrase

The first group on the left gives tools to personalize your vocabulary. The first option, **Add a New Word or Phrase**, opens a window where you can enter the new word or phrase and the way it is spoken.

1. Say **Click Add a New Word or Phrase** to open a window like the one at right.

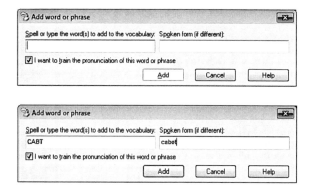

2. Think of a word not in your vocabulary set yet, that might be nice to add. For example, a person's name with an unconventional spelling, or an acronym you use frequently would be good choices. (In the example at right, "CABT" is a department name—it stands for Computer Applications/Business Technology—but it is usually spoken as "cabot".) Enter your text in the two fields, then click **Add**. In the training window, click **Go** to train your voice saying the new vocabulary item. When you are finished, click **Done**. (Notice that this is the Train Words window introduced in Chapter 2 to train a word or command.)

Personalize Your Vocabulary: Open the Vocabulary Editor

1. Say **Open the Vocabulary Editor** to open a window like the one at right.

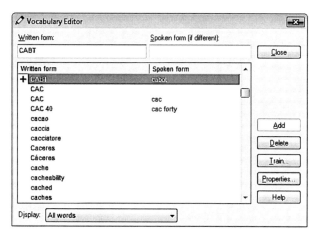

2. In the "Written form" field, type in your custom vocabulary word section above. You should see it appear proceeded by a red plus sign. This window shows the built in vocabulary, with the spoken forms (if different).

Exercise 5.13, Continued

3. Any custom vocabulary you have added will be shown (with the plus sign in front). In this window, you can delete a word from the vocabulary, train a word in the vocabulary, adjust the properties of the word (including the spacing before and after the word) and get help.

Note: the Vocabulary Editor is where you can remove words you do not want recognized, like vulgarities. Or, you can add these words to the Vocabulary if you choose.

4. Click or say **Close** to close the Vocabulary Editor.

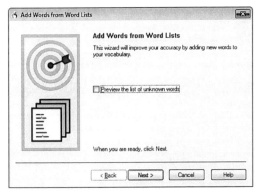

Personalize Your Vocabulary: Import a List of Words or Phrases

1. Say **Import a List of Words or Phrases** to open a window like the one at left.

2. **Click Next**, and a window opens where you can upload files (they must be .txt format!) from which you would like Dragon to learn vocabulary (see image below). The text files can be lists of words, or sentences.

3. As you created at .txt file with Exercise 5.2, click **Add File**. When a window opens for you to browse to your file, locate your Exercise 5.2 and click the **Open** button.

4. When you see your file in the "Add Word Lists" field, click **Next**. Dragon will now upload new vocabulary from the document. (You could return to the Vocabulary Editor and see the proof of this, but for now continue with the exercise.)

5. Dragon will let you know when the process is done and how many new words or phrases were added. Close the window when finished.

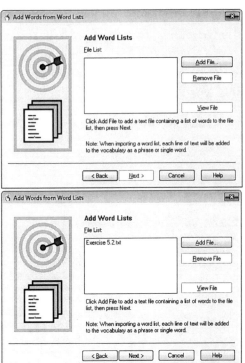

Exercise 5.13, Continued

Personalize Your Vocabulary: Learn From Specific Documents

1. This item works much like the previous item, except that you can use file types beyond .txt, and Dragon will learn more about your personal writing style.

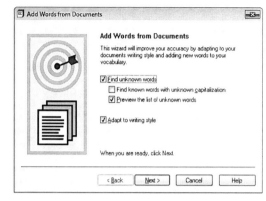

2. At the Accuracy Center window, say **Learn from Specific Documents** to open a window like the one at right.

3. **Click Next**, and a window opens where you can upload document files (or folders of documents) from which you would like Dragon to learn your writing style and vocabulary.

4. Click **Add File**. When a window opens for you to browse to your file, locate an exercise from Chapter 4 (4.5 and 4.12 are especially good choices) and click the **Open** button.

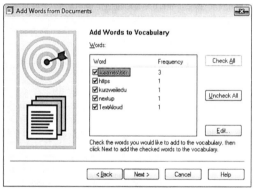

5. When you see your file in the "Add Word Lists" field, click **Next**. Dragon will now upload the vocabulary from the document, and adapt to your writing style.

6. When uploading has completed, a list of new vocabulary words is displayed. Any that you want added to your vocabulary need to have a checkmark in the box next to the word. Click or say **Next**.

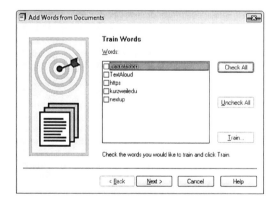

7. The "Train Words" window opens. Check any words you would like to train to your voice. Click or say **Next**.

8. At the word summary window that opens, click or say **Finish** to close.

Exercise 5.13, Continued

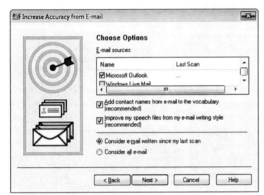

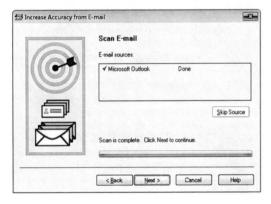

Personalize Your Vocabulary: Learn From Sent E-mails

1. From the Accuracy Center window, say **Learn from Sent E-mails**.

2. The window at left will open. Click or say **Next**.

3. If you use one of the e-mail programs listed (on the computer you are currently using), check the box next to its name and then click or say **Next**.

4. Dragon will scan for your contact names and email writing style to adapt.

5. When the scan is complete, click or say **Next**. (See image below.)

6. Click or say **Finish** to close the window.

Set Options and Formatting: Open the Options Dialog

1. From the Accuracy Center window, say **Open the Options Dialog**.

2. A window with seven tabs opens.

3. The Options dialog box is covered in depth in Chapter 8, so close this window by saying **Click Cancel**.

Set Options and Formatting: Open the Auto-Formatting Options Dialog

1. From the Accuracy Center window, say **Open the Auto-Formatting Options Dialog**.

2. This window is discussed on page 128. Say **Click Close** to close the window.

Adjust Your Acoustics: Check Your Microphone

1. From the Accuracy Center window, say **Check Your Microphone.**

2. This link opens up the audio check you completed when you first trained Dragon. It checks the audio level and the sound system.

Exercise 5.13, Continued

3. The microphone and audio checks are discussed on page 12 through page 14. Say **Click Close** to close the window.

Adjust Your Acoustics: Launch Accuracy Tuning Now

Note: The Acoustic Optimizer should be run every so often, as it "optimizes" (improves) your user profile. However, it takes quite a while to complete and you shouldn't do much else with the computer while you are running the Optimizer, so plan to do this at a time when you don't need to use your computer for any resource-intensive tasks.

1. From the Accuracy Center window, say **Launch Accuracy Tuning Now.**

2. A window will open like the one pictured. Running accuracy tuning now is inconvenient (unless you want to wait 10-40 minutes to move to the next section) so close the window now by saying **Close Window**.

3. When you ARE ready to run accuracy tuning, come back to this area and say **Go**. Accuracy tuning is good to run after you have given the computer several hours of input, in order to improve your user profile.

Adjust Your Acoustics: Read Text to Train Dragon to Your Voice

1. From the Accuracy Center window, say **Read Text to Train Dragon to Your Voice.**

2. A window will open with the phrase "Welcome to General Training" ready for you to train.

3. This area is covered on page 16. Close the window by saying **Click Cancel**. If a window appears asking if you want to quit without saving changes, say **Yes**.

Note: Use this link when you need to tune up your recognition. Some experts recommend doing this every week or two to keep your recognition at its best, but most users just do it when their recognition isn't as good as it should be. This link opens up the training readings, like the one you did when you first created your user profile. Note: You don't need to complete a whole training to see the benefit. Even 5 or 6 screens, closed without saving, will help. Really!

Exercise 5.13, Continued

Find or Train Commands: Open the Command Browser

1. From the Accuracy Center window, say **Open the Command Browser.**

2. The Command Browser will open. The Command Browser is discussed in the final section of this chapter.

3. Close the window by saying **Close Window.**

Get More Information: How to Manage and Personalize Your Vocabularies

1. From the Accuracy Center window, say **How to Manage and Personalize Your Vocabularies.**

2. The Dragon Help file opens to the section on vocabularies. Read as much or as little as you feel will be useful to you in this window. A good command for moving down the page by voice is **Page Down.**

3. Close the Help window when you are finished by saying **Close Help.**

Get More Information: Visit the Nuance Website

1. From the Accuracy Center window, say **Visit the Nuance Website.**

2. The Nuance website will open in your default browser. Speak the names of links or tabs to visit them. (Try at least one item, to see how it goes.)

3. When you have finished exploring the website, close the window by saying **Close Window.**

Close the Accuracy Center

4. Close the Accuracy Center window with the command **Close Window.**

Review: This long exercise contained tools new to you, and ones you have learned about already. Open a word processor and answer the following questions: 1) What was one new item for you in the Accuracy Center? 2) What is one item you plan to explore further in the future? 3) Did you add any new words to your vocabulary in this exercise? 4) Did you have any difficulties with any of the items in the Accuracy Center? Save your work as "Exercise 5.13" and print if needed.

The Command Browser

The Command Browser shows Dragon command combinations that are available globally (in all programs) or in specific applications (or contexts), such as Microsoft Office Word. Commands you have created through the MyCommands Editor are also displayed here. To look and see what commands are available, go to the **Tools** menu, and select the **Command Browser** option.

When the Command Browser opens, the "Browse" option is usually displayed by default. In the Browse option, you can look at the different commands available in different contexts.

In the "Context" list at the top of the screen, Global Commands are usually displayed upon opening. However, to change the context—for example, to see the commands list available in Microsoft PowerPoint (pictured at right)—click the down-pointing arrow and choose another context.

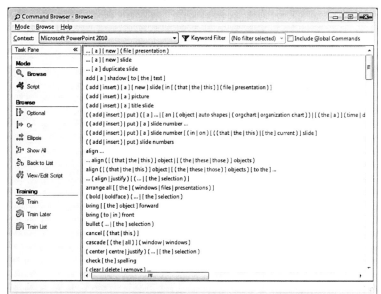

In the main window area, command combinations are displayed, which shows the various ways to command a certain action. For example, if you see "close [the] window" this means that the command can be spoken as **Close Window** or **Close the Window**. The word in brackets [ ] is optional, but the words *not* in brackets are required. This command combination is fairly easy to decipher; however, some of them are quite complex.

Using and understanding the Command Browser can be challenging; this is certainly an advanced feature. To get an introduction to understanding commands available in the Command Browser, look at the sample command combination on the next page.

Study the example below to learn how the Command Browser shows command combinations.

For Example: (go | move) to [the] (bottom | end) of [the] (line | document)

The words in ( ) parenthesis show options: you must choose one of these words in the command. The words in [ ] brackets are optional—use them if you wish. The words not in parenthesis or brackets are required. So, what does this mean for the example above? There are 30 possible commands that can be made from this combination!

The following 30 commands are possible from the example above:

Go to Bottom of Line	Move to Bottom of Line	Go to the Bottom of Line
Go to the Bottom of the Line	Move to the Bottom of Line	Move to the Bottom of the Line
Go to End of Line	Go to the End of Line	Go to End of the Line
Go to the End of the Line	Move to End of Line	Move to the End of Line
Move to End of the Line	Move to the End of the Line	Go to End of Document
Go to the End of Document	Go to End of the Document	Go to the End of the Document
Move to End of Document	Move to the End of Document	Move to End of the Document
Move to the End of the Document	Go to Bottom of Document	Go to the Bottom of Document
Go to Bottom of the Document	Go to the Bottom of the Document	Move to Bottom of Document
Move to the Bottom of Document	Move to Bottom of the Document	Move to the Bottom of the Document

Isn't this amazing? There are thirty different ways to put the cursor at the end of a line or the bottom of a document. (This is why Dragon tells users to "try it and see" when it comes to commands; so many combinations will work!)

On the next page, practice parsing a simpler command combination. This skill is helpful when you are looking in the Command Browser for a command, and you encounter something that looks like a word puzzle!

Exercise 5.14: Find Four Commands

DIRECTIONS: Decode a command combination to find at least 4 different commands.

1. Look at this (real) command combination:

    delete [the] (character | line)

2. Find four possible commands that can be made from this command combination. Use the information on the previous page to help you decode the command if you have trouble.

3. Open a new document and dictate the four commands, holding down the Shift key while speaking to force the dictation mode.

4. Dictate your name, the date, and **Exercise 5.14**. Save the document as "Exercise 5.14" and close the document.

Review: Exercise 5.14 is the final exercise in Dragon NaturallySpeaking. Beginning in Chapter 6, use the speech recognition skills you have learned so far with Windows Speech Recognition.

QUESTION TIME!

Is Windows Speech Recognition going to be as complex (and difficult) as Dragon?

Not at all. Windows Speech Recognition will be much easier to use. There are two reasons for this: first, WSR does not have as many options as Dragon, so there is less information to remember; and second, you won't be starting as a speech recognition beginner—bringing your experience with Dragon to WSR makes it much easier.

Why should I bother with Windows Speech Recognition if I know Dragon?

WSR is available on millions more computers than Dragon NaturallySpeaking, as it is built into the Windows operating system. This is helpful when you can't work on your Dragon computer. Also, it is helpful to see a second speech recognition system in order to solidify your speech recognition skills. Generalizing your experience to another program will make you better at dictating, and better to face any new speech recognition programs that come along. (Don't we all know a person who learned one version of a program, and is now afraid to try a new or different one? You won't be that person.) Finally, the last reason: it is fun!

Command Review

New commands in this chapter:

Dictation Box
Show Dictation Box
Transfer

Screen Shot
Press Print Screen
Press Alt Print Screen

Viewing Web Pages
Start Internet Explorer
Start Mozilla Firefox
Stop Scrolling
Start Scrolling Up/Down
Speed Up/Slow Down
Page Up/Down
Move Up/Down 10 Lines
Go To Top/Bottom
Line Up/Down
Press Alt F4

Clicking Links on Pages
Click [*name of link*]
Click Link
Click Text
Click Image
Choose [3]

Addresses
Go To Address
Press Alt D
Switch to Spell Mode
Switch to Normal Mode

Navigation
Click Go
Go There

Go Back
Back
Go Forward
Forward
Refresh Page
Press F5
Go Home
Home

Favorites/Bookmarks
Click Favorites
Add to Favorites
Click Bookmarks (Firefox)
Bookmark This Page (Firefox)

Buttons, Boxes and Lists
Click Text Field
Click Check Box
Click Radio Button
Click List Box
Show Choices
Open List
Hide Choices
Close List

Searching:
Search the Web For [*item*]
Search [*site*] For [*item*]
Find a Website on [*topic*]
Search [category] for [*item*]

Screen Shot
Press Print Screen
Press Alt Print Screen
Paste That

Web Browser Tabs IE:
Open New Tab
Switch to The Next/Previous Tab
View the 3rd Tab [1–8]
Close Tab

Web Browser Tabs Firefox:
Add a New Tab
Go to the Next/Previous Tab
Close Tab

E-mail Commands
Start Mail
Check for Mail
Open Mail
New Mail
Write Mail
Write E-mail
Reply to Mail
Reply to All
Forward Mail
Send Mail
Send E-mail

Send an e-mail to [*Name*]
Send an e-mail about [*Subject*]
Delete Mail
Delete E-mail
Print Mail
Print E-mail
Close Mail
Click [*name of link or button*]
Go to [*name of*] Field

Gmail commands: *see list on page 193*

Facebook and Twitter Commands
Post to Facebook
Post That to Facebook
Search Facebook for [*topic*]
Post to Twitter
Tweet That

Accuracy Center
Start Accuracy Center
Improve My Accuracy

6 CHAPTER 6
Beginning Windows Speech Recognition

Introduction to Windows Speech Recognition

Windows Speech Recognition is built into the Windows 7 and Windows Vista operating systems. This has several advantages. First, no more wondering if the version you get will work with the version of Windows you are running: if you have it, it will work. Second, there is nothing to install. Finally, Windows integrated speech recognition into its existing support systems; the primary access to Windows Speech Recognition is through a control panel and help is found in the Windows Help file.

That said, it is important to remember that Windows Speech Recognition is a relatively new program; it doesn't have as many features as Dragon NaturallySpeaking, and it doesn't do some things you might expect it to. It does, however, allow the computer user to dictate documents and e-mail, control windows and programs, and use the desktop (and, to a limited extent web browsers) by voice.

There are **fewer commands available** with Windows Speech Recognition (also called WSR) than with Dragon NaturallySpeaking, but Windows SR works around this by numbering items in many locations, including the desktop.

People who use Dragon NaturallySpeaking often want to know if they can just use the Dragon commands they already know. The answer is yes and no. Many commands are the same between Dragon and WSR, but this is by no means universal. For example, both programs use the command MouseGrid to open up a numbered grid for making choices. However, commands to format text are different. This chapter will make comparisons wherever they seem useful.

In This Chapter

- ✓ Introduction to Windows Speech Recognition
- ✓ WSR Set Up and Tutorial
- ✓ Train the Computer to Better Understand You
- ✓ Making Corrections
- ✓ Dictating into WordPad
- ✓ Working with the Desktop and Multiple Windows
- ✓ Open the Speech Reference Card
- ✓ Feature Comparison: WSR and DNS
- ✓ 8 Exercises
- ✓ Frequently Asked Questions

Windows Speech Recognition seems best suited for using the **combination method** to computer use; that is, using speech recognition to dictate text, including letters, papers and other documents and e-mail, and using the mouse and keyboard to format text and to control programs and the desktop. Chapters 6 and 7 tackle features of Windows Speech Recognition.

Are there differences between Windows 7 WSR and Windows Vista WSR?

There are differences, but they are minor. While the screen shots and discussion are based on Windows SR in Windows 7, you can use the instructions in this chapter for Windows Speech Recognition in both Windows 7 and Windows Vista. Where there are differences, they will be noted. A few improvements in the program were introduced in Windows 7, including an Input Panel (a basic dictation box) for windows that are difficult to dictate into.

What if I haven't read the Dragon chapters because I only want to know about Windows Speech Recognition?

While you can begin with Windows Speech Recognition, it is helpful to read through the first five chapters of this book in order to understand the Speech Recognition Method. Working with a computer by voice uses a different workflow, and different techniques, than using a keyboard and mouse alone. If you find a concept confusing, flip to where the concept is first covered—there will be a fuller explanation there.

Set Up and Tutorial

User training with Windows Speech Recognition involves setting up the microphone, taking the Speech Tutorial, and training the computer to better understand you.

Open the Speech Recognition Options Menu

To begin, go to the Start menu, and type *speech* into the search box in the Start menu. A list of items related to speech recognition will populate the left side of the Start menu. Click on the option for "Speech Recognition" under the Control Panel heading (see illustration).

Control Panel

🎤 Speech Recognition

Another way to get there is to click on the "Control Panel" item in the Start menu, then choose the "Ease of Access" area and click on "Speech Recognition". (In Windows Vista, "Speech Recognition" is labeled "Speech Recognition Options". It opens the same window.)

This window contains in one place the speech recognition options and features for Windows SR. The

Configure your Speech Recognition experience

 Start Speech Recognition
Start using your voice to control your computer.

 Set up microphone
Set up your computer to work properly with Speech Recognition.

 Take Speech Tutorial
Learn to use your computer with speech. Learn basic commands and dictation.

 Train your computer to better understand you
Read text to your computer to improve your computer's ability to understand your voice. Doing this isn't necessary, but can help improve dictation accuracy.

 Open the Speech Reference Card
View and print a list of common commands to keep with you so you always know what to say.

first item in the list, "Start Speech Recognition", can be used to turn on the SR microphone. It also takes you through all of the Speech Recognition items the first time it is run if they haven't been completed already. Begin by setting up your microphone, using the directions below.

Set Up Microphone

Begin by setting up your microphone, using the directions below.

Exercise 6.1: Set Up Microphone

DIRECTIONS: Follow the steps below to set up your microphone to work with Windows Speech Recognition.

1. Begin by connecting your microphone headset to the computer, if it is not connected already.
2. Open the **Speech Recognition options** window (see instructions above). Choose "Set Up Microphone".
3. In the window that opens, choose the kind of microphone you are using and click "Next".
4. Read the "Setup Your Microphone" window that opens, then click "Next".

211

Exercise 6.1, Continued

5. In the next window, dictate the sentence on the screen regarding Peter and his preference for speech recognition. The bar should stay in the green range most of the time for best recognition.

6. Click "Next". The final window will ask you to click "Finish" to close the wizard. Your microphone is now ready to use with the Speech Tutorial and Windows SR.

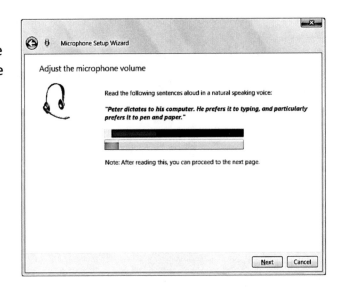

Review: Did you have any trouble setting up your microphone? If so, try unplugging it and plugging it back in. If you still have problems, see the recommendations on page 8.

Train WSR: The Speech Tutorial

The Speech Tutorial is a rich interface designed to give a good introduction to speech recognition and to train your user file. It matches your speech to printed text in order to develop your user file. Plan to spend **20 to 30 minutes** with the tutorial the first time in order to read carefully and follow the steps precisely.

The Tutorial covers dictation, correction, and working with windows. Don't worry about memorizing all of the new commands at once; the commands are all located in the Speech Reference Card and are covered in this text.

IMPORTANT: The Tutorial has no pause or minimize button. If you need to take

a brief break or get to the desktop of the computer, but do not wish to close the Speech Tutorial and start over later, **press the Alt + Tab keys** together. This keyboard combination cycles between the desktop and open windows.

Exercise 6.2: The Speech Tutorial

DIRECTIONS: Follow the steps below to take the speech tutorial. These instructions explain the Tutorial and guide you through it. Refer back to these instructions later as needed to review concepts introduced in the Tutorial.

Open the Speech Tutorial

1. Go to the **Start** menu and type *speech* into the search box.
2. Click the "Speech Recognition" item under the "Control Panel" heading (see illustration at right).

3. Click the link in the Speech Recognition options window that says "Take Speech Tutorial." A Tutorial window will appear like the one pictured below.
4. Notice the tabs across the bottom of the screen:
   - Welcome
   - Basics
   - Dictation
   - Commanding
   - Working with Windows
   - Conclusion

The screen you are viewing now (pictured below) is the **Welcome** area.

Welcome

1. Read the text on the right side of the window (not aloud).
2. Note that this tutorial is a simulation—and you will need to follow the Tutorial **exactly as directed** or your recognition will suffer.
3. Click the "Next" button or say **Next**.

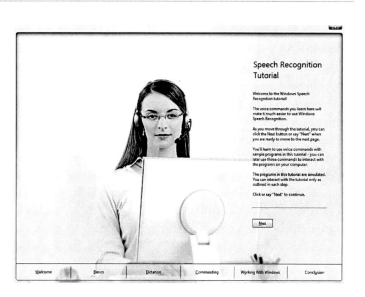

Exercise 6.2, Continued

Basics

The Tutorial advances to the **Basics** area. This area has an opening screen, and then the following topics:

SWITCHING ON AND OFF:

1. In this window, the microphone commands are given. These are **Start Listening** and **Stop Listening**. (In Windows Vista, this area is called **Microphone Button**).

2. You can choose whether you want to the two microphone commands to be microphone on and off commands (Manual Activation Mode), or if you want them to be microphone sleep/standby and on commands (Voice Activation Mode).

3. After the tutorial, a window will appear where you can select the Activation Mode you prefer. (If you want to control the microphone primarily by voice, choose Voice Activation Mode; if you plan to use the mouse to control the microphone, choose Manual Activation Mode.)

AUDIO METER:

4. The audio meter shows the microphone input level. You should see it change as you start and stop speaking.(If not, your microphone might not be plugged in or working properly.)

FEEDBACK:

5. The feedback area displays messages to tell you how the microphone is functioning ("Listening") or to give you other status messages. It will display helpful commands as well.

SPEECH OPTIONS:

6. **Show Speech Options** is the command to show the speech recognition options menu. **Hide Speech Options** will close the menu. (Don't say **Exit** to close the speech options menu—it closes the speech recognition program.)

Exercise 6.2, Continued

CLOSING AND HIDING:

7. **Hide Speech Recognition** and **Show Speech Recognition** are commands used to minimize and restore the SR Bar.

8. **Close Speech Recognition** will close the SR Bar, and turn off speech recognition. (In Windows Vista, this area is called **Minimizing Speech.**)

SUMMARY:

1. The summary tab describes and asks you to demonstrate the **What Can I Say?** command. This command opens the WSR Help file.

Dictation

The **Dictation** area covers how to dictate text into **WordPad**, how to press keys by voice, and how to make corrections. Topics in the Dictation area are:

INTRODUCTION:

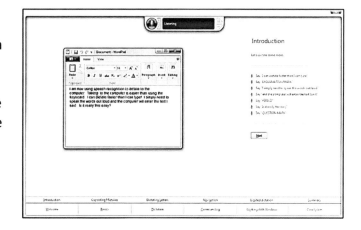

1. Key points in this area are to dictate in sentences or "meaningful sentence fragments", to dictate punctuation, and to speak clearly.

2. Notice how well your dictation is recognized—this is because it doesn't have to guess what you are saying, as you are matching the text on the screen. So, recognition here usually looks good!

3. Remember that you must dictate exactly as directed. WSR is training to your voice, so don't get creative—be precise!

CORRECTING MISTAKES:

4. Say **Correct [*wrong word or phrase*]**, and then choose the correct item from the list by saying its number, then **OK**.

5. If it isn't in the list, you say it, and see if it appears in the list.

6. Change your mind about some dictated text? To delete text you don't want (not a recognition error), say **Undo, Undo That** or **Delete That**.

Exercise 6.2, Continued

7. For longer selections, select the text with a **Select** command, then say **Delete That**.

8. To cancel a text selection, say **Clear Selection**.

DICTATING LETTERS:

9. Using **New Line, New Paragraph**, and saying **Spell It** in the Alternates Panel (a Correction box) to spell out a new word and add it to the vocabulary are demonstrated here.

NAVIGATION:

10. **Go To [*word*]** inserts the cursor before a word, and **Go After [*word*]** inserts the cursor after the word.

11. Other commands to move the cursor include, **Go to the End of the Document**, and **Go to the Start of the Document, Select [*item*], Delete That** and **Delete [*word*]** commands.

LIMITED DICTATION:

12. In areas where dictation is difficult, use the Input Panel (a basic type of dictation box).

13. Pressing keys: You can use keypress commands like **Press End** and **Press Control Home**, and spelling commands like: **Press [*letter*]** as in [*word that starts with that letter*].

14. Other keypress commands given in this section include: **Enter, Space, Backspace, Tab, End, Press Shift A, Press Capital B, Press c as I close, Press Down Arrow**, and **Press y Three Times**. Notice that some can be spoken without the word "Press", although all will work with the word "Press" spoken first.

SUMMARY:

15. Reviews commands in this section.

Commanding

The **Commanding** area covers how to control windows, start programs, switch between windows, work with menus, and click on buttons using speech recognition. Areas are:

INTRODUCTION:

1. Introduces commands in Windows Speech Recognition.

Exercise 6.2, Continued

SAY WHAT YOU SEE:

2. Speak the names of visible items in windows, including tabs, menu items and file names.

3. If more than one item matches that name, the multiple items will be numbered. Say the number of the correct item, followed by **OK**.

CLICK WHAT YOU SEE:

4. Say **Click**, **Double-click** or **Right-click [*item name*]** to perform the action.

DESKTOP INTERACTION:

5. How to use voice commands to work with the desktop, using commands like **Show The Desktop**.

SHOW NUMBERS:

6. Numbers the clickable items in windows, toolbars, and webpage links.

7. Numbers flash slowly until you speak a number and then say **OK**.

SUMMARY:

8. Windows SR calls this "Say What You See". Lastly, the Commanding area demonstrates how to number items using the **Show Numbers** command.

Working with Windows

In the **Working with Windows** area are commands for scrolling in windows, switching between programs, starting programs, and more. Included are:

INTRODUCTION:

1. Use scrolling commands like: **Scroll Up, Scroll Down, Scroll Up 10, Scroll Down 20**.

CONTROLLING WINDOWS:

2. Say **Minimize That, Restore That, Close That, Maximize That**.

FORMS:

3. **Go To [*field name*]** moves between field in windows; for example, e-mail windows. Then dictate the desired text.

SWITCHING:

4. **Switch to [*window name*]** moves between program windows.

Exercise 6.2, Continued

STARTING:

5. **Start [*program name*]** will start any installed compatible program; to close a window say **Close That.**

SUMMARY:

6. **Restore [*program name*]** is used to bring a window back from minimizing.

Conclusion

The **Conclusion** gives a brief review of commanding and dictation. Areas are:

COMMANDING:

1. Give commands one at a time, speaking clearly.

DICTATION:

2. Speak in full sentences or meaningful phrases.

WHAT CAN I SAY:

3. Opens the Speech Reference Card (list of commands).
4. Say **Finish** to close the Tutorial.

Review: How did it go? At the end of the tutorial, the software will recommend training the computer to better understand you. Do this in **Exercise 6.3**. (This is similar to the Dragon user profile training, in that there is a script that you dictate, and the software adapts your user file from this input.)

 ## QUESTION TIME!

Wow, that was easy! Uh, what did I do again?

Many people are pleasantly surprised at how easy it is to train WSR. It is an easy interface, but the simplicity can be misleading: there is a lot of important content in the tutorial, and absorbing it all at once is difficult.

Refer back to the preceding pages when you need to remember what was covered in the tutorial—everything that is important is written down there.

That felt so much easier than training Dragon! Was it easier?

If you look at the combination of text instructions and commands, it is probably more difficult. But once you have learned to use speech recognition, and you understand the concepts and best practices, **learning a second speech recognition program is much easier**. (It makes sense, doesn't it? Just as learning how to make chocolate chip cookies is easier once you know how to make sugar cookies.)

Can I stop now and come back to this later?

Yes. To have the most consistent result, close the **Speech Recognition Options** window with the mouse. When you are ready to continue, go to the Start menu and type "speech" into the search box.

The Start menu will display a number of choices; click the one under "Control Panel" that says "Speech Recognition". This will re-open the "Configure Your Speech Recognition Experience" window you had open previously pictured on page 211 (and not do something unexpected).

Control Panel
🎙 Speech Recognition

Then, do Exercise 6.3 and click "Train your computer to better understand you".

About Exercise 6.3: Train the Computer to Better Understand You

Windows Speech Recognition matches your voice to a script; this will improve your speech recognition.

Exercise 6.3: Train to The Script

DIRECTIONS: Follow the instructions to train Windows SR to understand your speech more accurately. Read the entire phrase before you begin speaking in order to speak more fluently.

1. To start this process, click the "Train the Computer to Better Understand You" item in the Speech Recognition options window. (If you aren't sure how to get this window open, read the instructions under "Can I stop now and come back to this later?" above.) After clicking on the item pictured below, the training window opens.

	Train your computer to better understand you
	Read text to your computer to improve your computer's ability to understand your voice. Doing this isn't necessary, but can help improve dictation accuracy.

Exercise 6.3, Continued

2. The first window is titled "Welcome to Speech Recognition Voice Training". Read the text, then say **Next**.

3. The first sentence or phrase of text will appear. Speak the text, and when the computer has processed it, you will see the next phrase displayed.

4. If you need a short break, say **Pause**. To begin again, say **Resume**.

5. The script window doesn't let you know if your speech has been understood as you are working, so if it doesn't work right away, wait a few seconds and then repeat the phrase. If it gets really stuck, you can click or say **Cancel** and restart it.

6. Continue until you have finished the entire script. (You may be offered a second script; feel free to decline). This usually takes 10–15 minutes. In the future, if your recognition doesn't seem to be very good, go back to this training area and dictate a script again.

7. You might see a window appear after training, called "Share Speech Data with Microsoft." Read the window and make the choice you prefer. This will not affect your recognition one way or the other.

8. When you have finished, restart your computer. (If you don't restart your computer, your recognition may not work as well, so this is highly recommended.)

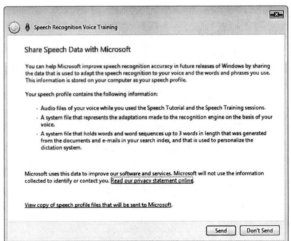

9. While the computer restarts, drink some water and read the review section of this lesson on the next page.

Review: How did this work for you? Did it feel familiar, like the Dragon training? In order to document your work, **take some notes now** about how this worked for you, and any parts you would want to review in the future. You will write up a reflection of your experience in **Exercise 6.5**, after practicing microphone commands and choosing a few settings.

Starting Speech Recognition After Training

After you have trained WSR and restarted your computer, go to the Start menu and look for a Windows Speech Recognition item in the left pane (where frequently used programs are listed.) If you see it, click on it. If you do not, type *speech* into the search box. Click on either "Start Speech Recognition" or "Windows Speech Recognition" (both will open the program). What happens next will vary by computer, but either:

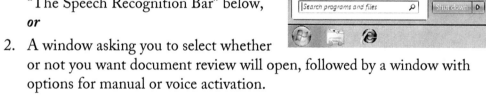

1. The Speech Recognition Bar (containing the microphone icon) will open—if so, go to the section titled "The Speech Recognition Bar" below, *or*

2. A window asking you to select whether or not you want document review will open, followed by a window with options for manual or voice activation.

What is the "Enable document review" option all about?

This is a feature to adapt Windows SR to your writing style by reviewing documents and e-mails stored in your computer (just for your user, not other users' profiles). If you have documents and e-mails stored on the computer you are using, it is a good idea to click the button next to "Enable document review" and let Windows SR learn your writing style. Then, click "Next".

> ◯ **Enable document review**
> ◯ **Disable document review**

Is it better to have manual or automatic activation selected?

This depends on your preferences. If you prefer to have the **Stop Listening** command turn off the microphone (like Dragon's **Microphone Off** command), choose "manual activation mode".

⦿ **Use manual activation mode**

⦿ **Use voice activation mode**

For a more hands-free experience, select "Use voice activation mode" to make the command **Stop Listening** have a 'standby' function (like Dragon's **Go To Sleep** command). To turn the microphone back on when using "manual activation mode", you must manually click the microphone button or press the **Ctrl + Windows** keys.

To turn the mic back on when using "voice activation mode" just say **Start Listening**. After making your choice, click "Next" to continue. Click "Finish" in the last window.

Tip: If you have difficulty deciding which mode to use, choose "voice activation mode" as it is the setting used in this book, and it gives the most flexibility. (In "manual activation mode" there is no voice option to sleep the microphone.)

The Speech Recognition Bar

By now you are ready to use Windows SR with text dictation (including corrections), controlling the desktop, and opening and closing windows. But first, turn on the Speech Recognition Bar, use voice commands to wake and sleep the microphone, and learn a few essential options.

Exercise 6.4: Microphone Commands

DIRECTIONS: Follow the steps to use microphone commands and the Speech Recognition Bar.

1. In the Start menu, type *speech* into the search box. Click on either "Start Speech Recognition" or "Windows Speech Recognition". (Both will open the program.)

2. The Speech Recognition Bar (SR Bar) will open, covering the top-most center area of the screen. The microphone will be sleeping.

Exercise 6.4, Continued

3. To turn on the microphone, say **Start Listening**. The message area should say "Listening" as in the picture at right.

4. To put the microphone to sleep, say **Stop Listening**. The microphone should say "Sleeping". In this mode, it only listens for the command **Start Listening**.

5. Try the manual way of waking and sleeping the microphone. Click once on the microphone icon, and the microphone should say "Listening". Wait a moment, click it again, and it should say "Sleeping". Manually pressing the keyboard command **Control key + Windows** (the Windows logo key) does the same thing.

6. Other features on the SR Bar are: a volume level indicator to the right of the microphone icon; a message area in the middle of the window to alert you to the status of the microphone or of your recognition; and, a close button and a minimize button on the right side of the SR Bar. Locate these now.

7. Say **Stop Listening** to put the microphone on standby.

Review: How did it go? **Start Listening** and **Stop Listening** are the only microphone commands for Windows SR; no alternate commands exist. If you have any trouble getting them recognized, remember to speak "commandingly", especially at first.

Note: The instructions in Exercise 6.4 presume that you are using the "Voice Activation Mode". If you are using "Manual Activation Mode" instead, you can turn the microphone off by voice, but not back on—use the mouse or manually press the Control key + Windows Logo key for this.

Can I move the Speech Recognition Bar?

Yes. If the Speech Recognition Bar is covering something you need to get to, or you would just prefer to have it positioned in a different location, you can move it by voice or manually. To move it with voice commands, say either **Minimize Speech Recognition** (to shrink the SR Bar to the Taskbar) or **Move Speech Recognition**, which moves the SR Bar to the bottom middle of the screen. The message thoughtfully displayed while this process occurs says "Moving out of the way".

To manually move the SR Bar, click and hold with the mouse, then drag it to any location on the screen where you would like it to be. The SR Bar has only two display modes—displayed, and minimized. Finally, the SR Bar can also be moved using MouseGrid—see instructions in Chapter 7.

About Exercise 6.5

In this exercise, use **WordPad,** a simple word processing program included with Windows. Expect several recognition errors with this exercise. You will correct the errors in Exercise 6.6, so don't erase them. As with Dragon NaturallySpeaking, making corrections increases accuracy.

Use **New Line** and **New Paragraph** commands as needed. Finally, you can use the command **Scratch That** to remove the last bit of text.

Exercise 6.5: Dictate into Microsoft WordPad

DIRECTIONS: Starting from the desktop, dictate into WordPad, then save and print your work. Make sure you don't have any other windows open before you begin. You do not need to correct recognition errors in this exercise, as the errors from Exercise 6.5 are corrected in Exercise 6.6.

1. Turn on the SR microphone. Say **Start WordPad**. WordPad opens.
2. Say, **I am using Microsoft Windows speech recognition to dictate a short document.** (Say **period.**) Say **New Line**.
3. Say, **I have completed the training tutorial. I also matched my voice to the script.** (Say **period.**) Say **New Line**.
4. Dictate a short (2 or 3 sentence) paragraph about how this went for you. What was easy, what was difficult, and comparing it to your Dragon user training experience are all appropriate topics for this paragraph. (Remember to think through the phrase or sentence before speaking it for best recognition accuracy. Be tolerant of errors.)
5. Say **New Paragraph**, then dictate your name. You will likely have several words that need correcting. Do not fix them yet—you will do this in Exercise 6.6.
6. Say, **Date and Time** to open up the date and time feature.

Exercise 6.5, Continued

7. From the Date and Time list, choose one of the formats by saying **Move Down 7** (or some other number) to get to the one you want. If you need to move back up the list, say **Move Up [*number*]**.

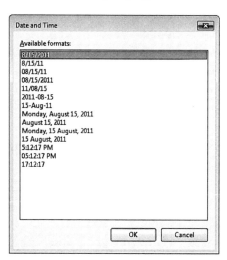

8. Say **OK** when the focus is on your choice. The date and time should now appear in the document.

9. Save the document. Say **Press Control S**. After the Save As dialog box opens, dictate or type in the "File Name" field, naming your document "Exercise 6.6" and adjust the save location if needed. Say **Click Save**.

10. Print the document. Say **Press Control P**. The Print dialog box should open. Choose the correct printer if needed, check that only one copy will be printed, then say **Click Print**.

11. **Read carefully** over your printed exercise for recognition errors and circle or underline them. This makes it easier to see them when you go to make corrections in the next exercise. (But don't feel too bad about it—you and Windows Speech Recognition are just getting to know each other!)

Review: This exercise is usually challenging, as it is your first time dictating into WordPad with Windows SR, you are dictating your own composition (the paragraph) and your recognition may not be very good yet. (If your recognition was excellent in Dragon NaturallySpeaking, poor recognition in Windows SR can feel discouraging, or even insulting!) Hang in there, and remember, recognition quickly improves when you make corrections.

Why use the keypress commands for printing and saving?

The easiest way to avoid confusion and extra steps in WordPad (especially because Windows Vista and Windows 7 have different versions of WordPad) is to use keypress commands. For example, if you use a command like **Click Print** and a menu has both a Print and a Print Preview command, they will be numbered. You then need to say the correct number, and **OK**. Using **Press Control P** makes it clear that you want the Print command, without the intermediate steps.

Use Best Practices

Best practices for dictating text apply, whether you're using Dragon NaturallySpeaking or Windows Speech Recognition. First, begin using any new speech recognition program by dictating printed text. It doesn't matter if it's a memo you wrote to your boss last week or an article from a newspaper. Reading pre-printed text is the easiest way to **free your mind to focus upon your vocal delivery**, and to make it easy to see what needs correcting.

Second, always dictate unformatted text first, make corrections, save the work, then return and format the text last. Follow core instructions (below) for keeping your voice healthy, preventing injury and aiding your speech recognition. Finally, do make corrections to misrecognized text, so your recognition will improve (and not get worse), but always finish the sentence you were dictating before correcting. These are not just efficient work habits, they help make your speech recognition better. For more on best practices, see page 54.

Follow Core Instructions

These instructions are key to keeping your speech recognition, and your voice, in tip top shape: 1) do a warm up exercise before launching into your main work (see Exercise 7.1 on page 242), 2) take frequent sips of water (to keep your voice as healthy as possible), 3) take regular breaks (e.g. 5–10 minute break each hour), 4) read the step before you do it *or* plan ahead what you mean to say and do, and 5) make corrections as needed. Core instructions are discussed in depth in Chapter 7.

About Misrecognitions and Making Corrections

Was your name properly recognized in Exercise 6.5? If your name is common in English, like Susan Jones or Tom Davis, it probably will be easily recognized. If not, you will need to correct it.

Corrections to misrecognized text are a fact of life for speech recognition users; just as manual typists become accustomed to correcting their typing errors. However, the number of corrections needed with speech recognition software is reduced over time as words are trained and the user file gets better calibrated to the way you speak. (For a review of what causes misrecognitions and how best to dictate text and commands, see page 59 in Chapter 2.)

Making Corrections

There are two levels of correction in Windows SR: the **Alternates Panel**, which is similar to Dragon's Correction box, and the **Spelling Panel**, which works like Dragon's Spelling box.

Level	Type of Correction	Commands
1	Alternates Panel	**Correct [*word*] ,[3] , OK***
2	Spelling Panel	**Spell It, Spell It Again**

*Instead of **Correct [*word*]**, you can double-click with the mouse on the incorrect word, then say **Correct That** to open the Alternates Panel.

Windows Speech Recognition does not have the Select and Replace correction option; that is, you cannot select a misrecognized word with the **Correct [*word*]** or **Select [*word*]** command and then say the replacement word and see it appear in the document directly. Instead, the **Correct [*word*]** command brings up a correction box, called the Alternates Panel. Then, you choose the correct word from the list, or say the correct word.

If the correct word is not in the list, say the correct word again and see if it appears. If not, say **Spell It** and use the Spelling Panel.

Alternates Panel: An Example

If you say "My name is Cindy Keith" but you get "My name is sin dee Keith" correct this by saying **Correct *sin dee***.

The Alternates Panel will open. Choose the correct item by saying the number next to it and then **OK**, as in **Number 1, OK**.

If the word you need isn't in the Alternates Panel, try saying the correct word or phrase again, and the list of options will change. It may be there now.

The Spelling Panel

If you still don't see the word, say **Spell It**. In the Spelling Panel, dictate the letters one at a time until the word is spelled out.

Tips for the Spelling Panel:

1. If the word starts with a capital letter, say **Capital C** (or other letter) at the beginning.
2. If it isn't spelled correctly, say **Spell It Again** to delete what you have and start over.
3. To correct a specific letter in the word, say the number above that letter, then say the correct letter.
4. Windows SR recommends that if you have trouble getting certain letters recognized, you should use a format such as "a as in apple." You can use the Radio Alphabet (i.e. "a as in alpha"), or Windows SR suggests you use any word that starts with the letter, such as "f as in flexible".

Moving the Cursor after a Correction

When you make a correction, the cursor moves to that place in the document. To get it back to the end of the text, so that you can continue dictating, use these commands (many of which should be familiar):

Go to End of [*item*]	moves to end of the item
Go to Beginning of [*item*]	moves to beginning of the item
Go to Start of [*item*]	moves to beginning of the item
Go To Top	moves to top of document
Go To Bottom	moves to bottom of document
Go To [*word*]	moves to *before* the word spoken
Go After [*word*]	moves to *after* the word spoken

Note: Items that can be spoken include **Word, Line, Sentence, Paragraph, Page** and **Document**. (For example, **Go to End of Sentence** and **Go to Beginning of Line** are valid commands.)

The commands **Go To [*word*]** and **Go After [*word*]** are equivalent to Dragon's **Insert Before [*word*]** and **Insert After [*word*]** commands.

Exercise 6.6 Correct Misrecognitions

DIRECTIONS: Follow the steps to correct misrecognitions from Exercise 6.5.

1. Open Exercise 6.5 if needed (make sure it is open in WordPad and not Word). Say **Press Control S** and save your work as "Exercise 6.6".

2. Look over the text on the screen and locate the first error in recognition. Use your printout of Exercise 6.5 to aid you.

3. Say **Correct [*wrong word*]**, using the incorrect word in the command. (Alternately, click on the incorrect word with the mouse and say **Correct That**.)

4. The Alternates Panel will open.

5. If the choice you want is in the list, say its number, then say **OK**.

6. If the choice you want is not in the list, say the correct word (or words) and see if it appears in the list now. If so, say its number, then **OK**.

7. If the correct text does not appear, say **Spell It**.

8. In the Spelling Panel, spell the word or phrase, one letter at a time, until done.

9. Say **OK** and the text will be replaced in your document.

10. Correct any other recognition errors following steps 3-9, as needed.

11. Say **Click Save** to update the document's save.

12. Say **Press Control P** and print the exercise. Compare it to Exercise 6.5 to see the corrections you have made.

Review: How did this work for you? If you like Dragon's options and methods of correction, it can be difficult to get used to a different approach. However, some people prefer the simplicity of the Alternates Panel and they appreciate the additional options in the Spelling Panel, such as the option to speak a number over any letter in a word, and to say *a* **as in** *anything*.

If you had more than three or four corrections, this exercise can be time-consuming. However, more practice with the Alternates and Spelling Panels will make it that much easier to use later.

About Timed Writing Exercises and Exercise 6.7

 A timed writing exercise gives instant feedback on your dictation speed and recognition. Expect to see many recognition errors in this first timed writing in WSR; your speed and recognition will improve as you work with the software. You will need a reliable timer handy.

- ✓ The timed writing passage (on the next page) is 150 words long. **Do not try to finish it in one minute**; in fact, it was written so that you likely do not complete it. (Just stop speaking when the timer goes off.)

- ✓ However, if you do complete it, say **New Line** and then start dictating again from the beginning.

- ✓ If you have trouble reading the text aloud (you skip words, get lost in the text, etc.) try the old grade school trick of focusing on each word, one at a time.

- ✓ You may have many errors. Think of this first timed writing as a kind of pre-test—before you have honed your user profile by dictating text and making corrections.

- ✓ Feel free to try this exercise more than once. Often, it takes a try or two in order to get used to speaking normally while a timer is running!

- ✓ Punctuation spoken in this timed writing is **period** and **dash**. Your dash may look like this (--) or like this (—). For this exercise, both are fine.

- ✓ Note: This timed writing exercise is adapted from Exercise 1.6 on page 42. If you completed this exercise previously, compare your two timed writings after you finish Exercise 6.7 and see how your early Dragon recognition compares to your WSR recognition currently.

Go to the next page to begin Exercise 6.7.

Exercise 6.7 WSR Timed Writing I

DIRECTIONS: Read the steps below before beginning.

1. Set a timer for one minute, but do not start timing yet.
2. Turn on your microphone and say **Start WordPad**.
3. Say **Stop Listening** to put your microphone to sleep.
4. **Pre-read** the timed writing passage, to make your speech more fluid and less error-prone. Notice where the commas and periods are.
5. When you're ready to begin, turn on your microphone and start the timer.
6. Dictate at your normal rate of speech, or just a little more slowly and deliberately. Remember to dictate punctuation.
7. When the timer goes off, turn off your microphone immediately by saying **Stop Listening** or clicking on the microphone icon.
8. Look over your work, and count how many words you dictated (use the guide at the right-hand side of the page to help you).
9. Subtract the number of errors (wrong words) from the total number of words. This is your adjusted WPM (words per minute).

WSR Timed Writing 1 *Dictate the text below*	Words Per Line	Total Words
New users of speech recognition software are often surprised	9	9
that it can be difficult to work with the computer in a new	13	22
way. There are several reasons for this. For someone who has	11	33
been typing for years, it takes a while to get used to how	13	46
quickly you can dictate e-mail and create documents.	8	54
Learning the right commands for any situation, and	8	62
remembering them when you need them, is challenging at	9	71
first. If you frequently reach for the mouse or revert to typing	12	83
on the keyboard, stop and dictate the command to learn what	11	94
you can say. Finally, it's easy to become irritated or frustrated	11	105
with the computer when it misunderstands. After all, we tend	10	115
to become irritated or frustrated with people when they	9	124
misunderstand us. Don't take it personally. Just keep in mind	10	134
that you're talking to software, not a person, and that it will	12	146
get better with practice.	4	150

Total words − errors = adjusted words per minute

Exercise 6.7, Continued

Review: How did it go? If you had a lot of errors, it can be disappointing. Choose three or four errors and correct them using the techniques you learned in Exercise 6.6. If you have many errors, choose ones that seem relatively easy to correct. (If you don't have three or four errors, congratulations!) After you practice with WSR and make corrections to misrecognitions, your recognition will improve significantly. Follow the directions below to save, print and close your work.

Save and Print Your Work

Turn on your microphone and say **Press Control S** to open the "Save As" dialog box. Save your work as "Exercise 6.7". Say **Press Control P** to open the Print dialog box. Print your work if needed (this can also make it easier to see errors).

Close WordPad

Close WordPad by and dictating the command **Close Window** (or, **Click Close**).

How many words per minute should I expect?

You should have somewhere between 70 and 150 words per minute. If you have more, then you were probably speaking very quickly (perhaps too quickly). If you have fewer than 70 words total, consider why: do you have difficulty reading or speaking? If so, you may want to try a timed writing with some text that you know by heart and can speak easily. (See the True Story below for an example.)

How many errors are normal and acceptable?

The number of errors depends upon many factors, but it comes down to two causes: the software has misrecognized what you said, or you misspoke. Five to 10 errors in this exercise is typical. Be patient, make corrections, and you will have fewer errors.

True Stories

Kurtis was one of my first speech recognition students, at a time when speech recognition software took many hours to train. He has Multiple Sclerosis, which makes it difficult for him to speak clearly. He had an idea, though: he would use the "Pledge of Allegiance" as his timed writing text. "Heck, I've been saying it since the first grade," he told me. He closed his eyes after he started the timer, to avoid watching the screen and making mistakes. He dictated the "Pledge of Allegiance" three times in one minute (93 words), with a few (correctable) errors, which pleased him greatly. He used it for his warm-up exercise from then on.

Select Sentence, Delete That vs. ~~Select Line, Scratch That~~

When you work with Dragon NaturallySpeaking and you dictate into any text box (like a search box), if the word (or words) you dictate is misrecognized, you might choose to correct the misrecognized text. Or, you might just say **Select Line**, then **Scratch That**.

With Windows Speech Recognition, the **Select Line** command is replaced by the **Select Sentence** command (even if the text is just a phrase, not a complete sentence). Additionally, while the **Scratch That** command works well in word processing programs, in text boxes the command **Delete That** works better.

In the next section, you will encounter text fields. If you have any misrecognitions in those text fields, say **Select Sentence**, then **Delete That**. To make a correction instead, say **Select Sentence**, then **Correct That**.

True Stories

Some people really love correct grammar. Mary Benson is one of those people. When she heard that she should say **Select Sentence** for a phrase, she was displeased. She refused! "What else can I say?" she asked. Well, the other option is to be precise in the number of words. Some examples of this precision in commanding would be **Select Last 3 Words**, **Select Previous 6 Words**, or something similar. Then, when the text is selected, say **Delete That**. Or, do it in one step: **Delete Last 3 Words** or if it is just one word, **Delete Last Word**. Mary would be pleased!

Open the Speech Reference Card

The Speech Reference Card, a part of the Windows Help file, makes available a list of voice commands for Windows SR and "how to" instructions for common tasks, organized by categories.

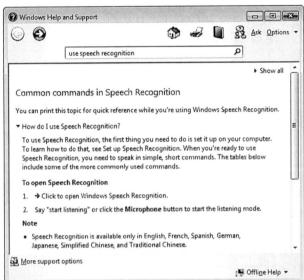

To open and close each category, speak the name of the blue text links. To open all the categories at once, say **Show All** to activate the link in the upper-right corner. Using the word **Click** in front of a link makes it much more likely to be recognized.

To get started, say **What Can I Say** to open the Speech Reference Card. (You can accomplish the same thing with the command **Show Speech Options** and then say **Open The Speech Reference Card**.)

Exercise 6.8 Speech Reference Card

DIRECTIONS: Follow the steps to get familiar with features in the Speech Reference Card, to practice clicking a link in a window, to open and close a subtopic, to move up and down a window, and to search for a particular item in a window. If you give a command, and the wrong thing happens, click on the left-pointing "Back" arrow in the upper-left corner of the window (you can also try saying **Click Back**) and try the command again.

1. Say **What Can I Say** to open the Speech Reference Card.
2. When the Speech Reference Card opens, say **Click *How do I use Speech Recognition***. (You do not need to dictate the question mark.)
3. Look over the information that appears. It should roughly match the window above.
4. Say **Click *How do I use Speech Recognition*** again to close this subtopic.
5. Say **Click *Controls*** to open the Controls subtopic. Move down the page by saying **Move Down 5** until you have reached the bottom of the topic (usually three times).

Exercise 6.8, Continued

6. When you are ready to move back up, say **Move Up 15** (or the correct number) until you are back where you started and can see the top of the window.

7. Say **Click *Show All*** and all of the subtopics will be displayed in the window.

8. Move up and down the page, experimenting with these commands: **Move Down [*number*], Move Up [*number*], Scroll Down [*number*], Scroll Up [*number*], Press Page Down, Press Page Up, Move to the Beginning of the Document**, and **Move to the End of the Document**.

9. Try keypress commands: **Press Control Home** and **Press Control End**. These commands move the focus to the top and bottom of the document. They work in some windows where the other commands do not.

10. It can be faster to find specific information by searching using a keyword. Say **Click Options** to open the Options item in the upper right-hand corner of the window. Say **Find** or **Click Find** to open the Find item (you do not need to say "on this page…").

11. Find box will open. Search for information about how to switch to another window. Say **Switch To** to type the words "switch to" into the box (some words may be capitalized—that's fine).

12. Notice how the words "switch to" are highlighted where they appear in the page.

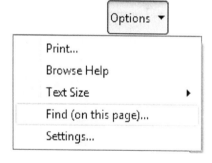

13. Say **Click Next** and the next instance of "switch to" is highlighted in the page.

14. Say **Click Previous** and the previous instance of "switch to" is highlighted in the page.

15. Say **Click Close** and the Find box closes.

16. Say **Press Control Home** and the focus moves back to the top of the window.

17. Say **Hide All** and the subtopics close.

18. Say **Close Window** and the Speech Reference Card closes.

Review: Did you make it through all 18 steps (*whew!*) without too much trouble? If you found this difficult, you may want to print the Speech Reference Card and study it. The entire Speech Reference Card can be printed easily if you first speak the **Show All** link and then give the **Print** command (it's about 8 pages long).

Note: As the Speech Reference Card is contained within the extensive Windows Help and Support area, it is easy to perform other Help searches from this window. For example, if you want to know how to print something, say **Search Help** to move the focus to the search box. Then, dictate search terms like "how to print" and then say **Press Enter**. A list of results appears in the window.

Windows 7 and Windows Vista Help and Support are filled with useful information written in clear language.

Feature Comparison: Dragon NaturallySpeaking and Windows SR

Feature	Dragon	Windows SR
Add a word to vocabulary	Yes	Yes
Add a list of words to vocabulary	Yes	No
Accuracy Center	Yes	No
Natural Language Commands	Yes	No
MouseGrid	Yes	Yes
Basic Word Processing Program	DragonPad	WordPad
Multiple Users on Same Machine	Yes	Yes—each must have a unique user profile in Windows
Custom Commands	Yes	No
Dictation Box	Yes	Input Panel instead
Recognition Modes	Yes	No

About Exercise 6.9 Working with Windows

Read all the steps before beginning so that you are familiar with what you will be doing. This exercise involves moving among several windows, performing functions, and moving copied text between windows.

If you have trouble in the calculator, say **Clear Entry** and start again.

Exercise 6.9: Working with Windows

DIRECTIONS: Open program windows, and use the **Switch to [*window*]** command to move between these items. Take a screen shot, paste it into Paint, resize it if necessary and print.

1. Turn on the SR microphone. Say **Start WordPad.** WordPad will open.

2. Dictate your name, and correct any misrecognitions. Say **New Paragraph** to move the cursor down to a new paragraph**.**

3. Say **Start Calculator**. The Calculator will open.

4. To enter this problem: 39 X 8472 and get the answer, say these numbers and functions slowly and clearly, with pauses in between: **3, 9, multiply, 8, 4, 7, 2, equals**. The answer appears in the Calculator.

5. Say **Copy That** and the answer gets copied to the clipboard.

6. Say **Switch to WordPad**. Say **Paste That**. The answer will be copied to the WordPad document. Say **New Paragraph**.

Calculator with Problem Entered

7. Say **Switch to Calculator**. Say **Press Alt Print Screen**. This takes a screen shot of only the Calculator.

8. Say **Switch to WordPad**. Say **Paste That**. The Calculator screen shot is pasted into WordPad. Resize the screen shot if necessary to keep the printout to one page.

9. Say **Press Control P** and speak items as needed in the Print dialog box to print the document.

10. Save your work as "Exercise 6.9".

Calculator screen shot in WordPad

Review: How did this work for you? It can be easy to get lost in the steps. If this happens, back up a step or two and try it again. To minimize all open windows, say **Show Desktop**.

 **QUESTION TIME!**

What about saving user files in Windows SR?

You don't do this manually, as user files are saved automatically in the hard drive of the computer you have trained. On the upside, this makes it easier to use. On the other hand, you can't save your Windows SR user file to a network location, or export it.

What else is there to know about Windows Speech Recognition?

In Chapter 7, you will learn how to use Windows Speech Recognition with Internet Explorer and Microsoft Word. Practice the warm up exercise with Windows SR, learn how to add a word to the Speech Dictionary, and how to click the mouse by voice and give MouseGrid commands in Windows SR. Learn your way around the Speech Options menu, accessed with the **Show Speech Options** command.

Can more than one person use Windows Speech Recognition on one computer?

Yes, several people can use Windows Speech Recognition on the same computer. Windows ties the user file to the Windows user profile; so, to have multiple users, each one needs a separate user profile.

To create a new user profile, go to the Speech Options Control Panel and look for an item that says "User Accounts". Inside of this area is usually a link to "Add a User Account". (The exact wording may vary—if you have difficulty finding this area, look in the Help file, accessed by pressing the F1 key on the keyboard.) Follow the steps to create a new user account for your computer.

You must have administrative access in order to create a new user account. Once the account is created, restart the machine and log on as the new user. Windows Speech Recognition can now be trained for the new user.

Note: In Chapter 7 is a discussion of the Advanced Speech Options. Within the Advanced Speech Options area is an option to add a second user file into the same Windows User Account. This is an advanced option, however, and not generally recommended. It is significantly easier, and less likely to have the unfortunate problem of one user dictating on another user's file, to make a new Windows User Account for each person.

Command Review

New WSR Commands:

Start Listening
Stop Listening
Show Speech Recognition
Hide Speech Recognition
Move Speech Recognition
What Can I Say?
Show Speech Options

Windows and Programs:
Show The Desktop
Switch to [*program or window name*]
Go to [*field name*]
Minimize That
Restore That
Close That
Press Alt Print Screen
Click Start (opens Start menu)

Selecting, Navigating and Clicking:
Go To [*word*]
Go After [*word*]
Move Down [7] (or other number)
Move Up [15]
Select Sentence
Select Last Word
Select Last [3] Words
Scroll Down [5]
Scroll Up [10]
Show Numbers
Click [*item*]
Select [*word*]
Undo That
Delete That
Go to the End of the Document
Go to the Start of the Document

Go to End of Sentence
Go to Beginning of Sentence
Go to End of Line
Go to End of Paragraph
New Paragraph
New Line
Copy
Paste
Print
Save

Correcting Text:
Correct [*word or words*]
Correct That
Spell It
Spell It Again

Keypress Commands:
Press a
Press Shift A
Press Capital B
Press C as in close
Press d as in daughter
Press Enter
Press End
Press Control Home

Notes:

CHAPTER 7
Working With Windows Speech Recognition

After training a user file, learning microphone commands, and how to dictate text and make corrections in WordPad with Windows Speech Recognition in the last chapter, Chapter 7 takes WSR further. Apply what you know about core instructions and the warm up exercise to WSR, use MouseGrid, learn the speech options, and use WSR with two essential Windows programs: Microsoft Word and Internet Explorer.

Core Instructions

These core instructions for speech recognition will increase recognition accuracy and help prevent injury. Get in the habit of following these few steps when using Windows SR.

1. Do a warm up exercise (2–5 minutes of generic practice, see below)
2. Take frequent sips of water
3. Take regular breaks (e.g., 5–10 minute break each hour)
4. Read the step before you do it (or plan ahead what you mean to say and do)
5. Make corrections as needed (but don't interrupt a sentence)

Start Windows Speech Recognition

Turn on Windows Speech Recognition by opening the Start menu and typing *speech*. Click on "Windows Speech Recognition". (If you set up Speech Recognition to start up automatically, as described on page 243, you can skip this step in the future.) When the Speech Recognition Bar appears in the top center of the screen, Windows SR is ready to go!

In This Chapter

✓ Core Instructions and Warm-Up Exercise
✓ Windows Speech Recognition Options Menu
✓ Adding a Word to the Speech Dictionary
✓ Clicking the mouse and MouseGrid
✓ Advanced Speech Options
✓ WSR and Microsoft Word
✓ Browsing the web with WSR and Internet Explorer
✓ 10 Exercises
✓ Frequently Asked Questions

Exercise 7.1 Dictate the Warm Up Exercise

DIRECTIONS: Click the microphone button or say **Start Listening** to turn on the microphone. Start WordPad by saying **Start** or **Click Start, WordPad, Enter.** Dictate the following exercise and leave your document open afterward. Items in bold are commands and should produce an action. Items in parentheses ( ) are for you to customize:

[Start Dictating]

Hello computer, are you ready to work today? **New Line**
I am using speech recognition software. **New Line**
Dictating is much faster than typing. **New Line**
(Dictate a favorite quote here.) **New Line**
(Your First Name) (Your Last Name) **New Paragraph, Stop Listening**

[Stop Dictating]

Make any needed corrections, and save your document as "Exercise 7.1".

Windows Speech Recognition Options Menu

With the command **Show Speech Options,** the main list of speech recognition options and features will open. (Right-clicking the mouse on the SR Bar will also open this list.)

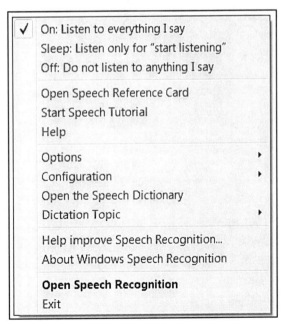

Using Speech Options

Turn on the microphone and say **Show Speech Options** (or press the right-mouse button over the SR Bar) and a context menu will open up similar to the one pictured. The first three options are **On, Sleep,** and **Off.** These refer to the status of the microphone. One of these will always be checked.

The second three options repeat those in the Speech Recognition Options window used in Chapter 6: they open the Speech Reference Card, the Speech Tutorial, and the Help file. (The Help file gives an overview of speech recognition information contained in other areas, and it also explains some terminology; for example, Windows SR calls a user file a "voice profile".)

Options

The **Options** item contains choices that allow the user to play audible feedback after making corrections, to have Windows SR run when the computer starts, to be able to speak the text in the Alternates Panel, and to enable the dictation scratchpad, also known as the Input Panel. The picture on the right shows the default settings. Turn any of these on by clicking on each one and waiting for the checkbox to appear. (If you change your mind later, you can always turn it back off.)

✓	Play audible feedback
	Run at startup
	Speak text in correction dialog
✓	Enable dictation scratchpad

What are the advantages to turning these options on?

Each of these options extends the functionality of Windows SR. If you like auditory feedback, you can turn this on. If you select "Run at startup" you won't have to turn Windows Speech Recognition on manually each time you wish to use it; it will be on already. If you check "Speak text in correction dialog" it will be possible to speak the words in the Alternates Panel, not just the numbers next to the items in the list. Finally, with "Enable dictation scratchpad" checked, the Input Panel will appear in useful locations, such as certain text boxes in web browsers.

Configuration

Configuration is an item which brings together the options that are designed to let users improve their recognition by setting up a microphone, performing additional training, and by opening the control panel for speech recognition.

Set up my microphone
Improve voice recognition
Open Speech Recognition Control Panel

Open the Speech Dictionary

Choosing **Open the Speech Dictionary** lets the user train a new word, which adds it to the user's speech dictionary (vocabulary) or train a word to ask the computer *not* to recognize. (Good for those who say "um" a lot or who tend to use choice language when frustrated!)

Help Improve Speech Recognition

The **Help Improve Speech Recognition** item opens a window which asks the user to choose to share information about the user's speech recognition with Microsoft. In this window, click "Send" if you choose to share information; otherwise, click "Don't Send".

About Windows Speech Recognition

The **About Windows Speech Recognition** item opens a window which displays the version of Windows and the Microsoft Speech Recognizer your computer is running. (In the Windows Vista version there is also a link to the Windows SR website, which has tutorials and other information.) The **Exit** item closes the program.

Open Speech Recognition

The **Open Speech Recognition** option has no action from the Speech Recognition Bar when the SR Bar is open on the desktop. When the Speech Recognition Bar is minimized, however, and a user clicks the Windows SR icon in the Taskbar, click this option to restore the SR Bar to its regular size.

A Work in Progress?

Windows SR is so new, that on the one hand it is impressive that it works as well as it does. On the other hand, it seems to be missing many features one might expect, such as the ability to train a command, or an option to switch between dictation modes. The **Dictation Topic** option in the list above doesn't seem to do anything, which suggests Microsoft put it there as a placeholder, to develop later.

My options don't look like the ones in this chapter—help!

If your speech recognition options menu is different, you probably have a different version of Windows Speech Recognition running on your computer. If you have Windows Vista, your options menu will be a little bit different.

Add a Word to the Speech Dictionary (or Remove One)

After spelling a word in the Spelling Panel, Windows SR will sometimes offer to add that word to the Speech Dictionary (the list of vocabulary). However, you can add a word to the Speech Dictionary anytime by saying **Show Speech Options** and then **Show Speech Dictionary**.

Exercise 7.2 The Speech Dictionary

DIRECTIONS: Follow the steps to add and remove a word from the Speech Dictionary.

Open the Speech Dictionary

1. Say **Show Speech Options**. The menu of options should open.
2. Say **Open the Speech Dictionary**. A window opens similar to the one pictured.

Add a New Word

3. Say **Add a New Word**, then say **Next**.
4. Type in the word you want to add to the dictionary. (Use a name of a place or a person; for example, Tahoe or Kayla.) Click or say **Next**.

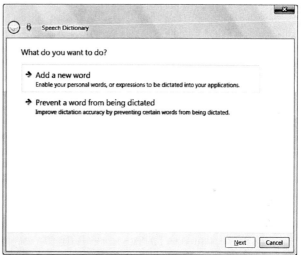

Train the New Word

5. In the following window select the option to record a pronunciation of the word (this is highly recommended).
6. If the word is sometimes or always capitalized, click or say the appropriate phrase. Click or say **Finish**.

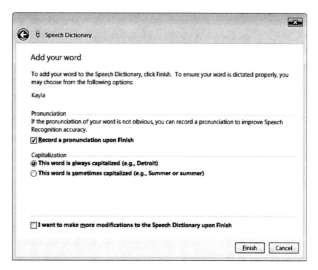

Exercise 7.2, Continued

7. In the next window, turn on the Windows SR microphone and record the pronunciation of the word.

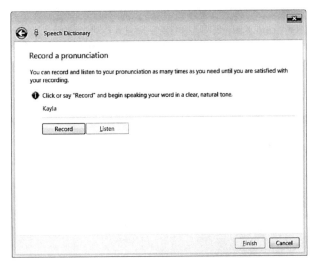

8. Say or click "Listen" to check the recording.

9. When the recording sounds acceptable, uncheck the box next to the option to make more modifications to the speech dictionary and click "Finish".

Remove a Word from the Speech Dictionary

10. Say **Show Speech Options** to open the menu of options.

11. Say **Open the Speech Dictionary**.

12. Say **Prevent a Word From Being Dictated**, then **Next**.

13. Type in the word you want to remove. (Use a nonsense word like "blahblah" if you don't have a word to remove.) Click or say **Next**.

14. The next screen confirms that the word will be removed from the speech dictionary. If it is correct, uncheck the box next to the option to make more modifications to the speech dictionary. Click or say **Finish**.

Document Your Work

15. Say **Start WordPad** and type or dictate a paragraph about adding and removing words from the Speech Dictionary. What word did you add, and what did you remove? Do you have difficulty with any particular word being dictated when you don't want it to appear? What did you find easy, and what was challenging, about this exercise?

16. Make any needed corrections to recognition.

Review: Save your paragraph as "Exercise 7.2" and print if needed.

Types of Speech Recognition Commands

There are four kinds of commands used in speech recognition: Correction, Control, Keypress, and Word Processing. These four types of commands (introduced in Chapter 2 for Dragon NaturallySpeaking) are also available in Windows Speech Recognition, just on a smaller scale as Windows SR has fewer commands (and very few alternate commands).

Command	Where Used	Examples
Correction	Anywhere text can be dictated	Correct [*word*], Correct That, Spell It
Control	In programs and on the desktop	Click File, Click Start, Scroll Down 6, Show Numbers
Keypress	Anywhere a keyboard command would work	Press Enter, Press Spacebar, Press Ctrl B, Press Ctrl E
Word Processing	Anywhere text could be typed or dictated	Caps [*word*], All Caps That, New Line, New Paragraph

Correction

Windows SR's two levels of correction, including the Alternates Panel and the Spelling Panel, were covered in Chapter 6. These include **Correct [*word*]**, **Correct That** and **Spell It.**

Control

A speech command to replace a mouse action is called a control command. Control commands are used to control the desktop, including the Start menu and windows. One example is saying **Click File** (or just **File**) to open the File menu in a program. **Show Numbers** and **MouseGrid** are specialized control commands which replace multiple mouse actions.

Keypress

Keypress commands are spoken versions of anything you can press using the keyboard. One example is saying **Press Enter** to activate the Enter key. Some keyboard commands can work without the word Press: **Spacebar**, **Tab**, and **Backspace**, for example. Keypress commands are especially useful with Windows SR in word processing and web browsing programs.

Word Processing

Word Processing commands are used for working within documents created by word processing programs. Some word processing programs that can be used with Windows Speech Recognition include Microsoft Word and WordPad. The category of word processing commands includes commands for editing, dictating text and numbers, capitalization and other formatting.

MouseGrid and Clicking the Mouse

Clicking the mouse by voice requires first having the pointer where you want it to be, then giving the correct command. Like Dragon NaturallySpeaking, moving the mouse pointer in Windows Speech Recognition is quickly accomplished with MouseGrid. Windows's MouseGrid looks a bit different, but it works in the same way. After giving a MouseGrid command, give the desired mouse action command.

Use the commands below to get started:

1. Say **MouseGrid** to bring up the grid, then focus on your target by saying the number in the grids until you are where you want to be.
2. Then say **Click, Double-click**, or **Right-click** to click the mouse.
3. To undo your last MouseGrid action, say **Undo That.**
4. To close MouseGrid, say **Cancel.**

For Example: **MouseGrid, 7, 7, 7 Click** (opens the Start menu)
MouseGrid 4, 4, 3, Double-Click
MouseGrid 5, 8, Right-Click
MouseGrid 2, 1, 3 Mark. MouseGrid 7, 2, Click (not Drag)

Exercise 7.3 MouseGrid

DIRECTIONS: Follow the steps to use MouseGrid with Windows Speech Recognition.

1. Get to where you can see the Taskbar and the Desktop. Notice the location of the Taskbar clock.
2. Say, **MouseGrid**. The grid appears.
3. Say **9**; the grid will shrink to cover the lower right corner of the screen.
4. Say the number closest to the clock, usually **9**.

Exercise 7.3, Continued

5. When the grid is on the clock, say the number and then say **Click**, and the mouse left click will occur. (**MouseGrid 9, 9, 9 Click** clicks the clock and usually shows a calendar.)

6. Choose another icon you can open, such as the Recycle Bin. Say **MouseGrid**, then the correct numbers until the focus is over the icon. Say **Double-Click** while the focus is on the icon and it will open.

7. Say **Close Window** to close the open icon window.

Move an Item with MouseGrid

Mouse Grid can be used to "click and hold" an item so that it can be moved to a different spot on your desktop. The commands for this are **Mark**, then **Click.**

8. Close or minimize any open windows so that you can see the Taskbar and the Desktop. Decide upon an icon you will move to another location on the desktop. (For example, the Recycle Bin.)

9. Say, **MouseGrid**. Say the numbers you need until the grid is over the icon.

10. Say **Mark**, and the mouse click and hold will occur.

11. Say **MouseGrid** and the correct numbers until the grid is over the new location. Say **Click**, and the icon should appear in the new location after a few seconds.

Move the Windows Speech Recognition Bar

12. Windows Speech Recognition Bar.

13. Repeat steps 8-10 to move the SR Bar to the upper-right corner of the desktop. (Refer to the instructions above as needed.)

Create a Screen Shot, Paste Into WordPad

14. Say **Press Print Screen** to take a screen shot of the desktop. Open WordPad and say **Press Control V** to paste the picture into word. Resize the screen shot manually, if desired.

15. Say **New Paragraph** or **Press Enter** to move below the picture. Dictate your name and the date.

Review: Are you feeling more comfortable moving between programs and pasting items? Do you find MouseGrid easier with Windows SR, since you have already learned to use it with Dragon NaturallySpeaking? Save your work as "Exercise 7.3" and print if needed.

Using Windows SR with Microsoft Word

Microsoft Word, with its advanced word processing features and ribbon interface, offers hundreds of options for document creation, layout, styling, formatting, and more. To access these features with Windows Speech Recognition requires trial and error to know which methods will work. When you want to use a feature, remember these techniques:

- Names of tabs (Home, Insert, etc.) can be spoken. This is most reliable with the command **Click** in front of the tab name, such as **Click View**.

- If the group has an icon for a dialog box (see picture at right), speak the name of the group to open the box. Some examples are **Click Font**, **Click Paragraph** and **Click Styles**.

- Speak the names of items in dialog boxes to move the focus to those items. Use commands like **Press Down Arrow** to move through a list box, and **Press Tab** to move among items in the dialog box or its options.

- For icons that don't have text titles, say **Show Numbers** to number them. Then, speak the number, and when it is selected, say **OK**. Watch the SR Bar's message area as you say **OK**—if there is a command that can be used with this icon, a message will say "Next time say [command]". For example, "Next time say **Clear Formatting**".

- If none of the above are successful, use MouseGrid to navigate to and activate an item.

- Finally, experiment! Many Windows Speech Recognition commands aren't documented in the Speech Reference Card. If you think a command might work, give it a try.

To Open Microsoft Word:
- From the desktop, say **Start Microsoft Word**. Wait 10 seconds for Word to open.

- If it does not, say Start to open the Start menu, then speak the exact text of the Microsoft Word item you see preceded by the word **Click** (for example, "Click Microsoft Word 2010").

Formatting Words, Numbers and Symbols

Windows Speech Recognition has commands for capitalization, spacing, dictating punctuation and symbols, and for dictating and auto-formatting numbers.

Capitalization and Spacing Commands

Caps [word] *or* **Select [word], Cap That**	To capitalize the first letter of a word or phrase
All Caps [word] *or* **Select [word], All Cap That**	To capitalize all letters in a word or phrase
[word] No Space [word]	To remove a space (i.e. FileMaker)
No Caps [word]	To remove capitalization

Exercise 7.4: Capitalization

DIRECTIONS: Read the explanation that accompanies the sentences below. Open Microsoft Word and dictate the indented text, adding formatting as directed. Make corrections, then save as "Exercise 7.4".

1. Say **Start Microsoft Word**. Wait 10 seconds for Word to open. If it does not, say **Start** to open the Start menu, then speak the exact text of the Microsoft Word item you see preceded by the word **Click** (for example, "Click Microsoft Word 2010").
2. When a new document opens, dictate your name, then **New Paragraph**.

The *Caps* Command

3. Use the **Caps** command before the word to be capitalized.

[Start Dictating]

> My friend Marty likes to be called **Caps** Spike. **New Line**
> He's a **Caps** Certified **Caps** Accountant. **New Paragraph**

[Stop Dictating]

Exercise 7.4, Continued

The *Cap That* and *All Cap That* Command—After Dictation

4. Dictate these sentences without the **Caps** command. Go back and select the words that need capitalization and say **Cap That** or **All Cap That**. Your sentences will then match the examples.

[Start Dictating]

> A Certified Public Accountant does my taxes.
>> Say, **Select Certified Public Accountant**, then, **Cap That**
>
> He's the one in the HOPE building downtown.
>> Say, **Select HOPE**, then say **All Cap That**.

[Stop Dictating]

To REMOVE caps, say No Caps [*word*]

5. When you see a word which should not be capitalized, say **No Caps [*word*]**.

[Start Dictating]

> He said it was time to Sally forth.
>> Say, **No Caps *Sally*.**
>> *Say, **New Paragraph** to move the insertion point down the page.*

[Stop Dictating]

Review: Turn off your microphone and check over your work. Did you notice how similar the capitalization commands are to the Dragon capitalization commands? Save your work as "Exercise 7.4". You can leave your Word document open and dictate the next exercise into the same document.

Exercise 7.5 Punctuation and Symbols

DIRECTIONS: Dictate these punctuation and symbols into your Microsoft Word document (pronunciations are also provided). Say **Tab** or **Press Tab** between each one. Say **Press Control S** after dictating this list to update your saved work. Save as "Exercise 7.5" and leave Word open for now.

Symbol	Say This...	Symbol	Say This...
,	Comma	}	Close curly bracket
;	Semicolon	[	Open bracket
.	Period; Dot; Decimal point	]	Close bracket
:	Colon	|	Vertical bar
"	Open quote	☺	Press smiley face
"	Close quote	☹	Press frowny face
'	apostrophe	;-)	Press winky face
'	Open single quote	¾	Three quarter sign
'	Close single quote	¼	One quarter sign
>	Greater than sign	½	One half sign
<	Less than sign	£	Pound sterling sign
/	Forward slash	&	Ampersand; and sign
\	Backslash	*	Asterisk
~	Tilde	//	Double slash
@	At sign	<	Open angle bracket
!	Exclamation mark; Exclamation point	>	Close angle bracket
		±	Plus or minus sign
?	Question mark	«	Open angle quote
#	Number sign; Pound sign	»	Close angle quote
		×	Multiplication sign
$	Dollar sign	÷	Division sign
%	Percent sign	¢	Cent sign
(	Open paren(thesis)	¥	Yen sign
)	Close paren(thesis)	§	Section sign
_	Underscore	©	Copyright sign
-	Hyphen; Minus sign	®	Registered sign
–	En dash	°	Degree sign
—	Em dash; Double dash	¶	Paragraph sign
=	Equal sign	...	Ellipsis; Dot dot dot
+	Plus sign	^	Caret
{	Open curly bracket		

Dictating Numbers

Windows Speech Recognition will auto-format many number uses, such as:

- Numbers 10 and under as words (seven, not 7) when they are in a sentence
- Numbers over 10 as numerals
- Money, including cents
- Time, including phrases such as "a quarter after"
- Dates and addresses
- Phone numbers

Exercise 7.6 Numbers and Number Formats

DIRECTIONS: Dictate the following numbers and commands into a Word document.

Numbers 1–9

DIRECTIONS: Practice dictating numbers 1-10. For the number 1, say **Numeral 1**. Give a brief pause and say **Spacebar** or **Press Spacebar** between each one.

[Start Dictating]

> 1 2 3 4 5 6 7 8 9 **New Line**

[Stop Dictating]

DIRECTIONS: Now try sentences that use numbers 1–10. Notice that the numbers will be spelled out as words. (If they are not, correct them.)

[Start Dictating]

> I will be taking four classes next semester. Last semester I took two classes. I also volunteer for six hours a week. **New Line**

[Stop Dictating]

Exercise 7.6, Continued

Numbers 10–99

DIRECTIONS: Numbers 10–99 are dictated exactly the way you usually say them. Dictate these numbers between 10–99 (say **Space**, **Spacebar** or **Press Spacebar** to put a space between each one):

[Start Dictating]

14 21 28 35 42 49 56 63 70 77 **New Line**

[Stop Dictating]

Larger Numbers

Dictate these numbers as you would usually speak them (for example, "Two thousand, eight hundred and fifty-one").

DIRECTIONS: Dictate these larger numbers. Say **Tab** or **Press Tab** to get tabs between them:

[Start Dictating]

439   2,851 3,765,842   14,980   **New Line**

[Stop Dictating]

Dates

Dates are dictated auto-formatted—no need to say punctuation.

DIRECTIONS: Dictate these dates. Say **Tab** after each.

[Start Dictating]

September 16, 1810   May 8, 1945   The 1960s **New Line**

[Stop Dictating]

Exercise 7.6, Continued

Telephone Numbers

Telephone numbers can be dictated quickly and easily if you speak the number in a smooth, continuous way, especially if you use the area code. Phone numbers will auto-format like this: (800)-475-5767.

DIRECTIONS: Dictate the telephone numbers below. Say **Tab** after each.

[Start Dictating]

      (408)-728-9394   (831)-477-6379   Try your phone number!

[Stop Dictating]

Dictating Money

Dictate money as you would normally speak it (for example, "thirteen dollars and seventy-five cents").

DIRECTIONS: Dictate these amounts (say **Tab** after each):

[Start Dictating]

     $4.25 $13.75 $288.09   24¢   **New Line**

[Stop Dictating]

Talking About Time

The time of day is dictated as it is normally spoken.

DIRECTIONS: Dictate times of day, saying **Tab** between each item.

[Start Dictating]

      9:30 ("nine colon thirty")   6:42 PM ("six forty-two pm")
      3:15 ("a quarter after 3")   10:25 AM ("ten twenty five am")
      11:00 ("eleven o'clock")   12:00 PM ("twelve o'clock noon")

[Stop Dictating]

Exercise 7.6, Continued

Addresses

To dictate a postal address, try to dictate it as you would a telephone number—that is, smoothly and continuously. If you do this, the address will likely be formatted properly.

DIRECTIONS: Dictate addresses as smoothly and continuously as you can.

[Start Dictating]

> 1280 Oak St. Los Angeles, CA 31050
>
> Now dictate your home or work address!

[Stop Dictating]

Review: Was that pretty easy, or were there some items that still are challenging for you? Save your Exercise 7.6 (say **Press Control S**) and print if needed. Get a new blank document before continuing.

Speaking Commands in Microsoft Word

Microsoft Office Word is a full-featured word processor which works well with Windows Speech Recognition. Word 2010 and 2007 organize the word processing features into groups of icons within tabs in the Ribbon interface. Earlier versions of Microsoft Word use menus and toolbar icons to access features. Unlike menus, which are opened by saying the menu's name and then the menu item, icons and groups in the Ribbon are selected one of three ways:

1. Dictate keypress commands (such as **Press Control B** to bold selected text).
2. Say the name of the tab where the feature is located, then say **Show Numbers**. Say the correct number, and when it is highlighted, say **OK**.
3. Discover commands! When saying **OK**, as in the previous step, watch the SR Bar's message area—if there is a command that can be used with this icon, a message will say "Next time say [command]". For example, "Next time say **Bold**".

Method 1: Use Keypress Commands

Select a sentence, paragraph or other unit. Use keypress commands (what you would press on the keyboard, but spoken instead) for best results.

To use keypress commands to make text bold, say **Press Control B**. For italics, say **Press Control I**, and for underlining, say **Press Control U**.

Method 2: Use Show Numbers

When you are not sure what command to use, say **Show Numbers**, and all items on the page are numbered. Say the number of the item you want, then **OK** to select it.

To change the font size, for example from size 12 to 14, select the text you want to change (all, or a sentence, paragraph or other unit). Say **Show Numbers** and look for the number over the item you want.

Say the number, for example, **33** (to select the icon over the font size box—yours may be different) then say **OK** to select it, **Press Down Arrow** (to open the list), then say **14**.

Method 3: Discover Commands!

To discover a command (so that you don't have to rely on **Show Numbers** for most actions), read the helpful command information in the message area of the SR Bar and, if you like, write it down for future reference.

For example, to change the line spacing (to make some text double spaced, for example), say **Show Numbers**. When the numbers appear, locate the one over the line spacing icon in the Paragraph group on the Home tab.

Say the number, then say **OK**. The SR Bar will tell you the command needed to get to this box in the future. (See the example on the next page.)

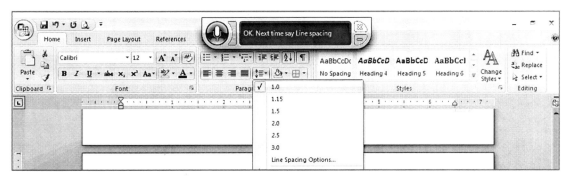

Note: The message in the SR Bar says "OK. Next time say **Line spacing**".

Within the line spacing menu, speak the item you want (for example, say "one point five" for 1.5 line spacing) and say **Press Enter** if needed to activate them. If you aren't sure how to speak a menu item, you can say **Show Numbers** again, and the list of items will be numbered.

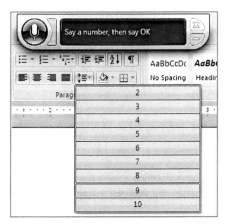

When you have discovered commands for yourself, write them down! This will save time later.

However, if you don't have a command handy that you need, don't hesitate to say **Show Numbers** again and discover for yourself what to say.

Practice using these three methods in Exercises 7.7, 7.8, and 7.9.

Exercise 7.7 Format Text in Microsoft Word and Discover a Command

DIRECTIONS: Follow the steps to format text style, size, and capitalization. In step 12, discover a command. In step 13, manually type that command. When dictating a command, such as **Save** or **Underline**, numbered options may appear. Speak the correct number, then say **OK**.

1. Turn your microphone on and Start Microsoft Word.

Dictate and Correct Text

2. Dictate (compose) three simple sentences, saying **New Line** between each. Make any needed corrections to recognition.

Exercise 7.7, Continued

3. Say **New Paragraph.** Dictate your name, say **New Line** and dictate today's date.

Save Your Work Now

4. Say **Save** or **Press Control S** to open the Save As dialog box, and save your work as "Exercise 7.7".

Move the Insertion Point and Select Text

5. Put the insertion point in the first sentence with a command like **Go to [*word*]**, filling in the blank with the first word of your first sentence. Or, say **Go to Top**.
6. Say **Select Sentence**. The first sentence should now be selected.

Underline the First Sentence

7. Say **Underline** or **Press Control U** to make the first sentence underlined.

Bold the Second Sentence

8. Select the second sentence. Say **Bold** or **Press Control B** to make it bold.

Italicize the Third Sentence

9. Select the third sentence. Italicize it by saying **Italics** or **Press Control I**.

Select Paragraph and Indent

10. Select the three sentences with the command **Select Paragraph**.
11. Use the **Show Numbers** command to select the icon (in the Paragraph group) to make the text indented.

Discover A Command

12. Watch the SR Bar display the command to do this directly in the future—and write down the command.

Document Your Work

13. Place the insertion point in a new paragraph.

Exercise 7.7, Continued

14. Dictate this sentence: "The command to make the text indented is [*type in command*]." Instead of [*type in command*], manually type in the words of the command. (Don't dictate it or Windows SR will perform the action!)

15. Say **Save** or **Press Control S** to update the document's save.

16. Print if needed by saying **Print** or **Press Control P**. Close the document.

Review: How did it work for you? Were the three methods—keypress command, Show Numbers and command discovery—equally easy for you? If not, review the instructions and plan to practice any difficult areas in the exercises that follow. Below are commands for the Font group in the Home tab.

FONT GROUP COMMANDS: From top to bottom, left to right, here they are: **Font, Font size, Grow Font, Shrink Font, Clear Formatting, Bold, Italics, Underline, Strikethrough, Subscript, Superscript, Change Case, Text Highlight Color** and **Font Color**. Saying **Font** also opens the Font dialog box. (Yours may vary.)

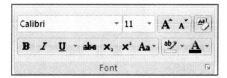

About Exercise 7.8

In the following exercise, use Microsoft Word to create a simple resume. This resume can be composed of your real information, which would make it more useful to you, or it can be made-up information, which is best if you have privacy concerns. However, the more realistic you make the resume, the better the exercise will be.

The exercise requires all capital letters, address and phone number formatting, and other elements covered in this chapter. Feel free to look back through the chapter for assistance.

Exercise 7.8: Create a Basic Resume in Word

DIRECTIONS: Open a new document in Microsoft Word. First, dictate resume information in the format below. Second, correct any recognition errors. Finally, add formatting as needed; do this as much by voice as possible. Make your name **Bold.** If you have difficulty thinking of what to type or how to format the information, look for examples in Word or on the Internet. Save your work as "Exercise 7.8".

[Start Dictating]

NAME

Street Address
City, State Zip

Phone Number
e-mail address

OBJECTIVE
    Type of position desired

EDUCATION
    Degree, School, Date

EXPERIENCE
    Position, Name of Employer, Dates of Employment (list most recent first)
        Primary Duties (one or two sentences or bullet points)
    Position, Name of Employer, Dates of Employment
        Primary Duties (one or two sentences or bullet points)

ADDITIONAL INFORMATION
(Any special skills, references available upon request statement, etc.)

[Stop Dictating]

Review: Save your work as "Exercise 7.8" after making any needed corrections. Print your exercise and look it over—is the formatting what you expected? Would you change anything next time? This is one of the last exercises in this book, and one of the most challenging for many students of speech recognition. How did it go for you? Did you find yourself needing to use the mouse or keyboard, or were you able to do most of the work by voice?

262

Exercise 7.9: Create a Form Letter with Formatting

DIRECTIONS: Dictate the following text (without formatting), make corrections, then save as "Exercise 7.9". Return to your document and make the formatting changes as shown. If you have difficulty remembering the commands you need, use the **Show Numbers** command to guide you.

[Start Dictating]

(Today's Month Day Year)

Angela Taylor
756 Walnut St.
Sacramento, CA 95043

Dear Ms. Taylor:

Have you ever thought about learning to type with your voice? We at Speech Recognition Pro Training would like to tell you why you should consider learning **speech recognition software** with us! Here are some reasons why you should choose us for your speech recognition training needs:

<u>Convenience</u>! Our trainings are available anytime at our website.

<u>Affordability</u>! The cost of this 10 lesson course is only $1200. After a payment of one half of the total, or $600, you will receive access to the first two lessons. After that, make **monthly payments** of $75 and get access to one lesson each month until you have completed them all.

<u>Support</u>! We are here for you. E-mail us your questions, or call us at 800-455-2681 between 10 AM and 5 PM Eastern time, Monday through Friday, and we will be happy to answer any questions you may have.

<u>Experience</u>! We have been in the distance education field for over five years! Please call today; we can't wait to hear from you!

Sincerely,

Michael Edwards, Director of Marketing
1285 Mission Dr.
Lancaster, CA 96752   **[Stop Dictating]**

Review: This challenging exercise uses many of the word processing skills described in this chapter. Save your work as "Exercise 7.9" and print if needed. Close Microsoft Word.

Using Windows SR with Internet Explorer

Internet Explorer (IE) is a Windows-native program, which means that Windows SR will work with it. However, only a few commands are available for use with IE, and those are commands designed to work with all windows; for example, **Scroll Down**, **Scroll Up**, and **Click Close**. Text can be dictated within form fields, but it is difficult to dictate into the address bar. Try these and see!

Say This	To Do This
Name of Link, or **Show Numbers**	Select links, including image links, on a web page
Show Numbers	Use to select form fields and most toolbar icons, select tabs, the address bar, etc.
Back, Forward, Home, Favorites	Go back a page, forward a page, go to the home page and click Favorites
Scroll Down 3, Scroll Up 5, etc.	To move down and up pages
Press Control Home	To move to the top of a page
Address	Go to the Address field
Page, Tools, File, etc.	Open their menus, speak items in list

Note: Windows SR works with some other browsers, such as Mozilla Firefox, but in more limited ways. Menu names and items can be spoken, but **Show Numbers** works only intermittently. If you use another browser, you are encouraged to experiment with it to see how Windows SR works with it.

About Exercise 7.10

In the exercise on the next page, use the commands given in the table above to move around a web page using WSR and Internet Explorer. If you have problems, say **Show Numbers** and select the number of the item you wish to activate.

Exercise 7.10

DIRECTIONS: Move around a web page using commands in this exercise.

1. Say **Start Internet Explorer**. Wait 10 seconds for it to start. If it does not, say **Click Start**, then **Internet Explorer**. (You may have to say **All Programs** if you don't see it in the Start menu right away.)

2. Internet Explorer will open. Look over the page.

3. Say **Scroll Down 2** (or, **Move Down 2**). Notice how far the page moves.

4. Say **Scroll Down 10**. Again, notice how far the page scrolls with this command.

5. Now, return the page to the top by saying **Scroll Up 12**.

6. Select a link on the page by saying its name. (Choose a simple text link.)

7. The new page should load. If it does not, say **Show Numbers**, say the number of the link you want, and say **OK**.

8. Repeat Step 6, choosing a different link this time.

9. Say **Click Back**. The browser should return to the previous page.

10. Say **Click Forward**. The browser should move forward one page.

11. Say **Click Home**. The browser should display the home page (the first one).

12. Say **Click Close** to close Internet Explorer. Say **Stop Listening**. The microphone should go to sleep.

13. Write a reflection of this exercise and print if needed.

At davidpogue.com: Using "Show Numbers" to shop for books

Review: Did this work well for you? Would you want to navigate web pages using WSR, or use the mouse and keyboard to do this? As you may recall from the discussion of using the web by voice in Chapter 5, this is one area where people who do not need a hands-free experience often work manually. Dictating email and web addresses can be especially tricky.

Command Review

Windows Speech Recognition commands in this chapter:

Show Speech Options	New Paragraph	Paste
Show Numbers	Go to [*word*]	Click Close
Correct [*word*]	Select Sentence	Close Window
Correct That	Select Paragraph	
Spell It	Press Control S	
Click File		
Press Enter	**Font Group**	
MouseGrid	**Commands**	
Double-click	Font	
Right-click	Font Size	
Mark	Grow Font	
Click	Shrink Font	
Click View	Clear Formatting	
Click Font	Bold	
Press Down Arrow	Italics	
Press Tab	Underline	
Clear Formatting	Strikethrough	
Caps [*word*]	Subscript	
Select [*word*]	Superscript	
Cap That	Change Case	
All Caps [*word*]	Text Highlight Color	
All Cap That	Font Color	
No Space		
No Caps	**Internet Explorer**	
Numeral 1	Scroll Up [*number*]	
Bold	Scroll Down [*number*]	
Press Control B	Back	
Underline	Forward	
Press Control U	Home	
Italicize	Favorites	
Press Control I	Press Control Home	
Line Spacing	Address	
Click Start	Tools	
New Line	Delete	
	Press Control V	

CHAPTER 8

8

Special Issues and Advanced Features

Ergonomics

Ergonomics is a critical, but often overlooked, area of computing. People who can tell you how fast their computer's processor is, and which version of each software they have, often have no idea about the state of their ergonomic set up. This may be because personal computing is still relatively new, or perhaps it has to do with the downplaying of possible injuries that exists in many computer fields.

Often, computer users come to speech recognition because of an injury caused in part by an ergonomic problem, whether it is due to poor positioning or overuse. However, speech recognition doesn't solve all of these problems, and it has its own ergonomic considerations as well.

Ergonomics and Speech Recognition

Speech recognition solves some computer use issues, and creates others. While computer users are no longer tied to a keyboard, and thus need not consider proper keyboarding position as stringently, it is also true that wearing a headset microphone can affect trunk position (it's easier to slouch back in your chair when your hands don't have to reach the keyboard), head and neck position, and other posture. Finally, there is a risk of strain to the vocal chords as the repetitive activity of speaking into a microphone is substituted for the repetitive activity of typing.

A good resource for information about computer workstation ergonomics, including photos of good working positions, is the U.S. government's OSHA

In This Chapter

- ✓ Ergonomics and Speech Recognition
- ✓ General Ergonomics
- ✓ Avoid Overuse Injury
- ✓ Troubleshooting
- ✓ Installing and Uninstalling Dragon
- ✓ Create a New User In Windows
- ✓ Advanced Dragon Skills
- ✓ User Profile on a USB Storage Device
- ✓ Import/Export a User Profile
- ✓ Command Browser
- ✓ Dragon Options
- ✓ Digital Recorders
- ✓ Other Issues and Resources

Ergonomic Solutions E-Tool site. Access this at:
http://www.osha.gov/SLTC/etools/computerworkstations/positions.html. The next
section discusses ergonomic body position from head to toes.

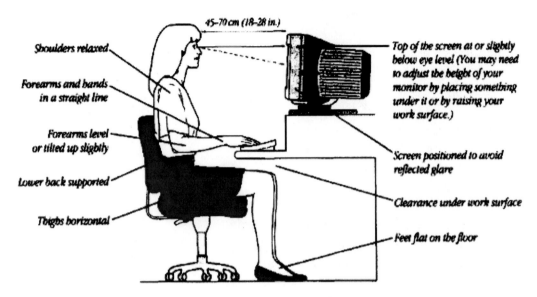

This illustration of computer ergonomics courtesy of Assistive Technology Network, a project of the
California Department of Rehabilitation.

General Ergonomic Principles

Use a healthy, neutral body position to prevent injury to the fullest extent possible.
Examine your mouse, keyboard, monitor and workspace furniture to see if they are
working in the best interests of your ergonomic positioning.

Good Body Position—90–90–90

Use good body position—beginning with your feet and working upward. Feet should
touch the floor, and ankles, knees and hips should be bent at 90 degree angles (this is
often referred to as 90–90–90). Your back should touch the back of the chair, and
your lower back should feel supported by the chair.

Try to avoid slumping as it will push your shoulders forward and cave in your torso.
Arms should be at your side, with elbows or forearms comfortably supported, if
possible. If your torso isn't stable, your upper body can't hold a proper position
either.

Keyboard Position

Even if you plan to rarely touch the keyboard or mouse and use speech recognition instead, it is useful to know correct keyboard or mouse position for those times when you must use them. Keyboard trays or desks (wherever your keyboard and mouse sit) are often too high for correct ergonomics. Elbows should be at a 90 degree angle or greater, never less. Wrists should be held parallel over the keyboard firmly, in "piano player" position. If needed, wrists can be gently supported, with a gel wrist rest or similar item, rather than slumping downward over the keyboard.

Not Recommended
Ergonomic Positioning

Hands should rest comfortably on the keys when typing does occur, with a minimum of strain with reaches. Often this means lowering a keyboard tray to a position that can feel as though the tray is sitting on your lap. In fact, some people find that they get a better ergonomic position when they put the keyboard on their lap, but this is trickier for a mouse! Finally, some experts recommend a keyboard without a number keypad to reduce the distance of reaches to some keys and to bring the mouse closer.

On Mice

The mouse is difficult to use ergonomically. For one thing, the nature of computing requires a high volume of mouse clicking, which uses muscles in repetitive ways that can be unhealthy. Add to this the shape of mice—often the wrist is put in a bent position—and problems are not far behind.

One solution is to use a trackball, or a foot-activated mouse, but this still risks injury. Clicking the mouse by voice takes the burden off one's hands or feet, but can cause other problems.

Another option is a head pointer, which lets a person select where to click on the screen by wearing a reflective dot or strip on the face or head which is detected by a receiver that sits on top of a monitor. The downside is that the device is slower than clicking by voice, requires practice, and is expensive.

The Popular Kensington
Programmable Trackball

To investigate mice and mouse alternatives, seek the expertise of an occupational therapist or experienced assistive technology specialist, and gather information from websites which feature mouse alternatives, such as enablemart.com.

Monitor Position

Consider the position of your monitor. It should be directly in front of you, not off to the side. The height should be such that when you look directly at the monitor

with your eyes focused straight ahead, you should be looking at the upper third of the monitor.

You should not have to bend your neck to look up at the screen or down at the lower part of the screen. (If you notice yourself raising or lowering your chin when you look at the monitor, watch out for neck strain.)

A recipe for neck strain!

Furniture

Take a good look at the chair you use. Most office furniture is designed for a person who is 5 feet 10 inches tall—which means that most women and many men will

need to adjust the chair downward, and possibly lower their desk or keyboard tray.

An alternate approach is to use a footrest to bring up your foot height. This may eliminate the need to lower the desk or keyboard tray and the monitor.

Footrest
(pumps optional)

Avoid Overuse Injury

Avoid overuse injury by following the healthy practices below.

Take Frequent Breaks

Every half hour or so, take a few minutes to walk around, raise and lower your shoulders, stretch your neck, and focus your eyes at a distance.

If you find this hard to do (you are so busy, after all!), think of little tasks you can accomplish at the same time. Walking to the printer is a little break, as is getting the mail. Maybe it's time for hot tea?

Or, some writers use the break time to focus their thoughts before sitting back down to write. You will find what works best for you if you experiment a little.

Take Frequent Mini-Breaks, Too

Even if you continue working (composing, reading, etc.,) take frequent breaks in your body position. Try dictating while standing if you usually sit. Try leaning back in your chair, or forward. Close your eyes while dictating to give them a little rest. (Dragon's dictation mode is useful if you are dictating without looking at the screen.)

Keep Your Vocal Chords Healthy

Take sips of water frequently while dictating and avoid speaking loudly or whispering when using a microphone. If you have a cold or a sore throat, you probably ought to reduce the amount of time you spend dictating.

Protect Those Peepers

Keep your eyes at their best by pausing to refocus across the room or out a window about every ten minutes. Glare can cause eyestrain, so look to see where your lighting is coming from and adjust it if needed. Light coming from behind which shines directly on the monitor surface causes the most glare and should be avoided.

Don't Tough It Out

It is far too easy to tell yourself that you will deal with an ergonomic problem when you get a minute. That minute is now. If you feel pain or stiffness, or parts of your body go to sleep while you are working, something needs to change. If you can't figure it out by yourself, get some help to diagnose your ergonomic need and fix it.

True Stories

People who have not been injured by overuse or computer workstations with poorly designed ergonomics may not understand how important it is to pay attention to pain signals that your body may be sending. However, those of us who have been injured wish that we had paid attention. Many students have told me that they wish they had **just stopped doing what they were doing when it hurt**— before they were too injured to continue. You only have one body, and you must practice good self-care.

Troubleshooting

There are some common problems in working with speech recognition. Some are caused by the computer's hardware, some by software, and some by other factors. Sometimes it is helpful to know what is causing a problem, but really, sometimes it is more important to know what to do about the problem. (Always restart your computer once each day you use it.)

Here are some suggestions for what to do when things go wrong.

Problem: Everything has suddenly slowed to a crawl, or frozen, or recognition has very suddenly become terrible.

 Try This:

Close speech recognition and restart following the steps below.

1. See if you can save your work before doing anything else. Turn off your microphone, if possible.
2. Close your speech recognition program with these methods. (Allow a minute for the method to work before moving to the next one.):
    a. Click "Exit" from the NaturallySpeaking menu, or click the close box (X) on the Windows SR bar.
    b. Press Alt+F4 (closes open program windows).
    c. Press Ctrl+Alt+Delete and click on the "Task Manager" button. Select an application, such as speech recognition, from the list and click on "End Task".
    d. If nothing works, press the power button on the computer and hold it down until the computer turns off.
3. Shut down the computer, wait at least one minute, then restart.

This process might cure the problem if it is due to a temporary glitch. Temporary glitches do happen, and often closing the program and restarting the computer is all it takes for things to work well again. However, some situations tend to pose more problems than others.

If you are dictating a long document, over 20 pages or so, you might get better recognition and faster processing if you break your long document into several shorter ones. Alternately, you could dictate a few pages at a time, then copy and paste them into the larger document.

Problem: Your speech recognition isn't *terrible*, but it isn't very good, either.

 Try This:

1. In Dragon NaturallySpeaking, go to the Accuracy Center (in the Tools menu) and choose the link that says "Which Tool to Use First?" and work from there. This will offer you options for more training, checking the audio levels, etc. One recommended tool is the Acoustic Optimizer. It should be set to run at a time when you do not need to use your computer, as the Optimizer is very resource intensive.

2. In Windows Speech Recognition, you can perform more training. To do this, right-click on the SR bar, choose "Configuration", then "Improve voice recognition".

Problem: Your user file, which used to work fine, hardly works at all!

 Try This:

1. Think back over the last few weeks. Did anything unusual happen with your computer? For example, did you install any new software that might be using a lot of memory that speech recognition needs to work well? Or, have you been having problems with other programs as well?

2. Consider your maintenance schedule. Is it time to run cleaning or defragmenting utilities, and update and run a scan using your anti-virus and anti-spyware software? If you don't do these regularly, you will have problems. (If you want to automate these processes, you can set them up to run at a particular time each day or each week.)

3. Are you trying to run too many programs while using speech recognition? Because speech recognition requires a lot of memory (RAM), it is important

to not run too many other programs which compete for RAM with your speech recognition.

4. Unplug your microphone, and plug it back in. Sometimes this helps. Also, look at the control panels that have setting for audio, speech and sound. If you aren't familiar with these control panels, you may not be able to tell if there is a problem, but it is worth a try.

5. Do you have a cold, or has anything about your speech changed? Remember: Never try to chew gum, suck lozenges, or eat and dictate—it just doesn't work.

6. Do some additional training to recalibrate your user file. Then, restart the computer, start speech recognition, and do some simple practice sentences in a DragonPad or WordPad document. If you are still having significant problems, create a new user file and train it. Then, delete the old one.

If none of these steps work, you will need to do some serious fixing. For Dragon NaturallySpeaking, this involves uninstalling and reinstalling the software. For Windows SR, you can't do this unless you reinstall Windows, but you can create a new user profile on the machine (from the User Accounts control panel) and train Windows SR there.

Uninstalling Dragon NaturallySpeaking

To uninstall Dragon NaturallySpeaking, go to the Start menu and select the Control Panel. From the Control Panel, look for an item that says "Uninstall a program." Depending upon your version of Windows and how your control panel is displayed, you may instead select an "Add/remove programs" item, or a "Programs" item. Once the Uninstall window is open, select Dragon NaturallySpeaking from the list of installed programs and click the button or link which says "uninstall" or "remove".

Make needed choices in any windows that uninstall or remove your program. A window will appear asking if you want to save the user files. If you want to keep the user files, choose this option. After you have uninstalled Dragon NaturallySpeaking, restart your computer before reinstalling it.

Installing and Activating Dragon NaturallySpeaking

Installing Dragon Naturally Speaking is usually fairly straightforward. To install Dragon NaturallySpeaking, put the disk into the CD/DVD drive in your computer. A window appears asking if you want to install Dragon NaturallySpeaking. Follow the instructions in the windows, entering your product serial number when prompted. Click "Next" as needed until the program installation is complete. Remove the disk from the drive and restart the computer.

After Dragon NaturallySpeaking has been installed, it must be activated. Usually, you can run and close the program five times before it requires activation. To activate Dragon, the computer needs an active connection to the Internet. When the window appears asking for activation, the easiest option is to click the "Activate Automatically" option. If your computer does not connect to the Internet, you will need to call Nuance to activate Dragon. (Use the phone number on the box your product came in.)

Create a New User In Windows

To create a new user profile, go to the Control Panel and look for an item that says "User Accounts". Inside of this area is usually a link to "Add a User Account". (The exact wording may vary—if you have difficulty finding this area, look in the Help file, accessed by pressing the F1 key on the keyboard.) Follow the steps to create a new user account for your computer. You must have administrative access in order to create a new user account. Once the account is created, restart the computer and log on as the new user. Windows Speech Recognition can now be trained for the new user.

Advanced Dragon Skills

What follows are options for backing up a user by importing and exporting a user file. If you aren't very comfortable working with your computer, you might want to get the help of a knowledgeable friend the first time you do any of these items.

Store a User Profile on a Removable Storage Device or Network Storage

When working with Dragon NaturallySpeaking on a home computer, you store your user profile on your computer's hard drive. However, if you are training your Dragon Profile at work or in a college computer lab, you may not be able to store your user profile on the local machine—or it might be inconvenient to do so.

User profiles can be set up to run from a USB storage device (flash drive, removable hard drive, etc.) by following the directions below. (Some versions of Dragon also allow you to designate a network storage location for your user profile.) To use this option, you must 1) remember to attach your USB device **before** starting the Dragon software, and 2) train the user profile with the USB device attached.

Create, Store and Use A User Profile on a USB Storage Device

Follow these Steps:

1. Attach the USB storage device to the computer you will be training. When the device is ready to use, go to the next step.

2. From the **DragonBar**, click the **Profile** menu.

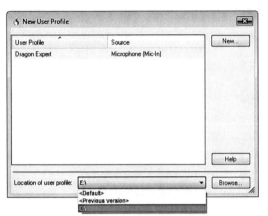

3. In the **Profile** menu, choose "New User Profile".

4. The **New User Profile** window opens.

5. Click the list box next to the words "Location of User Profile". A list of choices will open (see example at left).

6. From the menu of choices, select the location of your USB storage device (or network folder, if your computer is configured for this).

Note: "Default" is the storage location in the computer's hard drive. The option you are looking for will have a drive letter higher than "C" such as "E:\" as pictured in the example at left.

7. After you have selected the correct location, click the "New" button in the window to begin creating your new user profile.

8. Follow the steps to create a user profile (see the instructions beginning on page 9) and train a profile as usual.

9. No additional changes will be needed, except for the connection of the USB drive before starting Dragon each time you use the computer. (Therefore, it is critical that you do not lose the flash drive, or you will need to retrain a user profile.) You may also want to maintain a backup copy of your user profile.

10. Finally, do not remove your USB storage device until you have saved your user profile at the end of your Dragon session and closed the program. Be sure to eject the drive safely (don't just pull it out of the USB port). If you need information about safe removal of flash drives, search the Windows Help (press F1).

Trouble?

If these instructions do not work for you, the two most likely problems are: 1) you have a version of Dragon which does not allow this feature, or 2) the computer system may not be configured to allow this setup.

How much storage space do I need on a USB device?

The device needs to have sufficient storage space available, and a dedicated device may be best (buy a USB flash drive and use it only for this purpose). In informal tests, 2 GB of storage seems sufficient, but a 4 or 8 GB flash drive allows more space for storing data.

Backing Up A User—Exporting and Importing a User File

A user file gets better as you use it and make corrections. After putting significant time and energy into your user file, you should back it up in case it should ever become corrupted or your hard drive should stop working. (Having a regular system for backing up your saved documents and other items is highly recommended.)

While Dragon offers choices called "backup" and "restore", these work with the default storage location on your hard drive. It is preferable is **export** and **import** the user file because a copy is stored in a new location—just as you don't store copies of your important papers with your originals, it is a good idea to store backup copies of your user file somewhere other than in your computer's hard drive.

Another reason to back up a user file is to transfer it to another computer. This can work quite well, but as each machine has its own specific "machine noise" it may be equally effective to start over with a new user file (which is exactly what Windows SR requires you to do). Exporting and importing only work with Dragon NaturallySpeaking. To learn how to export and import Dragon user files, follow the directions below.

Exporting a User File

When you export a user file, you choose a location to copy the user file to. It does not get removed from the original location. First, open Dragon NaturallySpeaking and choose "Manage User Profile" from the Profile menu. Then click on the item on the right side of the window that says "Advanced" and choose "Export."

In the window that opens, **browse to the location** where you want to store the copy of the user file. An external hard drive is a good choice, in case the main hard drive should stop working. However, if you don't have an external hard drive, you could choose a **USB flash drive**. In a networked environment, you could back up the user file to a network storage area.

When you have chosen the backup location, click "Export", and copying of the file will begin. When it is finished, the window will close.

Importing a User File

To import a user file, open Dragon NaturallySpeaking and choose "Manage Users" from the Profile menu. Click on the button on the right side of the window that says "Advanced" and choose "Import".

In the window that opens, browse to the location where you have stored the backup copy of the user file. Remember, you must have export the user profile in order to have it available for importing—Dragon doesn't do it automatically.

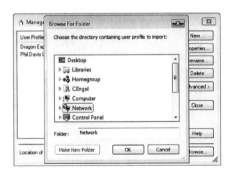

When you have chosen the location, click "Import", and the file will be imported. When it is finished, the window will close. In the list of users, you will see the user profile with the name it was given originally.

When you first open the imported user profile, Dragon will display a window that states that the user has not completed general training and that it needs to be done before the user profile can be used. Doing this training helps the user file calibrate to the new machine.

Working With Dragon's Options

Dragon organizes many of its options in the Options dialog box, which is found in the Tools menu of DragonPad. To open this area, say **Click Tools**, then **Click Options**, and then speak the name of the tab you wish to work in.

Correction Tab

This tab opens on top when the Options window is opened. The first four checkboxes let users set options about the **Select, Correct,** and **Spell** commands.

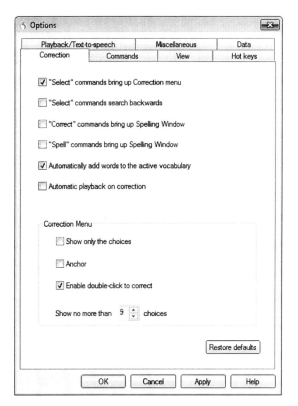

"Select" commands bring up Correction menu

This box makes the Correction box come up whenever you use a **Select** command. Turning off this option makes it impossible to say **Select** [*wrong word*] and then choose from the correction box. You can, however, still say **Select** [*wrong word*] and then say the correct word to replace what was selected.

"Select" commands search backwards

When this box is checked, **Select** and **Select Again** commands look for selected text backward from the insertion point.

"Correct" commands bring up Spell dialog box

If you prefer the Spelling box to come up when you say a Correct command, check this box.

"Spell" commands bring up Spell dialog box

For the Spelling box to come up when you say a **Spell** or **Spell That** command, check this box.

Automatically add words to the active vocabulary

When you correct a word, it can be added to your vocabulary automatically if this box is checked.

Automatic playback on correction

Set this option to have speech played back to you automatically when you make a correction.

Automatically add words to the vocabulary

If you would like to automatically add corrected words to your Dragon vocabulary, click this.

The Correction Menu Box

Show only the choices

To display *only* the correction options, and not the commands that usually appear underneath, check this box.

Anchor

The Correction box usually appears underneath the text being corrected. If you want to anchor it in a fixed location instead, click this box. To move it, drag it where you want it to be.

Enable double-click to correct

If you prefer to make corrections with a double-click of the mouse, check this box. (See Chapter 2 for more information on making corrections with the mouse and keyboard.)

Show no more than [9] choices

Sets how many choices will appear in the Correction box.

Restore defaults

If you would like to reset this tab to its default options, click this button.

Commands Tab

As its name suggests, this tab is about setting options for commands.

Pause required before commands

As you have learned, pausing before commands makes them more likely to be recognized as commands, and not as text to be typed. Adjust how long the pause needs to be with this slider. (The only commands that work without a pause are **New Line, New Paragraph**, and capitalization commands.)

Enable mouse motion commands

Checking this box gives you the option to move the mouse by voice. The Speed button opens a window that lets you set the mouse movement speed.

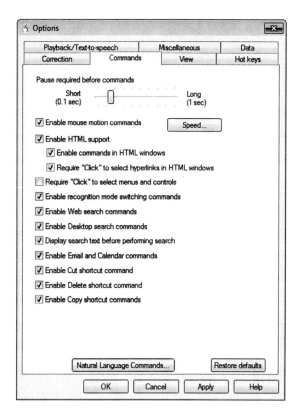

Enable HTML support

To use the commands for web browsers in Chapter 5, keep the first box ("Enable commands in HTML windows") checked. If the second box is checked, you must say **Click** in front of any link, for example, **Click** *About Us*.

Require "Click" to select menus and controls

If you would like to require the word "click" before selecting menu items and buttons, (for example, **Click File)** check this box.

Enable recognition mode switching commands

With this box checked, recognition mode commands are on, such as **Switch to Normal Mode.**

Enable Web search commands

When this box is checked, you can say the Web search commands introduced in Chapter 5, for example, **Search Videos for Home Repair.**

Enable Desktop search commands

When this box is checked, you can say desktop search commands such as **Search the Computer for** *Document Name*.

Display Search Text before performing search

With this command selected, you have a chance to edit any search command you give before the command is executed.

Enable E-mail and Calendar commands

With this box checked, you can say e-mail commands like **Send an E-mail to** [*contact name*].

Enable Cut/Delete/Copy shortcut commands

With these boxes checked, you can speak Dragon's shortcut commands for cut/copy/delete, for example, **Cut from** [*text*] **to** [*text*].

Natural Language Commands Button

Click this button, and a list of check boxes appears. With the boxes checked, you can say Natural Language Commands with Microsoft Word, Microsoft PowerPoint and selected other applications.

Restore defaults

If you would like to reset this tab to its default options, click this button.

View Tab

The View tab has options to set behavior and appearance of both the DragonBar and the Results box.

DragonBar

The modes area lets you select the way you want the DragonBar displayed. The modes are **Docked to Top, Docked to Bottom, Floating, Cling,** and **Tray Icon Only.**

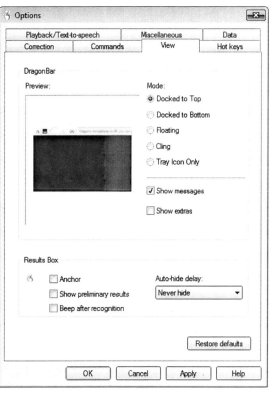

Show messages

Allows you to see useful hints that appear in the DragonBar periodically.

Show extras

Turns on the Extras toolbar, which is useful for transcribing dictation from a digital recorder.

Results Box: Anchor

If anchor is on, the results box is locked in its current location until you drag it somewhere else on the screen.

Results Box: Show preliminary results

Shows the Results box as it is processing your speech (all older versions of Dragon had this feature automatically). Otherwise, speech typed in the document after processing.

Results Box: Beep after recognition

Beeps when Dragon recognizes a word or phrase.

Results Box: Auto-hide delay

The amount of time the results box is displayed after recognizing text or commands can be controlled in this list.

Restore defaults

If you would like to reset this tab to its default options, click this button.

Hot Keys Tab

The Hot Keys tab shows the preset hot keys (specialized keyboard commands) for many Dragon functions. These can be changed by clicking on the item (button) and choosing a different key/key combo. (Use caution when changing hot keys to not choose a combination already in use for something else.)

This feature is especially useful with laptops, as they often lack number keypads! If you change the hot key and you then change your mind, you can change it back to the default with the "Restore defaults" button.

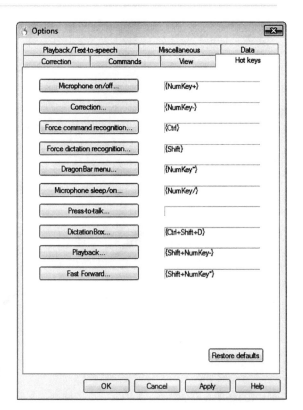

Microphone on/off

This hot key turns the microphone on or off.

Correction

This hot key opens the Correction menu.

Force command recognition

This hot key forces text to be recognized as commands and not as text to be typed.

Force dictation recognition

This hot key forces words to be recognized as text to be typed and not as commands to be acted upon.

DragonBar menu

This hot key opens the Profile menu on the DragonBar.

Microphone sleep/on

This hot key makes the microphone go to sleep or wake up.

Press-to-talk

This hot key turns on the microphone while you are holding down the hot key. The microphone turns off again when you let go of the hotkey.

Dictation Box

This hot key brings up the Dictation Box.

Playback

This hot key commands Dragon to play back your dictation aloud. Note: this works better with more recent dictation, as the playback memory stores dictation, then over-writes it with newer dictation as you continue working.

Fast Forward

This hot key makes the play-back speed faster.

Restore defaults

Clicking this button resets default options.

The Playback/Text-to-Speech Tab

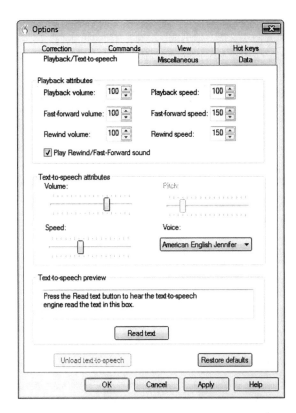

This tab changes settings when using playback features or text-to-speech. **Note:** To have selected text read aloud, say **Read That**.

Playback Attributes: Volume and Speed

Set the volume and speed of playback, fast playback and rewinding by saying the name of the item, then the number desired. If you wish to have the "rewind/fast-forward sound" played, check the box.

Text-to-Speech Attributes: Volume, Pitch, and Speed

Set these by adjusting the sliders manually or by voice. Commands to increase the volume, for example, are **Volume**, then **Move Right [6]**. (Say any number 1-20.)

Text-to-Speech Attributes: Voice

To change the text-to-speech voice, open the list box and click on a selection. Many selections may be displayed, but only the voices installed on your computer will work. (If you like text-to-speech, but you would prefer to have higher-quality voices, you can purchase additional voices from reliable TTS voice developers, like AT&T.)

Text-to-speech Preview

Click the "Read Text" button for a voice preview.

Unload text-to-speech

If your text-to-speech is loaded, and you wish to turn it off and save the processing power it takes, click this button.

Restore defaults

Clicking the "Restore defaults" button will reset this tab to its default options.

Miscellaneous Tab

This tab contains several very useful features. To set the behavior of the **Sidebar**, check or uncheck the first box. If you would like your **microphone** on, but asleep, when you **start Dragon**, check the second box. If, in addition, you would like **DragonPad** to start automatically when you start Dragon, check the third box.

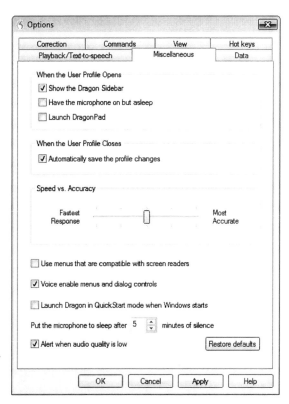

Automatically save the profile changes

Check this box to have Dragon save your user profile changes automatically when you exit the program.

Speed vs. Accuracy

If you have difficulty with accuracy, try sliding this slider bar to the right toward "Most Accurate". However, doing this will slow down the responsiveness of the software somewhat.

Use screen reader compatible menus

Makes menus accessible to screen reading software.

Voice enable menus and dialog controls

Allows you to speak menus and items in dialog boxes when checked.

Launch in QuickStart mode on Windows startup

Enables Dragon to start up automatically when you start your computer or log on. When using the QuickStart mode, a microphone icon will be visible in the notification area (near the clock on the Taskbar).

Put the microphone to sleep after [5] minutes of silence

This sleeps the microphone after a pre-set amount of time, if it is on.

Alert when audio quality is low

When this item is checked, you will be notified if audio quality is low.

Restore defaults

Clicking the "Restore defaults" button will reset this tab to its default options.

Data Tab

In this tab, set options that control how your user data is managed.

Store corrections in archive

A file of your corrections can be stored for later use by the Acoustic Optimizer. Click the "Archive size" button to get to a slider bar where you can select how much data is to be stored, from 30 to 180 minutes of corrections. It is highly recommended that you check this checkbox; otherwise, a file of your corrections will not be kept for optimizing.

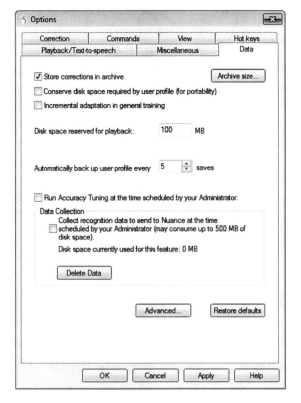

Conserve disk space required by user profiles (for portability)

If you need to limit the size of your user profile (to store it on removable media, for example) then check this box.

Incremental adaptation in general training

If you perform additional training with one of the scripts (see Chapter 1) this option allows Dragon to perform adaptation just the newly trained text.

Disk space reserved for playback

If you plan to play back your actual dictation (your voice, not the text-to-speech synthesizer), use this option to set how much space the computer should allow this file to use. If you never use this feature, you can set the value as low as 0 MB.

Automatically back up user profiles every [5] saves

Set how many saves before your user profiles are automatically backed up.

Run Accuracy Tuning at the time scheduled by your Administrator

Accuracy Tuning, which has to be run by a user with administrative rights, lets you set a time to run Accuracy Tuning automatically. Accuracy Tuning helps to ensure accurate speech recognition.

Data Collection

If you would like to give information about your use of Dragon software to Nuance, check the box to enable data collection. Nuance uses the data to improve Dragon; more information is available in Dragon's Help files.

"Advanced" Button

This button opens the Advanced dialog box, which has options to create a usability log, to always preserve wave data, to conserve the amount of disk space required by user profiles, and to enable Nuance to collect acoustic data. More information on these topics is available in Dragon's Help files.

Using a Digital Recorder

While using digital voice recorders can be extremely useful, especially for people who have difficulty writing manually, the initial setup can take quite some time, and no one set of instructions can cover all of the various recorders. What follows is an overview of the process for using a digital voice recorder.

If you are considering the purchase of a digital voice recorder, you should look at the compatibility list on the Nuance web site at http://support.nuance.com/ compatibility/default.asp.

The more Dragons in the rating, the better!

General Information about Using a

Digital Voice Recorder with Dragon NaturallySpeaking

1. Check to see what software came with the device, and then determine if it needs to be installed before or after the digital voice recorder is connected. If the digital voice recorder didn't come with any software, skip this, but check and see if it is compatible with Dragon.

2. Go to the Help menu and click on the "Index" tab on the left. Type in *digital voice Recorders* and press or say **Enter**. The right side of the window will have links to information for different brands and types of recorders. Select yours, and follow the instructions as given. (The following is an example.)

Digital Recorder (Sony)

3. Create a user profile for your recorder that is separate from your usual user profile. Go to the Profile menu on the DragonBar and choose "New User". In the window that opens, click on the "New" button. Then, type in a different user name, such as "Mary Smith's Recorder". Change the dictation source to match the recorder.

4. You will begin a process which involves several screens in Dragon NaturallySpeaking, which walks you through the process of dictating a text script into your digital voice recorder and then connecting it to the computer and downloading it into Dragon.

5. After your dictation is downloaded, Dragon will adapt your user profile. After this, you can use the user profile for downloading dictated text from files on the digital voice recorder.

Digital voice recorders use a limited command set. While you can dictate all of the text dictation you normally would, you can only dictate commands allowed while in Dictation Mode.

Commands Allowed in Dictation Mode

New Line	New Paragraph	Tab Key
Space Bar	Cap [word]	All Caps On/Off
No Space On/Off	Punctuation (!?,.)	Symbols (@&$%)

Other Issues and Resources

Many issues and technological difficulties still remain to be solved in speech recognition. For help with these as they evolve, visit usingspeechrecognition.com, or visit the Nuance.com site for Dragon NaturallySpeaking help at nuance.com, and the Windows Speech Recognition site for Windows SR. Also, pay attention to new developments—new versions, improved headsets, etc. There are a few bloggers who address speech recognition, but these come and go. Listed below are some resources for you to begin with. Best wishes for your success!

Dragon NaturallySpeaking:

http://www.nuance.com/naturallyspeaking/

Windows Speech Recognition:

Windows Speech Recognition Site: While this site was designed for Windows Vista Speech Recognition, the tutorials are also useful with Windows 7 Speech Recognition.
http://www.microsoft.com/enable/products/windowsWindows/speech.aspx

Windows Speech Recognition Profile Tool: This tool lets users backup and restore their user profiles (for Windows 7 and Vista). Note: If you aren't a techie, you may need a techie to help you!
http://www.microsoft.com/download/en/details.aspx?id=16296

Other Recommended Sites:

http://blogs.msdn.com/b/robch: Rob Chambers, part of the WSR team at Microsoft, maintains this blog.

http://www.usingspeechrecognition.com: The author's blog. Come say hi!

http://www.tau.ac.il/~itamarez/sr/index.html: Itamar Even-Zohar's speech recognition page. Best source of information on non-English speech recognition.

http://www.davidpogue.com: David Pogue's website also links to his blog and e-mail newsletters. Technology writer for the New York Times, David also reviews speech recognition software.

Dragon NaturallySpeaking Commands: Chapters 1-5

Chapter 1

Go To Sleep
Wake Up
Microphone Off
Listen To Me
Stop Listening
Start DragonPad
Open DragonPad
New Line
New Paragraph
Click Close
Scratch That
Strike That
Delete That
Undo That
Redo That
Close Window
Auto-punctuation On
Auto-punctuation Off
What Can I Say?
Give Me Help
Click Help
Close Help
Search Dragon Help for [topic]
Click [name of item]
Save User Profile
Click Profile
Exit Dragon

Chapter 2
Correct That
Correct [wrong word(s)]
Correct From [word] to [word]
Select [wrong word(s)]
Unselect That

Cancel
Escape
Spell That
Choose 1 (or the correct number)
Spacebar
Press Spacebar
Backspace
Press Backspace
Backspace 3 (or the correct number)
Letter Alpha
Click [item] (File, Print, etc.)
Press Right Arrow
Play That Back
Read That
Go To Bottom
Go To Top
Go To End of Line
Go To Beginning of Line
Insert Before [word]
Insert After [word]
Move Down 1 Line
Move Down [3] Lines (2–20)
Move Up 1 Line
Move Up [4] Lines (2–20)
Delete That
Delete Line
Delete Last [6] Characters (2-20)
Delete Last [7] Words (2–20)
Delete Next [4] Words (2–20)
Delete Paragraph
Delete All
Select Line
Select All
Select Next [2] Characters
Select Last Character
Select Next Word

Select Last [9] Words (2–20)
Select Last [5] Lines (2-20)
Open DragonPad
Start DragonPad
Print That
Click Maximize
Click Minimize
Click Restore
Click Close *or* Close Window
Switch to DragonPad
Switch to Dragon Bar
Switch to Dragon Sidebar
Switch to [*name of DragonBar*] Mode
Open Dragon Sidebar (*more sidebar commands on page 87*)

Chapter 3

Selecting:
Select Line
Select Last [2] Lines
Select Last [3] Sentences
Select Paragraph
Select Last [4] Paragraphs
Select All
Select Last Word
Select Last 6 Words
Select Last Character
Select Last [5] Characters

Capitalization/Spacing:
Cap [*word*]
Cap That
Caps On
Caps Off
All Caps On
All Caps Off
No Cap That
No Caps On
No Caps Off

No Space On
No Space Off
Compound That
Hyphenate That
Format That Strikethrough
Format That Strikeout

Numbers:
Numeral [6]
Roman Numeral [20]

Bold, Italics, Underline:
Bold That
Format That Bold
Bold [*word*]
Bold from [*word*] to [*word*]
Bold [*word*] through [*word*]
Press Ctrl + B
Italicize That
Format That Italics
Italicize [*word*]
Italicize from [*word*] to [word]
Italicize [*word*] through [*word*]
Press Ctrl + I
Underline That
Format That Underlined
Underline [*word*]
Underline from [*word*] to [word]
Underline [*word*] through[*word*]
Press Ctrl + U
Format That Bold Italics

Alignment:
Left Align That
Format That Left Aligned
Press Ctrl + L
Center That
Format That Centered
Press Ctrl + E
Right Align That

Format That Right Aligned
Press Ctrl + R
Justify That
Press Ctrl + J

Editing:
Cut [*word*]
Cut [*word*] through [*word*]
Cut That
Copy [*word*]
Copy [*word*] through [*word*]
Copy That
Paste That

Miscellaneous
Make That Size [14]
Format That Plain
Format That Regular
Restore That

Chapter 4

Navigating the Desktop
Press [*item*] (Spacebar, Tab Key, etc.)
Click Start
Start Menu
Start Recycle Bin
Start My Documents
Click Computer
Click All Programs

Working in Program Windows
Press Tab
Press Shift Tab
Press Escape
Open List
Close List
Click Application Tab

Using MouseGrid
MouseGrid

MouseGrid Window

Recognition Modes
Switch to ___ Mode
___ Mode On

Microsoft Word
Click File Tab
Click Office Button
Click [*name of tab*]
Click [*name of item*]
Undo That
Delete the Entire Document

Move Commands
Move This Line Down 2 Paragraphs
Move This Paragraph to the End of
    the Document
Move Up [ ] Lines
Move Down [ ] Lines
Move Up a Paragraph
Move Right a Character
Go to End of Document
Go to Previous Paragraph
Go to Beginning of Line
Insert Paragraph
Insert 8 Blank Lines
Page Up
Page Down

Save Commands
Click Save
Save That
Press Ctrl S
Save Changes

Print Commands
Click Print
Print That
Press Ctrl P
Print the Document

Spelling
Check Spelling

Bullet Style and Numbering:
Bullet That
Number That
Numbers Off
Unnumber That

Line Spacing
Double Space That
Single Space That

Font Name, Size and Style
Make This Paragraph Bold
Open a Document
Format That [*font name*]
Make That [*font name*]
Press Ctrl Shift F
Format That Size [*number*]
Format That Arial 12 Points
Make That Bigger
Make That Smaller
Set Font Arial 12 Points
Make That Blue

Switch To Commands
Switch to [*Program or Item name*]
Switch to Next Window
Switch to Previous Window

Table Commands
Add a Table
Add a 3 by 4 Table
Add a Row
Add 5 Rows
Add a Column
Add 2 Columns
Delete This Row

Unbullet That
Format That Bullet Style
Make That Numbered
Delete This Column
Delete This Table

**Custom Commands
(MyCommands Editor)**
Add New Command
Train

Chapter 5

Dictation Box
Show Dictation Box
Transfer

Screen Shot
Press Print Screen
Press Alt Print Screen

Viewing Web Pages
Start Internet Explorer
Start Mozilla Firefox
Stop Scrolling
Start Scrolling Up/Down
Speed Up/Slow Down
Page Up/Down
Move Up/Down 10 Lines
Go To Top/Bottom
Line Up/Down
Press Alt F4

Clicking Links on Pages
Click [*name of link*]
Click Link
Click Text
Click Image
Choose [3]

Web Addresses
Go To Address
Press Alt D
Switch to Spell Mode
Switch to Normal Mode

Navigation
Click Go
Go There
Go Back
Back
Go Forward
Forward
Refresh Page
Press F5
Go Home
Home

Favorites/Bookmarks
Click Favorites
Add to Favorites
Click Bookmarks (Firefox)
Bookmark This Page (Firefox)

Buttons, Boxes and Lists
Click Text Field
Click Check Box
Click Radio Button
Click List Box
Show Choices
Open List
Hide Choices
Close List

Searching:
Search the Web For [*item*]
Search [site] For [*item*]
Find a Website on [*topic*]
Search [category] for [*item*]

Screen Shot
Press Print Screen
Press Alt Print Screen
Paste That

Web Browser Tabs IE:
Open New Tab
Switch to The Next/Previous Tab
View the 3rd Tab [1–8]
Close Tab

Web Browser Tabs Firefox:
Add a New Tab
Go to the Next/Previous Tab
Close Tab
E-mail Commands
Start Mail
Check for Mail
Open Mail
New Mail
Write Mail
Write E-mail
Reply to Mail
Reply to All
Forward Mail
Send Mail
Send E-mail
Send an e-mail to [*Name*]
Send an e-mail about [*Subject*]
Delete Mail
Delete E-mail
Print Mail
Print E-mail
Close Mail
Click [*name of link or button*]
Go to [*name of*] Field

Gmail commands: *see list on page 193*

Facebook and Twitter Commands
Post to Facebook
Post That to Facebook
Search Facebook for [*topic*]
Post to Twitter
Tweet That

Accuracy Center
Start Accuracy Center
Improve My Accuracy

Your Custom Commands:

Windows Speech Recognition Commands: Chapters 6 and 7

Chapter 6

Microphone/Basic Commands:
Start Listening
Stop Listening
Show Speech Recognition
Hide Speech Recognition
Move Speech Recognition
What Can I Say?
Show Speech Options

Windows and Programs:
Show The Desktop
Switch to [program or window name]
Go to [field name]
Minimize That
Restore That
Close That
Press Alt Print Screen
Click Start (opens Start menu)

Selecting, Navigating and Clicking:
Go To [word]
Go After [word]
Move Down [7] (or other number)
Move Up [15]
Select Sentence
Select Last Word
Select Last [3] Words
Scroll Down [5]
Scroll Up [10]
Show Numbers
Click [item]
Select [word]
Undo That
Delete That

Selecting, Navigating and Copy/Paste:
Go to the End of the Document
Go to the Start of the Document
Go to End of Sentence
Go to Beginning of Sentence
Go to End of Line
Go to End of Paragraph
New Paragraph
New Line
Copy
Paste

Correcting Text:
Correct [word or words]
Correct That
Spell It
Spell It Again

Keypress Commands:
Press a
Press Shift A
Press Capital B
Press C as in close
Press d as in daughter
Press Enter
Press End
Press Control Home

Chapter 7

Show Speech Options
Show Numbers
Correct [*word*]
Correct That
Spell It
Click File
Press Enter
MouseGrid
Double-click
Right-click
Mark
Click
Click View
Click Font
Press Down Arrow
Press Tab
Clear Formatting
Caps [*word*]
Select [*word*]
Cap That
All Caps [*word*]
All Cap That
No Space
No Caps
Numeral 1
Bold
Press Control B
Underline
Press Control U
Italicize
Press Control I
Line Spacing
Click Start
New Line
New Paragraph

Go to [*word*]
Select Sentence
Select Paragraph
Press Control S

Font Group Commands
Font
Font Size
Grow Font
Shrink Font
Clear Formatting
Bold
Italics
Underline
Strikethrough
Subscript
Superscript
Change Case
Text Highlight Color
Font Color

Internet Explorer
Scroll Up [*number*]
Scroll Down [*number*]
Back
Forward
Home
Favorites
Press Control Home
Address
Tools
Delete
Press Control V
Paste
Click Close
Close Window

Index

CPSIA information can be obtained at www.ICGtesting.com
Printed in the USA
LVOW132130090212

267715LV00002B/100/P